A

Jewish Bishop

in

Jerusalem

Kelvin Crombie

Nicolayson's Ltd
Christ Church, Jerusalem.

First published in 2006 in Israel by
Nicolayson's Ltd,
Christ Church, Jaffa Gate, Jerusalem 91140
betnic@netvision.net.il

Website: www.itac-israel.org

ISBN 965-90941-0-8

Printed in Israel by
Yanetz Ltd
P.O. Box 10382
91103 Jerusalem.

Sponsored by:
Alexander College,
Christ Church, Jerusalem, Israel

Bishop Michael Solomon Alexander

Dedicated to the memory of
Reuven Achimeir,
part of the modern day legacy of
Michael Solomon Alexander.

Contents

page

Acknowledgements
Foreword
Introduction   i
Visual

Part One: 1799-1841
1	Son of a Prussian Rabbi	1799-1820	1
2	Seeking Refuge in England	1820-1824	12
3	The Messiah He is	1824-1825	19
4	The Irish Connection	1826-1827	26
5	Journeys in Central Europe	1828-1830	34
6	Labours in London	1830-1839	41
7	Time for Israel's Restoration	1838-1841	56
8	The Protestant Bishopric	1841	73
9	A Jewish Bishop for Jerusalem	1841	96

Visuals

Part Two: 1842 – 1845
10	A Jewish Bishop in Jerusalem	1842	105
11	The Sultan Intervenes	1843	138
12	The *Kingdom* Expands	1844	180
13	Death at the Moment of Victory	1845	205
14	The Day After – Alexander's Legacy		234

Bibliography   247
Index   251

Acknowledgements

The genesis of this book was in mid 2002. Quite unexpectedly, I was invited to deliver a lecture about Bishop Michael Solomon Alexander at a conference, entitled 'Confessional Conversions' in Germany. This conference was organized by the Simon Dubrow Institute of Jewish Studies attached to the University of Leipzig.

The purpose of the conference was to study why communities converted from one faith group to another. But it was also decided to add a few interesting individual stories of people who had a conversion experience. Somehow they got hold of my name, possibly because I had previously written an article about Alexander. I then had several months to locate my materials and put together something that I thought was presentable.

At the conference all thirteen or so speakers except two of us were professors or heads of departments from universities. I learnt at that conference that my knowledge was quite basic and superficial. I had only just scratched the surface relating to the story about this fascinating man.

This experience never left me, and thereafter, where opportunity afforded itself I began tracking down further details of the life of Michael Solomon Alexander. This search took me to various archives and sources in England, Ireland and Israel particularly. I also tried to locate as many as possible of the actual places where he had lived and ministered.

Many have assisted me in this project. These included, not in any particular order: David Pileggi, Director of Alexander College at Christ Church, Carol and Shira Pileggi; Murray Dixon, Ray Lockhart, Tony Higton, Michael Neil Cohen and Alfred Sawyer, present and former ministers of Christ Church Jerusalem; John Wood; John and Joyce Luscombe; Bob Brennan; Peter Darg; Rodney and Katherine Stafford; Derek Langram; Gershom Nerel; Alison Marchant, Sybil Parry and others.

Most of this work was done on a small desk in a corner of my bedroom. Special thanks then to my wife Lexie for putting up with this oftentimes inconvenience. To God for the privilege of being able to do this project.

And I hasten to add, this is by no means the full story. There is much more to 'dig up' and learn about this 'Jewish Bishop in Jerusalem.'

Foreword

For many of us, Bishop Michael Solomon Alexander (he is usually given his full name) is a shadowy figure from the past. We come under his spell only when we visit Jerusalem and stay at Christ Church guest-house within the walls of the Old City or call at the house of the present Bishop in Jerusalem alongside St George's Cathedral. His robed portrait is everywhere. As the first Anglican bishop in Jerusalem, he was the cornerstone of the work of the CMJ (then the London Jews Society) in the Holy Land, and it is fitting that his short life should be celebrated in the writing of this book a hundred and sixty years after his untimely death.

The impact of Alexander's life was out of all proportion to its length. Converted and baptized at the age of 26, ordained at 28, a university Professor of Hebrew and Rabbinic Literature at 33, consecrated Bishop of Jerusalem when only 42 and dying a mere four years later, he nevertheless became a significant part of Israel's recent history and his memory lingers on.

Kelvin Crombie tells his story, with all its struggles, first as a young rabbi exploring the New Testament and the messianic claims of Jesus, and then as a Christian missionary to his fellow-Jews in his native Germany, and overcoming many a health problem both in his wife and in himself that would have daunted a man of lesser dedication to his calling. His struggles and frustrations continued in the seemingly never-ending battle with Turkish bureaucracy over the permission needed to build a Protestant church in Jerusalem, but eventually he was successful and Christ Church still stands as a monument to his faith and persistence, and as a haven currently for four separate congregations of Romanians, Filipinos, Hebrew-speaking Messianic Jews and the large English - speaking "rump" of locals, short-term workers and visitors to the land.

He was not the first Bishop Alexander of Jerusalem. That privilege goes to the Alexander who survived the persecutions of the Roman emperor Severus but eventually fell foul of Decius and was martyred around 250 AD. He was the contemporary of those giants of the faith, Clement and the great Origen of Alexandria, of whom Eusebius writes in the sixth book of his Ecclesiastical History. But there were striking similarities between the Jerusalem bishop of the third century and the Anglican bishop of the nineteenth. Not least that they both paid with their lives for their faith - as Kelvin Crombie illustrates only too well.

The reader will be for ever indebted to him for these information-packed chapters about a hero of the Evangelical Movement in the Church of England whose story needed to be told.

Bishop John B Taylor

Introduction

Life in Jerusalem has always been characterized by its various communities zealously safeguarding their personal interests. Often this zeal is manifested in the unwillingness of a community to relate to or respect another.

For centuries there was a clear distinction between the Jewish and Christian communities. Christians mostly saw themselves as the new people of God, the new Israel, the new recipients and custodians of God's covenanted blessings. As such, they viewed the Jewish community as the old covenant people, whom they believed were a living testimony and warning to the world of God's judgment on a disobedient people. Some Christians even went so far as accusing the Jewish people of deicide, blaming them for killing Jesus of Nazareth, the Son of God.

For some 1,800 years these two communities were at enmity with each other concerning two issues of faith. Firstly, concerning Jesus of Nazareth: is He the Messiah or not?

Secondly, concerning the redemption of Israel. The Jewish community believed, albeit with some differences of interpretation, that when the Jewish Messiah came to Jerusalem Israel would be restored and redeemed. Their belief is based on their covenant relationship with God as promised to the patriarchs, Abraham, Isaac and Jacob.

Conversely, Christians generally believed that God had finished with the Jews, therefore, they would not be restored to the Land of Israel[1] and would not become a nation again.

These two communities held quite fast to these positions for centuries. Then suddenly, beginning in the 1820's, this rigidly held *status quo* was challenged. This challenge of the 1820's and 30's was preparatory to a massive assault upon the established order of life in Jerusalem in the 1840's. And that assault, which resulted in a religious or cultural

---

[1] The Land of Israel, *Eretz Yisrael*, was primarily referred to as Syria and occasionally as Palestine during the period under discussion. The name Palestine was first consistently used to describe the Land of Israel following the Bar Kockba Revolt in 135 CE, when the victorious Romans wanted to erase any Jewish connection to the Land. I will use any of the above derivations.

revolution, came about primarily through the presence of one man – Michael Solomon Alexander.

In the 1820's, Jerusalem was under the autocratic rule of Ottoman Turkey via its local rulers or governors (*pashas*) in the Holy City. There was an established *status quo,* an established rule of living, practiced almost without change for some 600 years since the end of the Crusader period. And this rule of life was this: 'we the Muslims are in control, and every other community (*millet*), beginning with the Orthodox Christians downwards to the Jewish people, are below us. This system, (known as the *dhimmi*[2] system), will not change.'

In the 1820's Protestant Christians, both British[3] and American,[4] began arriving in Turkish Palestine, and in particular, Jerusalem. Their task was an impossible one. Foreigners, (and this they were as they did not belong to a recognized *millet* or community) were forbidden to reside or even purchase land there. Added to this was the Muslim prohibition against the building of new churches.

Undeterred, these Protestant Christians, sometimes referred to as evangelicals,[5] resorted to prayer and patient endurance. Their strategy worked. Slowly situations changed, so that by the late 1830's evangelical Protestants were living with a certain degree of security in Jerusalem.

One of the major reasons for the perseverance of the Protestant Christians, especially the British, was a certain ideology they upheld - the restoration of Israel. These people belonged to a relatively large and

---

[2] A *dhimmi* is a person or community living in a Muslim state who is a member of an officially recognized non-Islamic religion. In particular it refers to Christians and Jewish people, but indeed all non-Muslims fall into this category.

[3] Several British Christian groups had previously ventured into the region, notably the British and Foreign Bible Society, the Church Missionary Society, and especially the London Society for Promoting Christianity among the Jews. This later Society, which was founded in 1809, and also known as the London Jews Society, LJS or today CMJ, was the first Protestant society to settle permanently in Palestine. The LJS sent it's first worker to the Levant in 1820.

[4] The Americans all belonged to the Boston based American Board of Commissioners for Foreign Missions, which was formed in 1810. The American Board sent it's first workers to the Levant in 1819 and they arrived in Palestine in 1821.

[5] Name given to group of Christians initially in Britain, both Anglican and non-Anglican (non-Conformist) who held similar views, based upon firm belief in the atoning death of Jesus; firm belief in the Bible; firm belief in social action emanating from belief in the Bible; and firm belief that individual lives needed to be changed by personal belief in Jesus. See D. W. Bebbington, *Evangelicalism in Modern Britain,* (Unwin Hyman, London, 1979), pp. 2-3.

vibrant movement within the British Church which desired to see the message of Jesus as Messiah restored to the Jewish people; to see the Jewish 'roots' of Christianity restored to the mostly Gentile Church; and to see the Jewish people restored to the Land of Israel. These they believed were to happen before the Second Coming of Jesus to Jerusalem.[6] This movement I refer to as the restoration movement.

These restorationist ideas in themselves were revolutionary. But while they remained just ideas they were virtually harmless. It was when they began to be put into practice that the 'revolution' became tangible. Those pioneer Protestant missionaries, Joseph Wolff, William Lewis, George Dalton and John Nicolayson working for the British,[7] and Pliny Fisk, Levi Parsons and Jonas King, representing the Americans,[8] laid a foundation.

Michael Solomon Alexander found himself being thrust onto that foundation – and in the process became possibly the main individual catalyst of a cultural 'revolution' in Jerusalem. Indeed Jerusalem was turned upside down in the 1840's, and there is no doubt at all, that it was the movement of restoration, often associated with Bishop Alexander, which was one of the main contributors to this upheaval.

What was it about Michael Solomon Alexander that enabled him to become such an important figure in this cultural 'revolution'? Was it because he was Jewish? Or because he was a rabbi? Or because he was a Jewish believer in Jesus as Messiah? Or because he was the first Protestant bishop in Jerusalem? It was all this – and more. Indeed Michael Solomon Alexander was also a firm believer in the concept of restoration. He was, what some may call today, a *Christian Zionist*, although that term, even in its secular form, was decades from formulation when he was going about his task in Jerusalem. But Alexander and his particular theological persuasion, and the ideology of his parent organization, the LJS or CMJ, only became of historical importance because of one important over-arching factor – geo-politics.

The Geo-political Background
Alexander came to Jerusalem as the first Protestant bishop, due to the establishment of the unique (some might say oblique) *Jerusalem*

---

[6] This belief was not held by all Christians, let alone all Protestants. It is based upon certain Scriptures, but primarily upon Zechariah 14:4 and Acts 1:6-10, both of which indicate that the Messiah or Jesus would come or return to Jerusalem.

[7] All working for the LJS. Wolff was from Germany, Lewis and Dalton both came from Ireland, and Nicolayson came from Denmark.

[8] The Americans belonged to the American Board of Commissioners for Foreign Missions.

Protestant Bishopric, a combined effort of the British and the Prussians. However it must be firmly understood, that this concept only came to the fore because of political events that occurred in Europe and the Levant.[9]

Significant political events had always been occurring in the eastern Mediterranean. Throughout many millennia there had always been large empires, usually one to the north, be it Assyria, Babylon or Persia, and one to the south, Egypt, vying for control over the strategic centre – Canaan, the Land of Israel.

These great empires rarely desired this land bridge for any of its natural resources. But what they did covet, apart from the strategic factor, was its position as the terminus of the trade routes that wound their way overland from Asia and ended at the various Levantine seaports.

Even during the period of Jesus, the region was regarded of great geo-political significance, as the Romans constantly feared invasion by the Parthian Empire on the east side of the Euphrates River. Hence the serious Roman concerns with the Jewish Revolts of the first and second centuries.

But there were other factors during the Roman period that would later influence Alexander's life. The Jewish nation was expecting and desiring a Messiah, deliverer, a redeemer, who would free them from Roman military, and spiritual oppression.

Thousands of Jewish people saw Jesus of Nazareth as being this promised deliverer, the Messiah. Jesus lived and ministered during the 30's of the first century. Within several decades after his ministry his followers, often known as Nazarenes, formed a considerable group within Jewish society. James, the brother of Jesus, was for a period the leader of this movement in Jerusalem.

Events surrounding the Roman destructions of Jerusalem in 70 and 135 CE and associated exile of the Jewish people from the land greatly affected the Nazarene movement. Within several hundred years there was very little trace of that original Jewish 'church' in Jerusalem, the church of St. James. Simultaneously, as more gentiles entered this Jewish messianic movement, the character gradually changed from its original Jewish character, to one virtually devoid of the Jewish component. The church in Jerusalem became a gentile church.

Control of Palestine changed in the fourth century from Rome to Byzantium. The Byzantine Empire was effectively the eastern half of the Roman Empire. The Roman Empire was Christianized by the fourth century and the eastern empire imposed Byzantine Christianity upon the

---

[9] The term often used to describe the eastern Mediterranean coastal area, stretching from Anatolia southwards to Syria, Lebanon, Israel and the Sinai.

Land of Israel. The main gentile church became the Greek Orthodox Church, which henceforth claimed hegemony among the numerous national churches then present in the Levant.

But by the seventh century a new power was descending upon the region – Islam. The followers of Mohammed coming from the desert of Arabia quickly established their control over the region, and forced the local inhabitants into submission. The surviving Christians were tolerated, but placed into subservient positions within the sphere of Islam. Orthodox Christianity remained the prime representative of the Christian faith.

Several Muslim Arab empires, the Umayyids based in Damascus, and the Abbasids based in Baghdad, controlled the strategic land between during the following centuries until the year 1099.

In that year 'Christian' Europe became intimately involved in the region, when the Crusader armies captured Jerusalem. This Crusader or Latin Kingdom challenged the established *status quo*, the supremacy of Islam, and the hegemony of the Greek Orthodox Church. The Latins, or Roman Catholic Church, placed a patriarch in Jerusalem, thereby challenging the authority of the Orthodox patriarch.

This European entity could not remain, as it was not unified and beset by countless internal, as well as external forces and opposition. Resurgent Muslim forces led by Saladin, an inspirational leader from Egypt, finally defeated the Crusader kingdom.

The returning Muslim rulers, primarily the Mamelukes from Egypt, permitted the Christian communities to remain, even the Latins or Roman Catholics, the spiritual representative of the Crusader powers. Jerusalem now had two rival claimants to Christian authority, the Greek Orthodox and the Latins, or Roman Catholics, represented by the Franciscans.

Early in their conquest of Jerusalem the Crusaders decimated the Jewish community. During the Mameluke period the Jewish community slowly recovered. One very interesting event soon after the Mameluke conquest was the visit of Italian Marco Polo, en-route along the spice route to China.

Indeed if there was one constant factor during all these upheavals, it was the continuing importance of the spice and silk routes, along which the precious commodities emanating from the east, came to the cities of Europe via the Levantine seaports. For several centuries following the departure of the Crusaders this trade was monopolized by the galleons of the Italian city-states, especially Venice and Genoa.

Modern Developments

In the year 1453 the Ottoman Turks captured Constantinople, the Byzantine capital. This was followed by the capture of Jerusalem in 1517 from the Mamelukes. A new and powerful force had now entered the scene, capturing extensive areas, including the regions of the northern empires, the southern empire (Egypt) and the land between.

The terminus of the spice trade was now completely in the hands of the Turkish Empire and its sultan, who was also the Caliph or spiritual leader of the Islamic world.

Although the Turks entered into trade agreements with several of the European powers[10] they nevertheless monopolized the spice trade. This monopoly engendered a response from the Europeans, especially the Portuguese who set out in search of the source of the Oriental spices.

Once Bartholomew Dias discovered a route around southern Africa in 1487 and Vasco da Gama landed in India in 1498, the Levantine coast lost its former importance, as the monopolization by the Turkish middle-man in the spice and silk trade was now being challenged.

In time large quantities of Oriental spices, silks and other precious commodities were being transported back to Europe by Portuguese fleets. Inevitably this Portuguese venture provoked European rivalry and competition as other major European powers coveted this trade for themselves. Initially the competition came from the British who set up an East India Company in 1599 and the Dutch who established their own trading company, the Dutch East India Company, in 1602. Then came the French, whose interests in the Levant were now in sharp decline due to the Portuguese, English and Dutch initiatives further east.

Each of these powers in time established trading stations, and then colonial empires. Britain ultimately concentrated its attention upon India, while the other powers carved out empires elsewhere. This colonial expansion, based primarily upon obtaining economic advantages, inevitably brought the European powers into conflict with each other. Occasionally such conflict was also due to political and economic tensions in Europe itself. Such competition and conflict led to the conclusion that whoever controls the quickest and most efficient route to the east has the greatest economic, and military advantage.

---

[10] These agreements, known as Capitulations, had been previously in effect between the Ottomans and the Italian city states, the first being with the Genoese in 1453. In 1535 France entered such an agreement, followed by England and other European powers. But France always claimed pre-eminence concerning trade with the Ottoman Empire.

With this dynamic in mind the French conceived a plan in the seventeenth century that the quickest and most effective way of obtaining a monopoly over the trade in the east was to conquer Egypt, which would be a springboard for a move to India via the Red Sea and Indian Ocean. But their plan never materialized.

However in 1798 Napoleon Bonaparte adopted the same concept. Napoleon was commissioned by his government to defeat Britain. He planned to conquer Egypt, establish a quick sea link to India – from where he planned to oust the British. The British Government was quick to respond by dispatching Admiral Nelson, who defeated the French fleet while in Egypt.

Stranded in the east, Napoleon then invaded the Land of Israel in 1799, from where he was again defeated decisively by a combined British-Turkish force at Acre in May 1799. However this was not before Napoleon, in view of Mount Tabor near Nazareth, made a proclamation in April 1799 encouraging the Jewish people to return to their homeland.[11]

The French invasion of Egypt and Palestine caused the British Government to cast wary eyes upon the activities of any rival power in that region. The link to India would have to be preserved at all costs. The security and well-being of the British Empire depended upon this.

The one Briton most anxious about this link was long-term Foreign Minister and Prime Minister, Lord Palmerston. Of this illustrious personality, the *Encyclopedia Britannica* wrote:

> The two great views he had in view were to prevent the establishment of Russia on the Bosphorus and of France on the Nile.[12]

A significant war occurred in the Land of Israel in 1840, in which Britain, Austria, Russia and Prussia sided with Turkey (the northern empire) and were pitted against Egypt (the southern empire), which was supported by France. Similar to today, every nation and high-minded individual had his or her opinion as to the future of the Holy Land in the aftermath of this conflict.

What is often not understood (or in certain quarters probably not wanted to be heard) is that a principle reason behind the establishment of the

---

[11] The original of this proclamation has never been found. However references to it were made shortly afterwards in various European newspapers. See *Moniteur Universal*, Paris, May 22, 1799, quoted in Simon Schwarzfuchs, *Napoleon the Jews and the Sandhedrin*. (London, 1979), p. 24. Also: H.A. Sacher, *A History of Israel* (New York, 1976), p. 22.

[12] *Encyclopedia Britannica*, (London & New York, 1926), p. 647.

Jerusalem Protestant Bishopric was the <u>official</u> British Government proposal for the future of the Land of Israel in 1840. It was no less than the restoration of Israel to her Land!

The Turks and the other Powers disagreed with this restorationist proposal and it was shelved. But it was foremost in the minds of prominent British statesmen and churchmen when the King of Prussia proposed to the British Government and Church the establishment of the Jerusalem Protestant Bishopric only a few months later. It may also be said that this proposal of 1840 influenced the agenda in 1917 when other statesmen, and fewer churchmen, re-introduced it and produced a profound document named the Balfour Declaration.

Perhaps the first authoritative book written on the Balfour Declaration was by prominent historian, Leonard Stein. Of this Protestant Bishopric, he wrote:

> What was in one aspect a move in the competition for prestige in the Levant and in another a symbol of a genuine Protestant claim to a recognized status in the Holy Land was mixed up with confused thoughts about the conversion of the Jews. The first Bishop, Michael Alexander, was a Jewish convert to Christianity and had, before joining the Church of England, been Minister of the Jewish Congregation at Plymouth. The choice was significant. So also was the comment of the Prussian envoy, de Bunsen, on the successful conclusion of his negotiations with Palmerston: 'So the beginning is made, please God, for the restoration of Israel.' The restoration of the Jews to Palestine under the auspices of the Protestant Powers, to be followed by their conversion to Christianity, would indeed be a triumph for the Protestant Churches.[13]

Many who adhered to the restorationist ideology now saw Alexander as the champion of their cause. In fact he carried on his shoulders the aspirations and expectations of two nations and two movements – the British hope of a Jewish restoration, and the Prussian hope of a worldwide Protestant union with Jerusalem as its centre and starting point.

In contrast to these expectations, Alexander was also berated and opposed by those who did not see value in these aims. Such opposition came from no less than Count Metternich of Austria, the French and Russian Governments, the Roman Catholic and Greek Orthodox Churches – and even the Sultan of Turkey himself. Not to mention almost every civil and ecclesiastical leader in Jerusalem. And on top of this there was the growing Anglo-Catholic movement within the Anglican Church itself.

---

[13] L. Stein, *The Balfour Declaration*, (London, 1961), p. 8.

Chapter 1

Son of a Prussian Rabbi: 1799-1820

Birth of Michael Solomon
At the same time that Napoleon Bonaparte was in the Land of Israel endeavouring to defeat both the Turkish and the British Empires, a second son was born to Rabbi Alexander[1] in the small village of Schonlanke,[2] in the Grand Duchy of Posen (then under the authority of Prussia).[3] That was 1 May 1799.

When the English-born rabbi named his son Michael after the Archangel, and Solomon, after Israel's wisest king, at his circumcision, little did he realize that his young son's future destiny was linked to those momentous events then occurring at Acre and Mount Tabor in far away Palestine.

Michael Solomon grew up as any other young Jewish child. His father, being a rabbi, would have had high expectations for his sons. Like other Jewish boys, Michael Solomon would have received a strong Jewish education through the synagogue. The Jewish community in Schonlanke was not large, possibly between 200-300. Being under Prussian control the Jewish community probably fared somewhat better than the typical *shtetl*, Jewish community, in east and south Poland.

Period of Change
The period in which Michael Solomon was born was one of tremendous change, not only for Palestine, but even more so for Europe, both for the Jewish people and for the Christian relationship to the Jewish people. The

---

[1] There is a bit of conjecture about his original name, that it was Pollack or even Wolff. For the purpose of this book however I will refer to him as Alexander.
[2] Now Trzcianka in Poland.
[3] A part of Greater Poland, known to the Poles as Wielopolska, was annexed by King Friedrich II of Prussia in 1772 during the first partition of Poland. Then in 1793, during what is known as the Second Partition, the remainder of this region was annexed to Prussia and was known to them as 'Southern Prussia.' After 1815 however it was referred to as Posen after the principal city.

French Revolution and subsequent Napoleonic Wars challenged the *status quo* that had for centuries determined how people were to live. Beginning in France, the power of established monarchies and the established Church was eroded.

In Germany, wrote Christopher Clark, the revolution strengthened 'eschatological hopes' and for many 'signalled that God had opened a new chapter in the history of salvation.'[4] Concerning Britain, the late Professor Meir Verete, stated '... it was the French Revolution which provided the starting point for the millenarian thinking of the 'nineties.' Several months after its outbreak Englishmen began to hear and to read that it was this great event that heralded the end of the generations and the impending advent of the kingdom of Christ.'[5]

Early Spiritual Awakenings
These 'eschatological hopes' resulting from the revolutionary period were, however, predated by spiritual awakenings in both Britain and Germany. Such an awakening, or revival, commonly known as the Pietist movement, took place in Germany during the late 1600's and the 1700's.

One name in particular is linked to this Pietist revival, Philip Jacob Spener. Spener desired to revive the Lutheran Church, not to start a new church, and he desired to see Jewish people acknowledge Jesus as Messiah. Several of the people personally touched by Spener's zeal were Count Zinzendorf[6] of Herrnhut and Hermann Francke of Halle.

As a young boy Count Zinzendorf was much impressed by Spener's theology and way of life. And while a student at the Francke Institute in Halle, he, in his own way, practiced this form of pietistic Christianity.

The Moravian Church or Brethren[7] was also involved in a spiritual awakening. About 1722 a group of Moravian Christians moved into southern Germany and lived on the lands of Count Zinzendorf at Herrnhut. Zinzendorf, now an active disciple of the Pietist movement, adopted the Moravians and together they pioneered the first Protestant missionary work overseas, heavily influencing the spiritual rebirth of John and Charles Wesley.

---

[4] Christopher Clark, *The Politics of Conversion*, (Oxford, 1995), p. 88.
[5] Meir Verete, *The Restoration of the Jews in English Protestant Thought 1790-1840,* Middle Eastern Studies, (January 1972, Frank Cass and Co, London), p. 5.
[6] Nicholas Ludwig, Count Zinzendorf, was born in Dresden in 1700. He died in 1760 at Herrnhut.
[7] Moravia is an historical region in the east of the present Czech Republic.

Another important Pietist was August Hermann Francke,[8] who operated a Christian institute named the *Franckesche Stiftungen* (Francke Institute) in Halle. Attached to his institute was the *Institutum Judaicum* operated by Johann Heinrich Callenberg,[9] which operated from 1728 till 1792. The *Institutum Judaicum* was unique in being the first concerted attempt by the Protestant Church to understand the Jewish people, and present the message of Jesus as Messiah to them.

Similar awakenings had occurred in Britain in the 1600's resulting from the Puritan 'revolution.'[10] An outcome of this revival was an increased desire to read and understand the Bible, a task previously undertaken by the privileged few of the clergy. As a result of reading the Bible openly, without having to interpret the Scriptures as the Roman Catholic Church had done for centuries, an automatic interest in the Jewish people and their restoration was engendered.

Much of the Bible story refers to covenants, promises and prophecies relating to the people and Land of Israel, which for many centuries had been interpreted by the established Church as relating not to the Israel of the flesh, but to the new or spiritual Israel – the Church. Many Puritans, desiring to understand and interpret the Bible in a literal sense, began to see that indeed there was still a divine purpose for the people and Land of Israel. A doctrine of the restoration of Israel then began to develop in the English and indeed the British Church from that time.

The Puritan revival of the 1600's was followed in the 1700's by an evangelical revival or awakening associated with John Wesley and George Whitefield. Throughout Britain and America individuals were challenged to have a personal 'saving or living' relationship with Jesus the Messiah.

Then, following the outbreak of the French Revolution there was an extension of that evangelical awakening in Britain. So radical were the political, social and economic changes occurring in Europe that many Bible believing Christians felt these were signs of the impending 'latter days.' Indeed Jesus had stated, as recorded in the Gospel of Matthew, that his return would be predated by 'wars and rumours of wars.'[11]

---

[8] Francke was born at Lubeck in 1663 and died in 1727.

[9] Callenberg, 1694-1760, is sometimes classified as the real father of modern Jewish missions.

[10] Initially a group of English Christians who desired to purify the English national church by eliminating every vestige of the Roman Catholic Church.

[11] Matthew 24:6-7.

Such a belief was also stimulated by the severe consequences of the revolution, the abolition in many parts of Europe of the established *status quo*.

In both Germany and Britain the spiritual awakenings of the 17th and 18th centuries brought a renewed interest in the Jewish people within sections of the church. There was considerable cross-fertilization between these European and British movements. It is ironic in a sense, therefore, that the unique and pioneering *Institutum Judaicum* closed down the very year that a new dynamic period of missions had its beginning in England.

Beginning of Modern Missions
In 1792 the Baptist Missionary Society was established. This Society was formed at a time of heightened interest in missions, stimulated, although not birthed, by the events of the French Revolution. Many evangelicals in Britain, believing they were entering into the last days, saw the need to obey the words of Jesus in Scriptures such as Matthew 24, and take the message of salvation to the ends of the world.[12]

This initiative was followed several years later by the formation of the London Missionary Society (LMS) in 1795, a society involving both Anglican and non-Anglican members. They were followed by the formation of the Church Missionary Society (CMS) in 1799, an evangelical Anglican society that was destined also to play a major role in the evangelization of the world.

During this very same period the interest in the Jewish people and their restoration grew. During the 1790's, numerous pamphlets and books were published on the subject, while sermons were continually preached. All this was within the context of the latter days and the events many believed must happen prior to the coming of Jesus.[13]

These events in Britain were felt in Germany. In 1796 Baron von Schirnding of Dobrilugk read an article in the *Hamburg Gazette* that the London Missionary Society (LMS) had been started. The Baron wrote an address entitled *Address to the British Nation* and sent it to Dr. Thomas Haweis, one of the LMS leaders.[14] Schirnding in his address drew

---

[12] See Verete, *ibid,* pp. 5 forward.

[13] See Verete, *ibid.*

[14] See Bridwell Library Manuscript and Documents Collection, British Manuscript Letters and Documents, Schirnding, August [Carl Friedrich] von, 1796, February 19, Dobrilugk in Saxony. "Oberforstmeister" [Chief Forestry Master] MS folio ("first doctrines of evangelical Lutheranism"), (II/2:149). Thomas Haweis Collection,

attention to the responsibility of taking the Gospel to the heathen. [15] The Moravian centre of Herrnhut was only some 60 miles from Dobrilugk, so their missionary attitude most likely influenced the Baron.

Schirnding's *Address* later appeared in the *Evangelical Magazine* in England in August 1796. Dr. Haweis' reply to Schirnding then found its way into the hands of Rev. Straecke, Lutheran pastor from Hatshusen, who then appealed to his German countrymen in 1799 to establish a similar institution as the LMS. The end result of all this exertion and interest was the opening of a seminary in Berlin on 1 February 1800 'for training promising candidates for missionary employ.' The Berlin Seminary commenced with seven students, 'for whose instruction a tutor was engaged.' [16]

Towards the end of that same year Rev. John Jaenicke, a Lutheran clergyman replaced Straecke.[17] From the outset the Berlin Seminary could only train the missionaries, and refer them to other societies. Those other societies were the LMS and the CMS, which thereafter received numerous candidates. Ironically these British missionary societies were staffed primarily by Christians from central Europe, who were candidates either from the Berlin Seminary, or the Basle Bible College in Switzerland.[18]

The Berlin Seminary encapsulated much of the pietist, missionary zeal of the German Church, both Lutheran and Moravian, in much the same way as the LMS and CMS encapsulated much of the Puritan and evangelical streams of the English Church.

In 1801 two events occurred at the Berlin Seminary which indirectly influenced the later course of Michael Solomon Alexander's life. In that year von Schirnding went bankrupt, and the institution came under the patronage of the King of Prussia, Frederick William III. Henceforth the royal family became more aware of German evangelical initiatives overseas. Also in 1801 one of the early candidates who went from Berlin to London to gain further training for overseas mission work was a Jewish believer in Jesus named Joseph Frey.[19] The LMS had requested three

---

www.smu.edu/bidwell/html/Manuscript Collection.htm#Thaweis.

[15] C. Hole, *Early History of the Church Missionary Society for Africa and the East to the end of AD 1814* (Church Missionary Society, London, 1896), p. 82.
[16] Hole, *ibid*, pp 82-3.
[17] At that time he was pastoring Berlin's Bethlehem Church.
[18] This Seminary was founded in 1816 by Christoph Gottlieb Blumhardt, as a training arm of the Basel Mission which he established in 1815.
[19] Joseph Samuel Christian Frederick Frey was born at Mainstockheim near Kitzingen in the province of Franconia in 1771. He had intended becoming a

missionaries to come to London for further training, and then to travel on to Africa to assist Dr. van der Kemp. Frey was one of the three chosen and left for England in July of the same year.

While in London Frey believed he was to remain there and bring the message of Jesus to the Jewish people in London's squalid East End. [20] He presented his vision to the LMS leaders, who permitted him to stay. Initially though Frey needed to study English, and was also sent to study under David Bogue, a LMS founder, at Gosport.

Frey and his vision, was in a sense a culmination of much which represented the German and the British evangelical, pietist streams, which now also included that interest in the Jewish people, which was espoused by the Puritans as well as Spener, Callenberg and the Moravians. It was a bridging of the British and the German evangelical movements.

From 1805 Frey entered upon his task in London, under the sponsorship of the LMS. It soon became apparent to him however that his philosophy of ministry differed from that of the parent society. He felt it was important to have a different approach to Jewish ministry from that applied to gentile based ministry.

With the support of several others he set up in 1808 a committee for specific work amongst the Jewish people. The parent society did not agree to this arrangement, so in 1809 the independent London Society for Promoting Christianity amongst the Jews (or London Jews Society) was established.

One of the first supporters of this pioneer initiative was William Wilberforce, MP, the prime agitator against slavery. Another pioneer member was the Rev. William Marsh[21] of Basildon, (later destined to play an important role in the life of Michael Solomon Alexander) who gave the anniversary sermon in 1812.

---

rabbi like his father, Samuel Levi, but instead heard about Jesus as Messiah from a Lutheran merchant, and confessed faith in 1798 in New Brandenburg. He initially worked under the Moravians before moving to Berlin. Frey moved to America in 1816 and became pastor of the Mulberry Street Congregationalist Church in New York in 1818. In 1820 he founded the American Society for Meliorating the Condition of the Jews. He died on 5 June 1850.

[20] Rev. J. Dunlop, *Memories of Gospel Triumphs amongst the Jews,* (London, 1894), p. 10.

[21] Marsh then became a Country Director (similar to area representative today) of the LJS in 1813. Marsh was regarded as a leading evangelical of the time, and was also an early speaker at the LJS annual meeting in 1812. By 1816 Marsh was a Trustee of the Society. By the early 1820's he was minister at Colchester in Essex.

The London Jews Society or LJS as it was commonly known, became the platform for all those, both Anglican and non-Conformist, who were interested in Israel's restoration. It was seemingly appropriate that a Jewish believer in Jesus, from Germany, with associations with the Lutheran and Moravian Churches, would be the initiator of this new and bold endeavour.

Almost immediately the LJS launched into a major project, the building of a large complex to be their centre known as Palestine Place. But this, and other projects, in the midst of the Napoleonic Wars, caused grave financial difficulties. It was decided that both parties, the Anglicans and the non-Conformists each had to raise a certain amount of money.

The non-Conformists failed to reach their objective, while the Anglicans, primarily through the benevolence of Lewis Way,[22] a devout LJS supporter, were able to raise their amount. This factor, combined with various theological issues, saw the Society in 1815 become fully affiliated with the Anglican Church.

Napoleon Invades the Eastern Mediterranean

Political life throughout Europe during this period was greatly influenced by the Napoleonic regime. Already in pre-Napoleonic France emancipation or freedom from the narrow confines of the ghettos had been granted to the Jewish people. Napoleon furthered this movement, emancipating the Jewish people of Italy following his victories there in 1797.

In 1798 Napoleon led a large force to the East, ostensibly to establish a base in Egypt, from where he would attack the British in India.[23] For politically motivated reasons he made numerous concessions to the minority groups, including the Jews, hoping to make them his allies.

But Britain was not going to allow the French to severe her vital link to India. Admiral Horatio Nelson was dispatched in hot pursuit of Napoleon's fleet. Napoleon had landed his ground forces and was

---

[22] Lewis Way (1772-1840), inherited a fortunate from John Way, no relation, and believed he was to invest much of this in a venture supporting the Jewish people. The LJS was the benefactor. He became an early spokesman for the LJS. In 1817 he spoke to the Czar of Russia on behalf of the Jewish people, and spoke on their behalf to the assembled leaders of Europe at the peace conference at Aix le Chapelle in 1818. He was involved in the LJS until his death, although the relationship became somewhat strained towards the end.

[23] See G. M. Trevelyan, *The History of England*, (Longmans, Green and Co, London, 1948), p. 576.

conquering a large Mameluke[24] force near Cairo when Nelson, in August 1798, located the French fleet nestling in the quiet waters of Aboukir Bay east of Alexandria. While Napoleon was gloating in a land victory near Cairo, Nelson surprised and destroyed most of the French fleet.

His fleet gone, Napoleon set out in early 1799 in command of a vast army, initially to conquer the Turkish Empire and then to march upon India. His quick movement north however was thwarted at the gates of Acre, the main seaport on the Levantine coast.

While awaiting the arrival of reinforcements, Napoleon defeated a large Turkish force at Mount Tabor[25] near Nazareth in April 1799. Gloating in this victory he then made his famous declaration calling upon the Israelites to return to the land of their forefathers.[26]

Napoleon was never able to put this plan into effect, as a British led force joined with the Turkish defenders of Acre and repulsed him. Nevertheless this Napoleonic decree furthered the call for Israel's restoration. Henceforth numerous British Christians began to sense that the time for Israel's regathering was close at hand.

One non-Conformist, a Baptist minister named James Bicheno, wrote:

> ... the result of the expedition of the French in the East may...not lead directly to the casting out of the Turks from Egypt and Syria, and to the restoration of the Jewish people to their own land; but these events [the casting out of the Turks and restoration of Israel] *may be brought about in a more circuitous way, and by means and instruments not thought of...*[27]

The French venture radically altered the geo-political situation in the Levant. Britain, incensed at how easily a rival European power could challenge her link to India, kept a watchful eye thereafter on events in the region. Britain's policy henceforth was to ensure the French never again gained access to that same region and that her other main rival, Russia, would never have easy access from the Black Sea to the Mediterranean via the Bosphorus and Dardanelles.

---

[24] The Mamelukes controlled Egypt from the mid 13th century until 1811. They were descended from freed Turkish slaves, and following the Crusader period, controlled the Land of Israel until conquered by the Ottoman Turks in 1517.

[25] A mount in the Jezreel Valley near to Nazareth where many believe the Transfiguration took place.

[26] See Note 11 of Introduction.

[27] James Bicheno, *The Restoration of the Jews, And the Crisis of all Nations,* (London, 1800), p. 111.

Conditions for Jewish People in Prussia and Posen

Napoleon's positive sentiments towards the Jewish people did bear fruit in Europe, for in areas occupied by French forces they received emancipation, or freedom from life in the ghetto to which they had been confined for centuries.

France's defeat of Prussia in 1812 dramatically affected this militarily proud nation. In consequence of these events a major Christian revival broke out in Berlin, influencing a large number of senior officials and army officers. It also led to King Frederick William III introducing an 'edict of emancipation' for the Jewish residents of Prussia.[28] Jacob Jocz wrote that this edict 'raised the Jews of Prussian citizenship and opened their way to greater opportunities.'[29]

Following the defeat of Napoleon in 1815 however, there was a rise of German nationalism, which caused distress to some Jewish communities in Prussia. Despite this setback greater opportunities opened for the Jewish people to be accepted into the host German culture. But in many cases such a radical move was synonymous to conversion into the host church, which in the German setting, was primarily the Lutheran Church.[30] Whether out of social necessity or personal desire, many Jewish people now became familiar with the New Testament and the teachings and doctrine of the German Evangelical Church.

Although Berlin was relatively close to the village of Schonlanke, it is doubtful if the effects of these changes ever influenced the small Jewish community there. Michael Solomon Alexander later confessed about his early life in Posen, 'that until that time I had not the slightest knowledge of Christianity, nor did I even know of the existence of the New Testament.'[31]

Nor did he know of Jesus, of whom he wrote:

> Strong impressions of prejudice against the very name of Christ was all the knowledge I possessed of him, and in blindness, and ignorance, I never felt curious to inquire the reason of that prejudice. I looked upon all other sects besides Jews, as the Gentile idolators mentioned by Moses and the

---

[28] Clark, *ibid,* p. 86.

[29] J. Jocz, *The Jewish People and Jesus Christ,* (London, 1962), pp. 100-1.

[30] It was during this period, especially in 1817, under the reign of King Frederick William III that a series of decrees were passed to combine the Lutheran and Reformed (Calvinist) Churches into a United Evangelical Church of Germany.

[31] J. Hatchard, *The Predictions and Promises of God Respecting Israel, (Appendix),* (London 1825), p. 37.

Prophets, from whom I found sufficient reasons and commands to abhor their practices.[32]

A later acquaintance, Rev. James Cartwright, recalled Alexander's boyhood observations:

Of Christianity he had no other idea than that which he had derived from the slanderous traditions of the Talmud,[33] occasionally illustrated by a passing view of a Romish procession in honour of some saint in his native town; and he regarded it accordingly as idolatry, to be abhorred by every faithful Israelite.[34]

It would appear therefore that Michael Solomon Alexander lived a traditional Jewish life in Schonlanke and was educated, in his own words, 'principally in the Talmud and in the strictest principles of Judaism.'[35] At age sixteen (in 1815) he was already a teacher of the Talmud and German language.[36]

In 1817 Rabbi Alexander died and his eldest son succeeded to the position of rabbi. This eldest son was, in the words of his niece, Deborah Ransom (nee Alexander) 'a terrible bigot.'[37] At this juncture Michael Solomon, being the second son, and perhaps somewhat disorientated, immersed himself in Jewish law in an attempt to determine his position within the family and community. He spent many hours pouring over the minutiae of Jewish law, and in the process he apparently became dissatisfied with his traditional faith system.

It seems that his eldest brother, now Rabbi Alexander, detected his younger brother's growing inquisitiveness and restlessness, and questioned him. Alexander the elder was horrified to hear that Michael Solomon dared question the authority of the Talmud. The elder Alexander gave his

---

[32] Hatchard, *ibid*, p. 37.

[33] Talmud is ancient Jewish commentary on Scripture and is comprised of two parts, the Mishna (the whole code of Jewish law) and Gemara (a commentary of Mishna).

[34] Sermon of Rev. James Cartwright, Episcopal Jews Chapel London, 28 December 1845, in *JI*, 1846, p. 58.

[35] Hatchard, *ibid*, p. 38.

[36] See Sermon of Rev. James Cartwright, Episcopal Jews Chapel London, 28 December 1845, in *JI*, 1846, p. 58; and Hatchard, *ibid*.

[37] D. R. M Ransom, *Life of Mrs. Ransom,* (London, 1913, unpublished manuscript, copy in author's possession), p. 5.

younger brother an ultimatum - desist from this questioning, or leave. Michael Solomon chose the latter.[38]

Leaving Posen, Alexander the younger chose to head to his father's homeland, England, where he hoped to teach German and the Talmud.

Prior to his departure Michael Solomon prepared himself for an uncertain future by attaining the position of *shochet* or ritual slaughterer. According to his own words this was 'given to persons peculiarly qualified, and who must go through the strictest examination by the High Priest.'[39]

---

[38] M. Corey, *From Rabbi to Bishop*, (London, 1956), p. 9.
[39] Hatchard, *ibid, (Appendix)*, p. 37. High Priest refers to senior or chief Rabbi.

Chapter 2

Seeking Refuge in England: 1820 - 1824

Arrival in England – Colchester and Norwich.
The young Michael Solomon Alexander arrived in England in 1820,[1] where he immediately encountered a set back. The anticipated work as a teacher of German and the Talmud fell through. He applied to Solomon Hirschel, Chief Rabbi of the Polish and German Jewish communities in England[2] for work. Rabbi Hirschel appointed him as a private tutor to the children of a Jewish family in Colchester, Essex. Of his future employer, Michael Solomon stated: 'My employer was a man of strict integrity, and strongly attached to the principles and ceremonies of Judaism.'[3] It would appear that Alexander's feet had fallen on solid traditional ground.

Such was not to be. His move to Colchester was one of those decisions that would radically alter Michael Solomon's life and future. It was here that he became acquainted with Rev. William Marsh, who was rector of St. Peter's Church in Colchester.[4] Marsh, unbeknown to the young Alexander, was a prominent and active member of the London Jews Society. No wonder then, that on one occasion Marsh spoke to Alexander about the New Testament. Alexander however claimed ignorance of both it and the English language.

Soon after, Michael Solomon saw an advertisement concerning the London Jews Society on a billboard. He thereupon asked his employer what it meant. Alexander wrote that his employer:

---

[1] According to Alexander himself [Hatchard, *ibid, Appendix*, p. 37], although according to Brian Taylor, *Alexander's Apostasy: First Steps to Jerusalem*, in *Christianity and Judaism,* Ecclesiastical Historical Society, (Blackwell Publishers, Oxford, 1992), it was 1819.

[2] Hirschel was in this position from 1802-1842.

[3] Hatchard, *ibid,* p. 37.

[4] Marsh was a close associate of the LJS and friend of evangelical and LJS stalwart, Charles Simeon. Simeon had influenced Marsh about interest in the Jewish people. Later, while rector of St. Thomas's in Birmingham, Marsh was affectionately known as 'Millenial Marsh.' Taylor, *ibid,* p. 365.

...was the first who acquainted me with the exertions which are making in England for the conversion of the Jews, but treated them with derision, and said that every Jew ought to read the New Testament, in order to be more convinced in his own religion.[5]

Alexander wrote of his response to this challenge:

This roused my curiosity, and not able then to read and understand English, I procured a German Bible. I was greatly struck with the first chapter of St. Matthew, and had no idea that Christians knew anything of our patriarchs; - I was still more struck with the character of Christ, and the excellent morals which he taught; but having gone no further than merely to admire them, it produced no particular effect upon my mind, though it considerably lessened my prejudices.[6]

Alexander now found himself in a similar situation to what he had been in Posen. He began reading the New Testament with the same inquisitive mind as he had the Talmud while in Schonlanke.

About 1822 the Chief Rabbi appointed Alexander to be Rabbi of Norwich[7] a move that Michael Solomon viewed as 'the Providence of God.'[8] Of his position as rabbi Alexander stated: 'This appellation is commonly given to those who are appointed in a Jewish congregation to perform their sacred duties, without any degree or order.'[9]

The small synagogue was located in the churchyard of St. George's Church, and opposite the local Anglican Cathedral. If Alexander thought

---

[5] Hatchard, *ibid*, p. 38.

[6] *ibid*, p. 38.

[7] Patrick Irwin, *Bishop Alexander and the Jews of Jerusalem*, in Studies in Church History, Vol. 21: Persecution and Toleration, ed. W.J.Shields, (Oxford 1984), p. 317 & Taylor, *ibid*, p. 366. Malcolm Brown contends that 'at Norwich he is more likely to have acted as no more than *hazan* and or *shocket* in the early 1820's.' Malcolm Brown, *The Jews of Norfolk and Suffolk before 1840* in Jewish Historical Society. Transactions of The Jewish Historical Society of England, volume 32, 1990-92 p. 231. Brown, refuting the reference to Alexander being a rabbi from the *Jewish Repository* 1840, p. 240, also likened him to being an itinerant or peripatetic.

[8] Hatchard, *ibid*, p. 38.

[9] *ibid*, p. 38.

he was escaping Christian contact by moving from Colchester, he was rudely awakened by this unlikely location.[10]

Alexander said of his time in Norwich that he also 'had opportunity and leisure to give lessons in Hebrew and German, as I had then obtained some knowledge of the English language.'[11]   His improvement in English he wrote, 'afforded me the means of access to many pious Christians.'[12] It would be hard not to, due to the location of the synagogue!

He now became even more familiar with the Christian faith, and he wrote: 'I was in an especial manner led to read the New Testament, and found many of the references there given to the Old Testament prophecies, incontrovertibly fulfilled.'[13]

In all likelihood one of those 'pious' Christians he met was a Miss Hancock. In latter years Miss Hancock of Norwich (who seemingly was an invalid, as was her mother) communicated consistently with Alexander, and by all accounts she was very well versed in the prophecies concerning Israel's restoration.[14]

The familiarity these Christians had with certain Old Testament prophecies that Michael Solomon knew well, and which the Christians believed as being fulfilled in Jesus, greatly perplexed him. More than perplexing him, he was becoming quite confused and disorientated by these new interpretations. Of this challenging period he stated that he 'endeavoured to shrink and turn away from the divine light which had thus begun to dawn upon me.'[15] More than merely shrinking from this challenge, Michael Solomon needed escape from it.

A Move to Plymouth

Just such an escape was provided by the Chief Rabbi, who in 1823 recommended Alexander for the position of *Shochet* and Prayer-reader in Plymouth.[16] This recommendation was made for a dual purpose. Firstly it

---

[10] The Synagogue was also located in the area rather unfortunately known as Tombland. It was not used after 1849. Today it is the offices of Saunders & Senior Solicitors.

[11] Hatchard, *ibid*, p.38. *Norwich Chronicle,* 6 July and 28 December 1822. See also Malcolm Brown, *ibid,* p. 233.

[12] Hatchard, *ibid, (Appendix),* p. 38.

[13] *ibid,* p. 38.

[14] See Hancock to Alexander, 1 October 1830, MSS 3397, 136-7, Alexander Papers, Lambeth Palace Archives. [Henceforth 'Lambeth'].

[15] Hatchard, *ibid,* p. 38.

[16] There was no official rabbi in Plymouth between 1815-1829. A *shochet* was appointed in 1822, perhaps Alexander's predecessor. His task was not only to

was seen as being more advantageous for him and secondly, in Alexander's own words: 'I felt to become reconciled to my former views, and regain my peace of mind, with a full determination to have no intercourse with Christians.'[17]

The *parnos* or head of the Synagogue at Plymouth was in London at the time Michael Solomon's appointment was under discussion. And while others also had an eye on employing the talented young German, the Plymouth representative succeeded in obtaining Alexander's services.

Alexander was very happy with the appointment, and was shortly en-route to Plymouth. On arrival, the *parnos* took him to the home of his mother-in-law, Mrs. Levi. It was at this first meeting that Alexander met Mrs. Levi's daughter, Deborah, a young woman to whom he obviously felt an immediate attraction. Deborah later wrote of this first meeting:

> I was in the drawing-room, and the moment I saw him, I thought how superior he was, and he thought the same of me, as he afterwards told me, he made up his mind to get me if he could.[18]

In fact only three months later Alexander gave her an official letter of proposal, in very good English. Three days later they were officially engaged.

Re-introduction to Messiah Jesus

For the first three months of his residence in Plymouth, Alexander kept strictly to his resolution to have no contact with Christians. But then he was asked to give Hebrew lessons to Rev. Benjamin Bass Golding, curate of St George's Church (or Chapel) in Stonehouse.[19] Together they studied the Old Testament, which eventually involved looking at the prophecies of the person and coming of the Messiah. It must have seemed like a bad dream initially to Alexander, considering it was for this very reason he wanted to flee from Norwich. Yet it was during this time that he came 'almost to the conviction that Jesus was the Messiah.'[20] Alexander now

---

slaughter animals but also to assist the *hazzan* or cantor, and teach the children for two hours on Sunday, Monday, Tuesday and Wednesday mornings. See Taylor, *ibid*, p. 367.

[17] Hatchard, *ibid,* p. 38.

[18] Deborah Alexander, *Autobiography*, MSS 3394, p. 8, Lambeth.

[19] St. George's Church in Chapel Street, Stonehouse, erected in 1789, no longer exists. It was partly destroyed in the Blitz and its remaining stones were used in the repair of St. Andrews.

[20] Hatchard, *ibid,* p. 39.

entered into a deep internal conflict. He would secretly go down to Stonehouse Church on Sunday evenings 'and under the shadow of its walls listen to the psalms and hymns.'[21]

He lost his contentment as he wrestled with the conviction of Jesus as Messiah. Finally while walking with Deborah at Stoke, he presented her a pamphlet explaining how a German Jew named Joseph Wolff[22] had come to believe that Jesus was the Messiah.[23]

Deborah told her mother about this unexpected development. Mrs. Levi was even more distraught than her daughter, which influenced Deborah in writing a letter to break off the engagement. Yet Alexander's love for her had not changed. In speaking to her mother he said: 'Did I believe the Christian religion to be the true one, I would embrace it at all costs.'[24]

When news spread of Michael Solomon's interest in Jesus, the family adopted a negative attitude towards him. Deborah's brother-in-law, the one who had introduced Alexander to Plymouth, declared that the marriage must not take place. Yet Michael Solomon and Deborah continued writing to each other. In these letters he asked her to read certain passages in Isaiah, which she did in secret. Deborah was slowly coming to the same realization as Alexander. Her mother detected a change in her daughter, and subsequently gave her a very difficult time. Mrs. Deborah Ransom, daughter of Alexander, wrote of this period many years later:

> Papa and Mama both suffered persecution for their faith. Mama was shut up a whole winter's night in the drawing-room with no covering but the hearth rug, as her mother vainly hoped that by that course Mama would give up her fiancé (Papa), who had been for many months unsettled in his belief.[25]

Deborah's brother and sister also tried to get her to give up Michael Solomon. At this point Deborah seems to have told them that they were going the right way to cause her to follow in Michael Solomon's footsteps. This apparently caused her relatives to change tactics and permitted her to

---

[21] Corey, *ibid*, p. 13.
[22] Joseph Wolff was born in 1795 in the Bavarian village of Weilersbach, his father being the local rabbi. He came to faith in Jesus in 1812 joining first the Catholic Church and later the Anglican Church. He was a pioneer missionary for the LJS. Wolff died in England in 1862.
[23] Corey, *ibid*, p. 13.
[24] Corey, *ibid*, p. 15.
[25] Ransom, *ibid*, p. 6.

see him again. Over the following thirteen months, consent to marry was given and withdrawn on several occasions.

This was indeed a trying time for Alexander. He wrote in July 1824 to Golding, who had moved to Kingston-upon-Thames, in response to a letter he had received from Golding:

> I can assure you my dear friend, that it [Golding's letter] was as a healing medicine to me, as it met me in the midst of affliction and trouble in body and soul, at the same time it did not less affect me, as it brought to my mind the happy and instructive intercourses which I enjoyed, while you were here, and of which I am now deprived of. I can impossibly express how much I did and do still feel your absence, for though I am happy and grateful to say, that the Lord is dealing graciously with me, in enlightening my understanding more & more; still at the same time, Satan is not backward in using his instruments & Power to raise difficulties & Doubts in my mind, in order to destroy my happiness and peace, which I am so far convinced is only to be found in true conviction and dependence on Him, who is gracious to all his followers.[26]

Marriage

In the same letter to Golding, Alexander indicated that Mrs. Levi's harsh attitude and interference had basically forced them to marry sooner than he would have desired. The marriage took place according to Jewish tradition under the *huppa* on 3 November 1824,[27] at the Crown Hotel in Devonport, a village across the waterway from Stonehouse and Plymouth. Forty-six guests attended the wedding and the ball that followed.

The Alexanders lived in Plymouth for several months. During this time Captain Thicknesse of the Royal Navy (Stonehouse Church was located close to the naval docks) often visited him. On one occasion Thicknesse loaned him an account of a rabbi who believed in Jesus as Messiah, named Rabbi Solomon Druitch [sic]. Alexander wrote: ' I derived much benefit by it, as it is very much according with my history.'[28] Alexander found himself going through a difficult period as he was confronted with breaking away from Orthodox Judaism. His despondency often returned.

Finally, Alexander confided his struggles in an old learned Jewish man. It was a mistake, as the old man exploded with rage. Before long the Chief

---

[26] Alexander to Golding, 23 July 1824, MSS 3393, 1-2, Lambeth.

[27] Taylor, *ibid*, p. 367. It was reported in the *Plymouth and Devonport Journal* on 11 November 1824.

[28] Alexander to Golding, 23 July 1824, MSS 3393 [1-2], Lambeth.

Rabbi became aware of Alexander's spiritual struggle. Rabbi Hirschel 'treated it as a temptation of the devil, and wrote to Alexander begging him to go before the Ark in the synagogue and curse the God of the Christians.'[29]

Pressure now mounted for Michael Solomon to return to the Jewish community. But Alexander's dilemma was accurately appraised by one Jewish man, Mr. Altmann, who asked him 'if he believed Jesus of Nazareth was the messiah.' Alexander replied: 'That is the difficulty, and on this I cannot make up my mind.'[30]

This sentiment summed up Alexander's predicament. Yet he was not without encouragement. During this difficult period he received letters not only from Golding, but also from Marsh, and he continued his correspondence with Miss Hancock to whom he wrote on 7 September 1824:

> I am only happy to say, that we are both growing stronger in the truths of Xnty [Christianity – ed] & in seeing our former Blindness, but I am sorry to say that I have not at present strength enough to open my mind publicly, our principal feast & the day Atonement will be in a fortnight and I shall have more opportunity then to declare my sentiments, whereas if I should do it now I should be too much persecuted, and I do not know how I should bear it myself.

Alexander also said that there were two or three people who knew of his sentiments, but they did not say anything publicly about them. 'I trust, in respect of that,' he wrote to Miss Hancock, 'the Lord will soon give me strength & Spirit that I may declare his name among my Brethren & unto kings and not be ashamed.'[31]

---

[29] Corey, *ibid*, p. 18.

[30] *ibid*, p. 18.

[31] Alexander to Miss Hancock, 7 September 1824, MSS 3393 [3-4], Lambeth.

Chapter 3

The Messiah He is: 1824 - 1825

Coming to Faith

Despite Alexander's previous disclosure that only two or three people knew of his present persuasion, it was soon apparent that the entire Jewish community was aware of it. Although they were loath to lose Alexander, action needed to be taken. The synagogue elders consulted Chief Rabbi Solomon Hirschel again, and Hirschel temporarily suspended Alexander from office. Michael Solomon wrote of this period:

> This was one of the most painful periods of my life; Satan stirred up every possible means to present fears and doubts to me.
>
> Those who are acquainted with human nature, and with the influence of early education, will easily be able to judge in what a painful situation I was then placed – by following the dictates of my conscience, I had nothing else to expect than to lose all that was valuable to me in this world, a comfortable and sufficient livelihood, together with the affections and friendship of all who were dear to me – but by yielding to the entreaties of my friends I should have inflicted a wound upon my conscience – in short, many painful ideas presented themselves to me...[1]

He added as a footnote to the above struggle, 'that so great was the struggle and so earnest the entreaties of my friends at that time, that I was even induced to appeal personally, and also by letter, to the leader of the congregation to say, that I should be happy to retrace my steps, if any means could be found to remove the difficulties by which I was encompassed.'[2]

To compound Michael Solomon's situation, Deborah's relatives now pressured her to leave him. On one occasion her mother came to Plymouth from Devonport to visit, and upon hearing that her daughter would not

---

[1] Hatchard, *ibid,* p. 40.
[2] *ibid,* p. 40.

leave her husband, the exasperated mother began wailing as if for the dead. Mrs. Levi left the house threatening to drown herself, but Michael Solomon followed her from a discrete distance and ensured she arrived home safely.[3]

Michael Solomon's search for spiritual truth led him more and more into the open. This search was in a sense determined for him by his suspension from office. He then regularly attended St. Andrews Church (located adjacent to the Synagogue) and heard 'a dear friend,' undoubtedly Rev. John Hatchard,[4] preach. Concerning the 'spiritual instruction' he received from this man, Alexander said he was 'greatly indebted.'[5] Then on Good Friday 1825 he walked with a friend, Lucit Rhind, to nearby Plympton and heard a sermon on the text from John 3:14: 'As Moses lifted up the serpent in the wilderness, even so must the Son of Man be lifted up.'[6]

Shaken by the rebuffs, and challenged by his quest for truth, Alexander continued to read through the *Tenach*[7] and New Testament, aided by Golding, Hatchard, Thicknesse and John Synge from Ireland.[8] By mid 1825 Michael Solomon came to the realization that Jesus fulfilled the Messianic prophecies.

The baptism was set for 22 June 1825. As could be expected tensions were high, especially considering that St. Andrews was adjacent to the Synagogue where Alexander had officiated. On the night before the baptism there was a failed attempt to kidnap Deborah. That same night the maid overheard two Jewish people say: 'If that apostate will be baptized, I will set fire to his house if I die for it. He shall not disgrace our holy religion.'[9] The Alexanders spent the night at the Hatchard's house. Several Jews came asking the maid if the Alexanders were home, and when told they were not, the visitors left.

---

[3] Corey, *ibid,* p. 19.

[4] John Hatchard had only recently arrived at St. Andrews in August 1824.

[5] Hatchard, *ibid,* p. 40.

[6] Corey, *ibid,* p. 19. Deborah Alexander, *ibid,* p. 19. There are two churches he could have visited, St Mary's or St. Maurice.

[7] Tenach, the Old Testament. Tenach is an acronym for T = Torah, N = the Neviim [Prophets], and CH = Chetovim [the Writings].

[8] John Synge was from Glanmore Castle in Ireland and was in Plymouth for the benefit of his wife's health. Synge was a member of the Church of Ireland Jews Society Committee since 1822. He was related to the famous Irish playwright, John. Millington Synge.

[9] Corey, *ibid,* p. 20.

Baptism

The service at St. Andrews, was very well attended. Rev. Robert Lampen read the prayers, while Captain Thicknesse and Rev. Benjamin Golding (temporarily back in Stonehouse) were his sponsors. Deborah attended the service, but was almost in a state of shock throughout.

Hatchard preached quite a powerful and challenging sermon, from Hosea 3:4-5, entitled: 'The Children of Israel shall abide many days ...' He then provided a profound historical analysis of the Jewish nation, of their receiving God's promises and mercies, and then turning away and provoking God to anger, culminating in the rejection of Jesus the Messiah, 'the man who was Jehovah's fellow.'[10]

But it was his in-depth description of the future restoration of Israel that was most stirring. Concerning the second part of Hosea's prophecy, 'they shall return in the latter days,' Hatchard proclaimed:

> It has been considered by some that the predictions and promises respecting the restoration of the house of Israel, received their full accomplishment in their return from captivity in Babylon, therefore, no further manifestation of mercy shall be made on behalf of those, who for so long a series of years, were the unthankful and rebellious recipients of the favours of the Lord of Hosts.
>
> The testimony of both the Old and New Testament scriptures expressly shows, that 'God hath *not* cast away his people which he foreknew' [Romans 11:2] for although 'as concerning the gospel they are enemies for your sakes; but as touching the election, they are beloved for the father's sake.'
>
> What saith the Holy Ghost by the prophet Jeremiah? 'I will gather them out of all countries whither I have driven them in mine anger, and in my fury, and in great wrath; and I will bring them again unto this place and I will cause them to dwell safely; and they shall be my people, and I will be their God: and I will give them one heart, and one way, that they may fear me *fore ever*...so will I bring upon them all the good that I have promised them.' [chapt. 32:42,47].
>
> This most gracious promise assuredly has not yet been fulfilled respecting our elder brethren, the Jews – for they *have* departed from the Lord – the *everlasting* covenant here promised to be made unto them, has *not* been entered into; and therefore we confidently anticipate the arrival of the period when the Jew and the Gentile shall be found in one fold under one shepherd, even Jesus Christ the mediator of this new, this better, this everlasting covenant.'

---

[10] Hatchard, *ibid,* p. 12.

Leaving Jeremiah, Hatchard turned to Ezekiel and addressed the issue of the dry bones of Israel, as well as explaining certain restorationist promises in Micah and Zechariah.[11] Hatchard then proclaimed:

> Thus too the apostle Paul, in the 9th, 10th and 11th chapters of his epistle to the Romans, most clearly demonstrates that he looked forward with delight and gratification to the period when his brethren should be saved – when the receiving of them should be, as life from the dead.[12]

Hatchard then addressed the issue of why they were gathered together in St. Andrews on that day. He continued:

> If the conversion of a soul from the ways of sin to the ways of righteousness is a matter upon which there is joy among the angels in heaven, surely when the vail which remaineth upon the children of Israel is done away in Christ, it is a cause for *peculiar* thankfulness unto him...Such an event, my Christian brethren, I have this day the delight to announce to you – A member of the house of Israel, will at this time 'Subscribe with his hand unto the Lord, and surname himself by the name of Israel [Isaiah 45.5].

Hatchard then challenged any Jewish people then present to be like the Bereans[13] of old and search the Scriptures – as Alexander himself had so painstakingly done over a period of years. He also challenged the Christians present to 'pray for the long neglected and widely scattered nation of Israel', stating, 'be assured, our Zion cannot become the praise of the whole earth, until the remnant of Israel and Judah be brought in – the language of prophecy, the signs of the times, the event of this memorable day, all conspire to animate the Christian heart, and ought to encourage us in the use of every means for the consummation of that era, when both to the Jew and the gentile, Christ shall be all and in all.'[14]

His final challenge was to Alexander himself, commissioning him to walk steadfastly before the Lord, and to 'give no rest day or night unto

---

[11] Ezekiel 37; Micah 4:42; Zechariah 8:10; 12:10. The prophecy of the dry bones refers to an Israel destitute of life, but when the Spirit of God comes upon these dry bones, Israel rises to new life.

[12] Hatchard, *ibid*, pp. 24-25.

[13] When Paul presented the message of Jesus to the Jewish people of Berea in Greece, 'they received the message with great eagerness and examined the Scriptures every day to see if what Paul said was true.' Acts 17:11.

[14] Hatchard, *ibid*, pp. 30-31.

God until he make Jerusalem the joy of the whole earth.' This however was followed by an admonition:

> Be assured your friends, your enemies, the world at large, angels in heaven, and the condemned spirits in hell, will be carefully marking the line of conduct you pursue, many I trust will follow you with their prayers, whilst others will not be deficient in zeal to draw you aside from the path into which you are now entering; but fear not, greater is he who is for you than all who are against you.[15]

Alexander was also encouraged to pray for his brethren according to the flesh.[16] The historical record indeed would reveal to us that Alexander would not forsake his people, and would continually labour and pray for the house of Israel, and that indeed all the parties mentioned would closely scrutinize his movements, especially after November 1841.

Concerning this most extraordinary service, the local newspaper *The Plymouth and Devonport Weekly Journal,* wrote:

> Mr. Alexander, late Reader to the Jewish congregation in this town, and who has held other offices of character and respectability among the Jews, was baptised in the Christian Faith, by the Rev. Mr. Hatchard, in the presence of an immense congregation who appeared to take great interest in the ceremony.[17]

Many Christians were intrigued by the event, but it shocked the local Jewish community. To an extent that shock remains until today. Brian Taylor, writing of the contemporary congregation at Plymouth, said:

> It is mortifying to the Hebrew congregation that its existence is mostly known not for its historic and architectural importance, but in connection with the defection of one of its ministers, Michael Solomon Alexander, in 1825.[18]

Michael Solomon Alexander had again challenged the established *status quo.*

---

[15] Hatchard, *ibid,* p. 35.
[16] *ibid,* p. 34.
[17] *ibid,* p. 40.
[18] Taylor, *ibid,* p. 363.

Exeter and Deborah's Baptism

That night the Alexanders stayed at the vicarage at Stonehouse with Golding. The following day they proceeded to stay with a Mr. and Mrs. Groves in Exeter.[19] This turned out to be a rather unpleasant ordeal as the hosts did not treat the young Alexander couple at all well. This deplorable situation resulted in Alexander writing to Golding, who in turn came to Exeter to visit them. Shortly afterwards, Alexander sold his books and furniture and gave up his house in Plymouth. They then moved into lodgings near St. Sidewell's parish church in Exeter.[20]

Not surprisingly Alexander's health began to decline. The stress and pressure of the preceding months must have been almost unbearable upon the young former rabbi. He wrote to Golding on 5 July 1825 that since coming to Exeter he had experienced much despair, 'my struggles of mind have been great since I came to Exeter. I do not find that spiritual comfort here,' he wrote, 'especially on account of Mrs. Alicarz [sic].' He continued and mentioned just how much he needed the Spirit and stated how much he missed the communications and instructions from Golding and Hatchard, and also made special mention of 'our dear friends Mr. and Mrs. Synge.'[21]

Alexander was now cut off from the Christians who had helped him through the difficult situation at Plymouth. It was indeed a testing time for his faith. Thankfully there were sympathetic people who could support the couple and a Miss Paget lent him her pony and he went riding each day for three months which assisted him in recuperating his health. It would not be the first occasion that Alexander would suffer health problems.

Meanwhile Deborah, obviously deeply impressed by the tremendous changes in her husband's life, continued her reading of the Scriptures. Michael Solomon wrote to Golding on 30 September 1825: 'I have much less earthly care and I find myself nearer to the Lord.' He wrote how appreciative he was of his wife's own journey of faith, and that she was:

---

[19] So states Corey, *ibid*, p. 24. Alexander himself wrote on one occasion that he was much in despair 'especially on account of Mrs. Alicarz [sic] (Alexander to Golding, 5 July 1825, MSS 3393 [5-6]), Lambeth. On another occasion he stated how he was very fond of Mr. and Mrs. Graves [sic Groves]. See Alexander to Golding, 30 September 1825, MSS 3393 [7], Lambeth.

[20] The original St. Sidewells, on Sidewell Street in the centre of Exeter is no longer extant.

[21] Alexander to Golding, 5 July 1825, MSS 3393 [5-6], Lambeth. It is hard to determine exactly who Mrs. Alicarz is. Perhaps he meant Mrs. Groves.

Much advanced in spiritual knowledge & comfort, I can truly say now, she is a great help for me, she is fully determined by the blessing of the Lord to dedicate herself to him by baptism, which I hope will take place a day or two before we leave Exeter, at the next Jewish meeting which will be on the 27th of October, when Mr. Hawtrey and Mr. Marsh will be here, and after that we expect to go to Dublin.[22]

The Alexanders were also expecting their good friends Mr. and Mrs. Hatchard and Mr. and Mrs. Synge at Deborah's baptism. Unfortunately this happy occasion had to be postponed for several months for on 11 October 1825 Deborah prematurely gave birth to twin girls. The stress of the events of the previous months, as well as childbirth then seriously affected her health, and she became perilously ill, almost to the point of dying. Unfortunately, though, the babies died and Miss Paget obtained a nurse who brought Deborah back to health.

Despite all of the suffering and anxiety, which included being separated from her family, Deborah, upon her full recovery became fully convinced that Jesus indeed was the promised Messiah. She was baptized at All Hallows Church in Goldsmith Street[23] in Exeter, on 9 November 1825 – some five months after her husband. Golding and Synge were present, and Hatchard assisted with conducting the service.[24]

In many ways this was the perfect setting for Deborah's baptism after all their ordeals. She was away from the scrutiny of family and friends in Plymouth and in the presence of so many of their friends and supporters.

---

[22] Alexander to Golding, 30 September 1825, MSS 3393 [7], Lambeth.

[23] This church was destroyed during World War II, but was located very close to the cathedral.

[24] In the Baptismal register she has the name Deborah Mary – probably taken at her baptism.

Chapter 4

The Irish Connection: 1826-1827

Dublin

Despite the improved conditions for the Alexanders in Exeter, it seemed right for them to have a complete change of scenery. Michael Solomon was then offered the job of Hebrew teacher in Dublin, his good friend John Synge providing him with the introductions to the necessary people in Ireland.[1] It also appears that he was offered work in the 'German' Church[2] in Dublin.[3]

In the early months of 1826 the Alexanders began a new chapter of their lives. They traveled from Exeter to Bristol, and stayed with Rev. Martin Whish, rector of St. Mary's Redcliffe. That was to be the easy leg of the journey. Shortly afterwards they travelled onto Ireland.

This would be a trip to be remembered. The sea that day as they travelled from Holyhead to Dublin was very rough, and when they finally arrived, Deborah recalled, 'We were all carried on shore by rough, strong men.'[4] And if that was not enough, they then stayed at the Hibernian Hotel[5] in Dublin, of which Deborah wrote with a touch of cynicism 'a more splendid dirty affair I never saw in Ireland.'[6]

---

[1] Deborah Alexander, *Autobiography,* pp. 33, 35, MSS 3394, Lambeth.

[2] The 'German' Church began circa 1779 and was located at 59 Poolebeg Street, for the German speaking community of the City. Oddly, in the *Dublin Register* of 1826 it is named the 'Danish & German-Lutheran Church' and in 1841 it is named as the Dutch Church. See *Dublin Register*, National Library of Ireland, Dublin.

[3] Alexander to Miss Hancock, 30 June 1826, Alexander papers, DS 125.3.A5, St. Anthony's College, Oxford, [henceforth St. Anthony's].

[4] Deborah Alexander, *ibid,* p. 32.

[5] On Dawson Street. It was demolished some years ago and replaced by Royal Hibernian Way shopping centre. In the source it is named the Hibernian Hotel, but more than likely it was the Royal Hibernian Hotel, and Mrs. Alexander's comment is a bit surprising as it was a hotel of high repute.

[6] Deborah Alexander, *ibid,* p. 32.

Very shortly however the young couple began to see the benefits of their friendship with the Synges in Plymouth. The day after their arrival they attended the Bethesda Chapel in Dublin,[7] of which Deborah Alexander wrote, 'our good friends Mr. and Mrs. John Synge gave us leave to occupy their Pew in that Chapel.' During the service they also met a Catholic man and spoke to him of their newfound belief in Jesus.[8]

The following day Alexander made acquaintance, through the recommendation of Mr. Synge, with Robert Newenham, a prominent banker. 'Nothing,' wrote Deborah 'could exceed the warmth of his reception. He sent a note to his dear wife who in the course of a few hours was at the door of our lodgings with her carriage and Cart for our luggage.'[9]

The Alexanders then became personal guests of the Newenhams for quite some time. Thankfully it was a friendly and welcoming home, for Michael Solomon had a relapse of poor health again while he was here. Despite this set back, they nevertheless made numerous new acquaintances. After some time they moved to a place of their own on Leeson Street in Dublin. It was here that they became acquainted with the Archbishop of Dublin, Dr. William Magee.

This acquaintance was mutually beneficial, for the Archbishop's second son took advantage of Michael Solomon's linguistic skills and studied Hebrew under him. While in Dublin the Alexanders also met and befriended Sir Richard and Lady Steele,[10] people well known in Dublin society. Another valuable contact was Mr. Arthur Guinness – of the famous brewery family.

Michael Solomon's Jewish identity assisted him in many ways during his stay in Ireland. One of these was with a new job – involvement with the Church of Ireland Jews Society.[11] Alexander began initially as an errand boy, working three hours in the afternoon as assistant to the secretary.

---

[7] Located on Dorset Street, Bethesda Chapel was built between 1784-86 by William Smith, as the Chapel of the Orphanage. Officially it was the Chapel of Ease of St. Mary's Parish, but is no longer extant.

[8] Deborah Alexander, *Autobiography,* pp. 33-34.

[9] *ibid,* p, 35.

[10] The Steele's later moved to Cheltenham, England.

[11] The Church of Ireland Jews Society was formed in 1810, one year after the formation of the London Jews Society, and thereafter became a very committed adjutant to the work of the LJS. Its official name was the 'Irish Auxiliary to the London Society for Promoting Christianity among the Jews.' The Church of Ireland is the name given to the Anglican Church in Ireland.

Shortly after beginning his new job, Alexander became acquainted with Rev. William Lewis – one of the pioneer LJS and Protestant missionaries in Palestine.[12] Lewis spoke at the Annual Meeting of the Jews Society on 11 April 1826, and informed everyone of the responsibility, challenge and difficulty of establishing a Protestant work in Jerusalem. It must have been interesting information for Alexander to hear, and who knows what challenge came to him when Lewis moved the following motion:

> … that not withstanding the difficulties which have hitherto retarded Missionary operations in Palestine, the meeting views with peculiar interest the Land of Israel & still calls upon the Xtian [Christian] Public to continue such assistance, as may enable them to carry out their Benevolent but Scriptural objects in that country.[13]

Alexander then became more active in his job with the Jews Society. In May he accompanied Lewis on a speaking[14] tour to Cork in the south of Ireland. This was soon afterwards followed by another speaking tour to the north of the country, to Armagh, Belfast and Ballymena. This tour was to be together with a fellow Jewish believer who was due in the country - Joseph Wolff. Later, when it became apparent that Wolff's arrival would be delayed, it was decided to defer this tour until his arrival.[15]

Wolff finally did arrive in mid August 1826, coming aboard the ship *Eblane* from Smyrna. Wolff was a classic eccentric. Not only had he openly proclaimed Jesus as Messiah to the strongly orthodox Jewish community in Jerusalem, but he had done the same to Jewish communities throughout the Mediterranean and Orient. He ventured to areas, often by himself, where others feared to tread.

His eccentricity and devotion to the Jewish cause is highlighted by his endeavours aboard ship, where he collected 2 pounds and two shillings

---

[12] Rev. William Bucknor Lewis, from Ireland, arrived in Jerusalem in 1823 following a decision by the LJS General Committee to establish a permanent base in Palestine. Although Lewis laboured alongside several missionaries belonging to the American Board of Commissioners for Foreign Missions, as well as LJS worker, Joseph Wolff, he, like all other Protestant missionaries, found the restrictions forced upon them as foreigners too difficult, and left Jerusalem. Lewis later worked for many years for the LJS at Smyrna in Turkey.

[13] Irish Jews Society [IJS] Minute Book, No 318 1.2, 11 April 1826, Representative Church Body [RCB] Library, Dublin. [Henceforth RCB].

[14] In Christian missionary circles known as a 'deputation,' informing churches of the work and vision of the society.

[15] See IJS Minutes for 24 & 31 July 1826, Minute Book 318 1.2, RCB.

from the crew 'in behalf of the Jews.'[16] Alexander and Deborah soon had to experience this eccentric man first hand. Wolff was ordered into quarantine for three weeks. Through the efforts of Alexander and a colleague, the time was shortened to three days. After his release, Wolff stayed with the Alexanders, which proved to be an experience never forgotten. Michael Solomon and Deborah had to keep their bedroom door locked as Wolff was in the habit of intruding upon their privacy very early in the morning informing the Alexanders that he wanted to read to them accounts from his journal.[17]

Wolff and Alexander then set out upon their deputation tour to the north, visiting Newry, Lisburn, Belfast, Ballymena, Coleraine, Derry,[18]Strabane, Moneymore, Tallymore, Dundalk and Drogheda. This was surely an exhausting, as well as exhilarating journey. It is not stated how Alexander fared – but no doubt he heard every one of Wolff's multitude of adventures from the land of their forefathers, and indeed wherever he had travelled.

Shortly after, Alexander accompanied Wolff and Rev. Thomas Kingston on another tour, this time to the south of the country. After returning from this tour, they were off again – this time he was to accompany Wolff to Liverpool to meet Hawtrey (the LJS Secretary) and Marsh.[19]

As busy as his work life was, Deborah was pleased for him. She wrote of his position: 'My dear husband...had to travel all over Ireland. My beloved husband was very much beloved and became very popular. It was very beautiful to watch how truly humble he was kept amid so much attention as he everywhere met with.'[20]

Alexander's busy schedule was matched by his domestic life. Another house move, to be nearer 16 Sackville Street,[21] offices of the IJS, was accompanied by an increase in work hours, and an elevation to assistant-secretary. Then on 10 November 1826 a daughter, Sarah, was born. Sarah was shortly afterwards christened at Sandford Church by Rev. Guinness,[22] and Mr. and Mrs. Synge were the child's god-parents.[23]

---

[16] IJS Minutes 15 August 1826, Minute Book 318 1.2, RCB.

[17] Deborah Alexander, *ibid,* p. 33.

[18] Although referred to as Londonderry by the Protestants of Ireland, in the source it is called Derry.

[19] IJS Minutes 22 September 1826, Minute Book 318 1.2, RCB.

[20] Deborah Alexander, *ibid,* p. 38.

[21] Renamed O'Connell after the British left in 1921.

[22] Which Guinness is a bit unclear. It could have been Hosea Guinness, who was stationed at St. Patrick's Cathedral in central Dublin at this time. It could also

Several days after the birth of his daughter the IJS Committee agreed to a request from Alexander, for himself and his colleague, Mr. Michael John Mayers, also a Jewish believer in Jesus, 'to avail himself of an opportunity that now presents itself of visiting his brethren in Prague, Breslau & Berlin ... to enable him to form a just estimate of the State of religion amongst the Jews in those places, two individuals having proposed to pay his travelling expenses.'[24]

It would appear that one of the sponsors was none other than William Marsh of Colchester. What is unclear is the name of the other sponsor, and also the results of the tour, if indeed they did proceed.

It was during this period that Alexander had an interesting encounter with Archbishop Magee,[25] whose son he taught Hebrew. Michael Solomon was preparing himself for entrance into the famed institution Trinity College.[26] Deborah wrote of this time: 'My dear husband studied for Trinity College Dublin, and was just about to enter when the Archbishop sends for him through Mr. Matthias of Bethesda Chapel.'[27]

Magee wanted to have Alexander ordained quickly, presumably for him to take over the 'German' Church. Michael Solomon on the other hand wanted first to study, and subsequently declined the Archbishop's offer. Not to be deterred, Magee sent his son to persuade Michael Solomon to meet the Archbishop. Michael Solomon relented. At the meeting Alexander stated his desire to study, and pleaded his lack of reading and preparation. To this Magee replied: 'I will give you six months to study deeply. If I knew Hebrew and German as you do, I should be very well satisfied.'[28]

Ordination

Alexander's studies were successful as he passed an examination at the Archbishop's Palace, St. Stephen's Green, Dublin. The following period was a very active and indeed stressful one for Michael Solomon. Deborah again was affected with bad health, and confined in a very weak state to

---

have been Arthur Guinness, who was acquainted with Alexander, and who was stationed at Chapelizod, north-west Dublin. The present Sandford Church on Sandford Road, Ranelagh was built in 1860.

[23] Alexander to Golding, 30 November 1826, MSS 3393 [9], Lambeth.

[24] IJS Minutes, 13 November 1826, Minute Book 318 1.2, RCB.

[25] William Magee (1766-1831) was a graduate of Trinity College and Archbishop of Dublin from 1822-1831.

[26] Founded in 1592 by Queen Elizabeth I.

[27] Deborah Alexander, *ibid,* p. 41.

[28] Corey, *ibid*, p. 28.

bed for several weeks.[29] Following her recovery Alexander made a journey to London 'whither I went for the purpose of many things connected with the German service I am to have.' While in London he also had occasion to meet Mrs. Levy, Deborah's mother, a visit which seemed to have been relatively calm. In a letter to Miss Hancock dated 5 June 1827 he commented on the benefits of the tour upon his health 'which was very precarious indeed before I went.'[30]

Michael Solomon was then ordained deacon on Trinity Sunday, 10 June 1827 in St. Anne's Church, and preached his first sermon in Sandford Church in the evening, taking as his text Psalm 51:15: 'Oh Lord, open Thou my lips.' His wife wrote: 'My beloved husband was much affected, and so was I, and felt deeply the responsibility and the honour conferred upon us.'[31] Of this occasion the LJS wrote:

> We have much satisfaction in stating, that Mr. Michael Solomon Alexander, formerly reader of the Jewish Synagogue at Plymouth, of whose conversion we have given an account, and who has since resided in Dublin, was admitted into Holy Orders on Trinity Sunday last, by his Grace the Archbishop of Dublin.
> Mr. Michael John Mayers, also a converted Jew, was ordained on the same occasion.[32]

This occasion was even the more special for the Alexanders as their special friends Mr. and Mrs. John Synge also attended.

Some could, and probably did, question the propriety of ordaining a man only two years a follower of Jesus. In response to this, a later acquaintance, Rev. James Cartwight, wrote of this time:

> His views of the great fundamental truths of Christianity were remarkably deep and clear, and often touchingly experimental. He had evidently learned much during his first years of sharp mental conflict. I believe that at that time he was eminently taught of God; and that if he was clear on the important subjects of a sinner's acceptance with God, of justification by the blood of Christ through faith alone, and of sanctification by the renewing influences of the Holy Ghost; it was because he had fought out,

---

[29] Alexander to Miss Hancock, 9 April 1827, MSS 3397 [134-5], Lambeth.
[30] Alexander to Miss Hancock, 5 June 1827, MSS 3393 [12], Lambeth.
[31] Alexander to Miss Hancock, 30 June 1827, MSS 3393 [14], Lambeth.
[32] *Jewish Expositor*, 1827, pp. 319-20. According to the IJS Minutes of 4 June 1827, Alexander was to be 'Minister of the German Church' and Mayers 'Curate to St. Lukes parish in Dublin.' IJS Minute Book 1827-1844, 318 1.3, RCB.

as. it were, these great questions in secret conflict and prayer; under deep conviction of sin, he had learned his need of the free mercy of the Gospel...Thus experience, temptation and prayer, had been his first commentaries on the doctrines of the Gospel; and, therefore, when in little more than two years from his baptism, Ordination was offered to him, entirely unsolicited and unexpected, by a prelate who was esteemed strict in his requirements from candidates for Holy Orders, he was found to possess suitable qualifications for the Christian ministry.[33]

Ill Health

After the hype and excitement of his ordination, Alexander encountered an immediate set-back. He wrote to Miss Hancock on 30 June 1827:

> I have so much to write and so little time that I must just briefly state that there are difficulties in the way of my getting the German Chapel appointed for me. I am sure you will be pleased to hear this, and I shall likewise view the Hand of God in it, if it should come to naught. It is wonderful that the Archbishop should grant me ordination on that idea. Of course I shall be more free. However I can and must say nothing about it. I must only wait for the opening of the Lord's ways. I desire to be resigned entirely to his Holy will.'[34]

The closure of one door – the 'German' Church – meant the opening of another – long-term involvement with Jewish people. Alexander had requested two weeks leave of absence in early July, and travelled to London with Deborah in order to meet Mrs. Levi. While in London he was invited to speak in the Episcopal Jews Chapel at Palestine Place on 8 July 1827, on the text, very appropriately, from Romans 1:16; 'The gospel is the power of God for the salvation for everyone, for the Jew first and also for the non-Jew.'[35]

On 1 August, soon after returning to Ireland, Alexander (and Mayers) set out on a deputation tour. Their first stop was Cork. Then another setback occurred. Alexander became very sick, and proceeded no further, and several days later returned to Dublin. Here he was taken care of by Dr. Cheyne, who diagnosed that the situation was very serious indeed.

---

[33] Sermon by Rev. James Cartwight at Episcopal Jews Chapel London, on 28 December 1845, in *JI*, 1846, pp. 60-61.

[34] Alexander to Miss Hancock, 30 June 1827, DS 125.3.A5, Alexander Papers, St. Anthony's; and Corey, *ibid*, p. 30.

[35] Corey, *ibid*, p. 29.

Alexander quoted Cheyne as saying to some common friends 'I (humanly speaking) could not be alive by next Spring if I remain in this Country.'[36]

Despairing to lose such a valuable part of their work, the Irish Committee at their meeting on 10 September 1827 stated that because of Alexander's 'very delicate state of health ... his Physician has declared that change of air is absolutely necessary for his re-establishment.' [37] From this point forward the parent society, the LJS in London became involved in shaping the destiny of the Alexanders.[38]

Dr. Singer, representing Alexander, enquired if the LJS Home Committee would consider employing Michael Solomon temporarily for service on the continent.[39] At this point the LJS was about to expand its operations in Germany, and Rev. W. Ayerst was being prepared to embark upon this venture. It was possible, they conceded, that Alexander could accompany him. The LJS Committee summoned an *ad hoc* meeting of all London Committee members willing and able to meet Alexander in late September 1827. So for the third time in just a few months Michael Solomon made the trip across the Irish Sea to London.

Michael Solomon was accepted to work alongside Ayerst on a twelve-month probation period.[40] It seems that at this point he returned to Dublin, where he was ordained priest by Dr. Lyndsay, the Bishop of Kildare, by letters emissary from Archbishop Magee. [41] Picking up his family, Alexander then departed for service on the continent.[42]

---

[36] Alexander to Golding [now in Edinburgh], 11 September 1827, MSS 3393 [16], Lambeth.

[37] IJS Minutes, 10 September 1827, IJS Minute Book 318 1.3, RCB.

[38] See Minute 563, 13 February 1827 and Minute 1044, 25 September 1827, in CMJ Minute Book c. 12, Bodleian Library, Oxford. [Henceforth Bodleian].

[39] Minute 1044, CMJ Committee Meeting, 25 September 1827, Minutes Book c. 12, Bodleian.

[40] Minute 1077, 16 October 1827, CMJ Minute Book c. 12, Bodleian.

[41] Corey, *ibid,* p. 29. Corey states he was ordained in December. There are no dates in the official records of the RCB Library in Dublin. Alexander was already on the Continent in December, so presumably he was ordained priest earlier or in absentia.

[42] Prior to departure however he spent some time on deputation work with Wolff in Lancashire.

Chapter 5

Journeys in Central Europe: 1828 – 1830

Mission Work in Germany.

The two LJS workers travelled to Germany via Holland, from where Alexander wrote to a Mrs. Vincent in Dublin on 5 November,[1] and also to the LJS Committee on the same day.[2]

Ayerst and Alexander made their way to northern Germany and spent the first weeks travelling to various locations.[3] Ayerst wrote to the LJS from Posen (now Poznan in Poland) on 4 December 1827, stating that he and Alexander had spent some time already in Berlin. Alexander further wrote that they arrived in Danzig[4] on 22 December 1827.[5]

Alexander himself later visited Posen, and wrote:

> I cannot describe my feelings on finding myself now in Posen my native country, when I reflect on the wonderful dealings of the Lord with me since I left this place nine years ago. I was then a wandering sheep from my Saviour's fold, walking in darkness, and in the shades of death, ignorant of the Lord that bought me. How did he lead me? The blind by a way I knew not. My soul doth magnify the Lord, because my spirit rejoiceth in my God, as my saviour, especially when I consider I am now engaged as a humble, but unworthy, instrument to preach the glad tidings of salvation, and to declare to my brethren, what the Lord hath done for my soul. When my prospects of usefulness are dark, I look to my Lord and say, "Thy grace is sufficient for me; thy strength is made perfect in my weakness."[6]

---

[1] Alexander to Mrs. Vincent, 5 November 1827, DS 125.3A5, St. Anthony's.

[2] Minute 1128, 13 November 1827, CMJ Minute Book c.12, Bodleian.

[3] Alexander wrote to LJS on 12 November 1827 from Elberfield.

[4] Present day Gdansk in Poland.

[5] *Jewish Expositor (JE)*, 1828, p. 259. This was the LJS monthly magazine.

[6] *JE*, 1828, p. 260.

Alexander also recorded that he had sent a letter to his brother, who 'is rabbi to the large Jewish congregation twelve miles from Posen' informing him of his arrival, 'and requesting that we might have a meeting.' The brother agreed and according to Michael the meeting was rather cordial. Michael was able to state to him 'the Gospel, and declared also to him an account of the hope that was in me.' Following this meeting Michael Solomon received a letter from his brother, which, Alexander wrote 'encourages me to hope that our meeting was not in vain.'[7]

It was not long before the two missionaries began their work in earnest in Danzig. Ayerst wrote on 29 January 1828 that they had 'commenced a regular service in the English church every Sunday' and that he hoped Alexander would soon begin a service in German on Saturday afternoon to accommodate the German Jewish people.[8] In the same letter Ayerst asked permission to set up a small school. Permission was granted, and although expectations were high, Ayerst stated in July 1828 that it 'was still unvisited by any Jewish children.' Jewish children did later attend the school, where instruction included needlework that was taught to the girls by Mrs. Alexander and Mrs. Ayerst.[9]

Alexander and Ayerst carried out numerous missionary journeys, sometimes together, sometimes individually. They undertook one such journey during June 1828 where they visited Stargard (now Szczecinski in Poland), Mewe, Nuremberg, Grandanz, Rehden, Lessen, Freistadt, Nydick, Rosenberg, Reisenberg, Stuhm and Marienburg (now Malbork in Poland). In all these locations Alexander and Ayerst made every attempt to interface with the Jewish people, and where possible to meet the rabbi. On some occasions they were given a positive welcome, while on other occasions they were met with derision.[10]

Prior to setting out on their next journey in August 1828, Alexander received notification concerning a request he had obviously sent to the parent committee, requesting, it seems, permission to remove himself from Danzig (perhaps to go to Warsaw to labour alongside McCaul, or perhaps to go to Berlin).[11] The committee informed him however that he was to remain at Danzig for the time being, at least until Ayerst was well equipped with the German language.[12]

---

[7] *JE,* 1828, p. 260.
[8] *ibid,* p. 260.
[9] *JE,* 1830, p. 67.
[10] *JE,* 1828, pp. 458-459.
[11] The author was unable to locate Alexander's original communication.
[12] Minute 1653, 12 August 1828, CMJ Minute Book c. 12, Bodleian.

During their missionary tour in August, Alexander and Ayerst visited Chrisburg, Osterode (in present Lower Saxony, Germany), Saalbeld (in present Thuringen, Germany), and Altmark (in north eastern Germany). Of Chrisburg, Ayerst wrote that they met the liberal minded rabbi and several others, who 'seemed to think that the writings of Mendelsohn[13] are most likely to benefit the Jews.' He strongly condemned the absurdity of the Jews praying in an ancient, and now dead language, 'which it is impossible for those who have not leisure to study, to understand in any tolerable degree.'[14] This comment indicates the struggle for internal emancipation then growing within the Jewish community, as many desired to follow the example of Moses Mendelsohn, and escape the narrow confines of Orthodox Judaism.[15]

Ayerst also wrote, concerning Alexander's contribution:

> It is a great advantage to Mr. Alexander, in speaking with these better informed Jews, that he has been brought up in their own way; and it has generally been a rule with us, when entering a strange place, to visit first the rabbi, who is often engaged as teacher, and thus we sometimes learn at once much about the state of religious instruction amongst them.[16]

It seems that Ayerst and Alexander never tired of these exhausting missionary tours. No sooner did they return from their latest tour, that they began planning their next one. In October 1828, during the period of the Feast of Tabernacles, they set out again. Their first stop was Mewe, where they were invited to speak at the opening of a new church. The next port of call however would possibly be Alexander's most challenging so far – Schonlanke.

They decided it best to stop at a Christian inn (most of the best inns were owned by Jewish people) in order as much as possible to minimize exposure. They then sought a meeting with Michael Solomon's sister, a widow, who agreed to come to the inn, not knowing the reason for the meeting. Ayerst describes what followed:

---

[13] Moses Mendelsohn, 1729-1786, was a former Talmudic scholar who became a philosopher of religion and greatly influenced Jewish thinking in central Europe, being regarded as the father of Jewish enlightenment or *haskala*.

[14] *JE*, 1828, p. 459.

[15] Ayerst later wrote of what he termed the 'new temple Jews' – 'the friends and followers of the celebrated philosopher Mendelsohn, have introduced into their service, not only the custom of preaching in German, but also singing with an organ, and many other things like those which we have.' *JE*, 1830, p. 5.

[16] *JE*, 1828, p. 459.

When she came, as it was uncertain how she would feel towards him, I spoke to her first alone, and when I asked her, whether she had not a brother, who some years since went to England, and whether she knew that he was now returned to Germany, she inquired after him mostly kindly; and when I asked whether she wished to see him and speak with him, I shall not soon forget the affectionate warmth with which she said, "If it be possible." This Mr. A. overheard in the adjoining room, where he had been waiting during this short but interesting interview, and you may easily imagine the grateful feeling with which he came forward to receive to his arms a beloved sister, from whom he had in the leadings of God's providence been so long separated.[17]

The following day Alexander and Ayerst visited the local Christian minister in the town, and Alexander also managed to briefly explain the message of Jesus as Messiah to his former Talmud teacher. At this juncture however several other Jewish people, when acquainted with whom this visitor was, became uncivil. This attitude upset Michael Solomon's relatives, and they took leave of him. Despite this small incident however, Alexander was more than pleased with the outcome of his visit. He later wrote of it:

... this journey has left a deep impression on my mind, that a wonderful change has taken place amongst my brethren of that part of the country, since the time I left it ten years ago. There is a general anxiety to converse about the truth of Christianity, which, when I left, was considered an abomination: and surely it may be considered no small proof of better feeling on the subject, that they now receive one of their brethren, who has gone over to the Christian religion and comes to declare the truth of it to them, and treat him generally with affection and kindness. This I have found, far beyond my expectation. I have found numbers of my former acquaintances and friends, who listened with great feelings of interest and sympathy, to my statement of how the Lord has led me and brought me to the knowledge of that Saviour ... I have read letters regretting that I did not spend longer among them, and that we might visit them soon again. Anyone that is well acquainted with the strong prejudices and hatred which the Jews have always manifested, especially towards one whom they consider an apostate, will look upon the fact, as decidedly favourable for the Gospel truth amongst them.[18]

---

[17] *JE*, 1829, p. 183.
[18] *ibid,* p. 184.

This emotional visit was followed by a period of some months back in Danzig where further efforts were made to consolidate the school, as well as general mission work in the port city itself and in the surrounding villages. Then in April and May 1829 Alexander made a visit to Poland, spending eight days in Warsaw. Although his letter abounds with some of the normal optimistic observations, he seemed most impressed by the work of one of the greats of Jewish mission work – Alexander McCaul.[19] Michael Solomon wrote:

> I have been astonished at the acquirements of dear brother McCaul, in Jewish and Hebrew learning, which can only be accounted for, besides his natural talents, by the zeal and love which he has for the Jews. His heart and soul seem engaged in the matter, and where this is the case, the Lord will not leave such endeavours unblessed. I was almost overwhelmed, when I heard him on Saturday address a considerable number of Jews in their own language, and place the Lord Jesus Christ powerfully before their understandings, in the Hebrew tongue.[20]

Alexander was drawn to McCaul, and as it turns out, this was the beginning of a long and very fruitful relationship between the two scholars.[21] They indeed had much in common – one had been a rabbi, the other, was lovingly called 'rabbi,' due to his abundant knowledge about Judaism and Jewish history and customs. And both had entered into the work of the LJS while in Dublin, and both had an unusual attachment to Rev. William Marsh. Later it was McCaul's foresightedness that led to Alexander being appointed as the first Protestant bishop in Jerusalem.

Another person that Alexander met while on his trip to Warsaw was the very young Elizabeth Anne McCaul, Alexander McCaul's daughter, who

---

[19] Alexander McCaul had been born in Dublin. He was a brilliant student and had earned his Masters degree at Trinity College by the age of eighteen. The professors of Trinity College had high hopes for him. In 1820 Rev. Lewis Way and Rev. William Marsh visited Ireland on behalf of the LJS and McCaul heard their presentation. At this point he felt called into Jewish ministry. McCaul then set out for Poland, arriving in 1821. See: E. A. Finn, *Reminiscences*, (London: Marshall, Morgan & Scott, 1930), pp. 18-19, & *JE,* 1820, p. 441.

[20] *JE,* 1829, p. 424.

[21] It seems that there had been a previous consideration of Alexander being stationed in Warsaw, but this was deferred in February 1829. See Minute 117, 24 February 1827, Minute Book, c.13, Bodleian.

in 1846 arrived in Jerusalem as the wife of James Finn,[22] second British consul in the Holy City.[23]

Upon their return to Danzig Alexander and Ayerst discovered another exciting way of forming relationships with Jewish people. During the summer period Polish Jewish traders would come down the Vistula River to the port of Danzig, to sell their grain. Many of these would live in temporary huts near the river. Alexander and Ayerst hired a room in this neighbourhood, and distributed Scriptures and other materials to these Jewish merchants.

Beginning in September 1829 Alexander set out again on a tour that included Marienburg, Stargard, Czersk (near Warsaw), Conitz (now Chojnice, south of Gdansk), Zempleburg (now Sepolno Krajenskie in northern Poland), and other towns and villages. In some places Alexander met with a reasonable and positive response, while in other locations he was greeted with derision and opposition. He wrote of one incident with a young Talmudic student:

> I found a young Jew sitting reading the Talmud aloud, at the same time smoking tobacco! Such darkness I have not found for a long time! This young man, though indeed, on the whole intelligent, was full of Talmudic stuff, and seemed to know no other source of bliss. I was very much reminded of my own days of ignorance, and could, therefore, feel for this poor young man. This was the fast of Gedaliah,[24] and in this manner the poor Jewish Talmudists spend the fast-day, and think of doing God service. I spoke to this young man with earnest and affectionate entreaties,

---

[22] James Finn was a member of the LJS Committee in the 1840's and also was well acquainted with the history of the Jewish people.

[23] Elizabeth Anne McCaul was born in 1825 in Warsaw. She began learning Hebrew from a learned rabbi at the age of three. She married James Finn in early 1846 and several months later found herself in Jerusalem, where they remained until 1863. The Finn's were responsible for founding the first agricultural settlements for Jewish people, as well as pioneering development outside the walls of the Old City.

[24] Gedaliah was the leader for the remaining Jewish people in Judah appointed by Nebuchadnezzar. However he himself was then assassinated by Yishmael ben Nesania. Fearing a Babylonian reprisal for this act the remaining Jewish people then fled to Egypt. The Gemara teaches that the death of a righteous person is almost on a par to the destruction of the Temple. In this context however it was the consequences of the death of righteous Gedaliah – the exile of the remaining Jewish people in Judah – that is the reason for this fast. This fast is held after Rosh HaShanah, the Jewish New Year.

but he seemed rather dissatisfied that anyone should tell him that this was not the way to heaven.[25]

One of Michael Solomon's last journeys in Poland and Germany took place in early 1830, again accompanied by Ayerst. They visited numerous locations, including Lessen (now a small Polish town named Lasin), where upon entering the inn he 'found the room full of drinking and drunken Poles, who had just come from their church, (that day being Epiphany).' Later on that day, after conversing with the local rabbi, the missionaries felt inclined to pass out tracts to the locals, as, 'This was a good opportunity to show the Jews that we are also endeavouring to promote true religion among those who are called Christians; several of them seemed greatly astonished at seeing us do this, and we became more deeply impressed with the importance of a Missionary to the Jews having an eye also upon those among whom they dwell, on that account.'[26]

This journey was Alexander's final sojourn in the land of his birth. Soon afterwards he was summoned to return to London. It seemed that the Society had financial problems, and required the workers to come to England and to speak on behalf of the Society's work and vision.[27]

[25] *JE,* 1830, p. 69.

[26] *ibid,* p. 84.

[27] Minute 805 & 806, 17 March 1830, CMJ Minute Book c.13, Bodleian.

Chapter 6

Labours in London: 1830-1838

Return to London

Alexander and his family returned to London in April 1830, whereupon Michael Solomon entered upon a dual role. The home missionary, Rev. J.C. Reichardt, would be absent for some months on a tour of duty to the LJS's scattered mission stations, and Alexander was temporarily to fill his position. He would also be involved in speaking around the country.

Alexander began his work quietly, but soon saw the need for a more regular plan for interacting with the Jewish people. He asked for, and received, permission to live in one of the houses at Palestine Place, one room of which he could use 'for the purpose of meeting & conversing with the Jews.'[1] Part of his work also involved delivering a lecture every Saturday afternoon.

Michael Solomon made numerous initiatives to make contact with the Jews of London. He circulated a *Notice* among the Jewish community informing them about this room and his availability to meet with them. During that period he also cooperated with the tutor of the seminary at Palestine Place[2] and was involved in meeting the Jewish people in sundry ways.

The other aspect of his task, deputation (speaking in churches), was not forgotten, and he made numerous tours including visits to both Plymouth and Bristol. One interesting tour took in Norwich, where his old friend and supporter Miss Hancock set up a meeting. She was insistent that Alexander present 'a fundamental lecture on the prophecies.'[3]

It soon became apparent that Michael Solomon was fulfilling an important task in England, and he was asked to remain until the spring of

---

[1] Minute 958, 19 June 1830, LJS Minute Book c.13, Bodleian.
[2] The seminary had originally been at Stanstead Park, the home of Rev Lewis Way. However in 1827 it moved to Palestine Place.
[3] Hancock to Alexander, 1 October 1830, MSS 3397 [136-7], Lambeth.

1831.[4] Then in early 1831 matters took a change. Initially, in February he was told to return immediately to Danzig, due, it seems, to Ayerst becoming ill.[5] Before he could set off however, Reichardt informed the LJS Committee that there was 'sufficient room for two home missionaries in England' and Alexander's name came to the fore. No doubt the Alexander family at this time was feeling quite restless, being caught in the middle of an official policy swing.

Matters were resolved for them in May 1831 when it was decided that Alexander would remain in England 'particularly for the purpose of visiting the various provincial Towns where they [Jewish people] reside.'[6] Reichardt was to take charge of the newly opened Jewish Operative Institution,[7] thereby permitting Michael Solomon to fulfill the position as second home missionary.

Alexander then returned to Danzig to pack and ship his belongings to England. He also took the opportunity to visit centres along the way, including Berlin, where, it seems, he again asked for a position. The Committee had to impress upon him that London was to be his 'general residence and principle scene of operation.'[8] It would appear that his two-year sojourn in central Europe had enthused Michael Solomon again to be actively involved amongst his own people in his native homeland.

Finally resigned to being placed in London, Alexander returned and took on this new challenge. At a special meeting of the LJS Committee on 5 November 1831, Alexander and other missionaries entering into new duties were prayed for and commissioned. One other Jewish believer present on that occasion was Frederick Christian Ewald, who was then entering the Hebrew seminary at Palestine Place.

The Alexander family moved into a house at No 7 Palestine Place close to the Episcopal Jews Chapel, and his office was also located on the same complex. Shortly after another daughter, Deborah, was born. She recalls later her impressions of Palestine Place:

> It was a peaceful, secluded spot, an oasis in the desert. Iron gates enclosed it, which were shut at night. A Chapel, a School for 50 Jewish girls, and one for 50 Jewish boys, a College, the Operative Jewish Converts Institution, the Chaplain's House, several good houses, two lodges, and a

---

[4] Minute 1091, 8 September 1830, LJS Minute Book c. 13, Bodleian.
[5] Minute 1297, 10 February 1831, LJS Minute Book c. 13, Bodleian.
[6] Minute 1424, 11 May 1831, LJS Minute Book c. 13, Bodleian.
[7] Minute 94, 8 November 1836, LJS Minute Book L, Bodleian.
[8] Minute 1506m, 13 July 1831, LJS Minute Book c. 13, Bodleian.

lovely double avenue of Lime trees, were the result of much effort on the part of the Society, and every May, for very many years, from far and near, came many visitors – friends to Jewish Missions – to hear what was being done.[9]

Professor of Hebrew & Rabbinic Literature

A man of Alexander's learning and experience would no doubt be sought after in a cosmopolitan city like London. And such was the case. The question would also be: 'Could the LJS hold on to a person of such character and learning?' The test would come sooner rather than later.

In 1831 a very new Christian institution, King's College, was established, centrally located on the Strand.[10] Shortly afterwards they offered Alexander the title and position of Professor of Hebrew and Rabbinic Literature. Alexander submitted this proposal to the LJS Committee, who responded negatively, stating it, 'would be incompatible with the performance of the duties of a Missionary of this Society' and asked Alexander not to give the matter further consideration.[11]

The LJS, however, was forced to modify its opposition in light of Alexander's desire to fulfill this position, and agreed to his request at their meeting of 12 July 1832. It was a wise decision. Not only did this position provide Alexander with numerous teaching opportunities, it also gave him exposure to a wider section of British ecclesiastical society than he would have encountered working only with the LJS. Richard Ehrlich wrote of this appointment:

> At that time he must already have been exceptionally learned, for a Chair of Rabbinical and Talmudic Law was specially created for him. His inaugural lecture, which appeared in print, had as its subject the importance of Hebrew and Rabbinical literature. He was granted the title of Doctor of Divinity.'[12]

---

[9] Ransom, *ibid*, p. 1.

[10] The College was founded in 1828, but the site was only given by the Government in 1829. It opened on 8 October 1831, with the inauguration sermon given by Charles James, Bishop of London.

[11] Minute No 153, 27 June 1832, CMJ Minute Book c. 14, Bodleian. According to F.J.C. Hearnshaw, *The Centenary History of King's College London*, (London, 1929), p. 110, Alexander was appointed to this position on 8 June 1832.

[12] Richard A. Ehrlich, *Michael Solomon Alexander, The First Evangelical Bishop in Jerusalem,* in AJR Information, April 1963, London, p. 13.

However, from the very outset there was a strain in the relationship between his two employers. Alexander was due to commence his King's College duties at the beginning of the 1832 academic year. But he wrote from Derby on 2 October 1832 to King's College that:

> With much regret I have just heard by a letter from the Secretary of our Society, that my labours in the Country are required for three weeks longer, consequently I cannot be at my post in the College, as you wished me, and as I expected, nor will it be possible for me to deliver my public introductory lecture in the 3rd week of this Month.[13]

The inaugural address of Alexander was finally delivered on 7 November 1832. He stated: 'The object of my present introductory address is, simply to point out the importance of Hebrew and Rabbinic Literature ...'[14]

Concerning Hebrew Alexander continued:

> ... The Jews ... universally believe that it was the language in which Jehovah made known his divine will to man ...
> ... it is acknowledged by all that Hebrew is the most ancient of all known languages ... Instead of its being, as some would have it, a mere dialect of the Semitic languages, we have every reason to view it as the mother of all the others, which easily accounts for the great similarity that exists between them.[15]

Alexander then explained, in brief, the importance of understanding rabbinic literature:

> The advantage of being able to read the rabbinical writings, on account of the light which they throw on the Scriptures. These are generally decried as worse than useless; but it can only arise from the ignorance of them. It is true, they contain much that is absurd and erroneous, and in many instances they even most awfully pervert the sense of the Scriptures; but nevertheless, they contain much that is most useful, and calculated to throw light upon them. [16]

---

[13] Alexander to H. Smith, 2 October 1832, in Correspondence A, 1832, King's College Archive.

[14] Introductory Lecture delivered on 17 November 1832, in *King's College Calendar*, 1832, p. 4.

[15] Introductory Lecture, in *King's College Calendar, 1832*, pp. 5 & 7.

[16] *ibid*, p. 25.

For that time, Alexander's perspective was quite progressive and forward looking. He was delivering a direct challenge for the church to understand the mind set of the Jewish people, especially the rabbinic trend, as well as gain a valuable understanding of their own Scriptures.[17]

Alexander's labours with two institutions would inevitably bring some minor tensions, especially as his main theatre of operation (and source of income) was the LJS. There was an occasion in mid 1833 when he was unable to take up an LJS related appointment due to his duties with King's College. This produced a stern censure from the LJS Secretary and Committee.[18]

McCaul joins the team

A move of far reaching significance, not just for Alexander, but for the Society and indeed for Christian work amongst Jewish people in general, occurred in 1833. Alexander McCaul had returned from Warsaw on sick leave in 1831 and it was decided he would not return to Poland. In fact the LJS Committee decided in July 1833 that 'his residence in England is very important to the progress of the work amongst the Jews of this country and requested him to occupy a house in Palestine Place.' [19] Thereafter Alexander worked alongside both McCaul and Reichardt.

These three talented men were involved in numerous projects, one being shared lectures, a very innovative form of outreach. These were held on Saturday evenings and became commonly known as the Aldermanbury Conferences. These lectures began in November 1832 and were intended as a forum for debate and discussion between Jewish and Christian leaders on matters concerning the Messiah, Judaism and similar subjects.

The *Eastern Question*

The beginning of Alexander's work in London coincided with another great turning in world affairs, and again, as at the time of his birth, it

---

[17] Some 180 years afterwards, these sentiments of Michael Solomon Alexander are being explored and taught through Alexander College and Shoresh Study Tours in Jerusalem.

[18] Minute 548, 24 July 1833, LJS Minute Book c. 14, Bodleian. Another similar situation occurred the following year (see Minute 700, 14 January 1834). It also seems that prior to the first conflict Alexander had requested either an increase in pay, or transfer to another foreign mission station where he would be better able to support himself and his family. See Minute 367, 13 March 1833, LJS Minute Book c. 14, Bodleian.

[19] Minute 94, 8 November 1836, LJS Minute Book L, Bodleian.

revolved around the Levant or the eastern Mediterranean. These affairs greatly influenced Michael Solomon's future, although he had little inkling of this in the early 1830's. This situation is known as the *Eastern Question.*

Napoleon's incursion into the East had radically altered European, and especially British, foreign policy towards that region. Thereafter Britain was determined to ensure that no rival European power would ever gain a toehold there again. Britain was particularly concerned lest the French again encroach near the area of Egypt and that the Russians would not come down from the Black Sea through the Bosphorus and Dardanelles and enter the Mediterranean.

In the 1820's Greece rose in revolt against her Turkish overlords. Britain felt obliged to come to Greece's aid, and on this occasion, she was joined by Russia. During this very same time a old-new entity began to rise on the horizon – Egypt. An Albanian named Mehmet Ali (or Muhammed Ali) had risen to power in the vacuum following the Napoleonic incursion, and gained power in Egypt. By the early 1830's he desired to gain territory. His forces invaded Syria in late 1831, seriously harming the political *status quo* of the region. In no time he had significant power, and was soon threatening Constantinople itself.

In desperation Turkey sought European assistance. The British Foreign Secretary, Lord Palmerston, was determined to offer assistance. Unfortunately for him the political balance in Britain weighed against him and he was unable to act. In desperation the Turks turned to their arch-rival, Russia, for assistance. Russia was only too keen to accept the invitation, and shortly a strong Russian military presence was evident in Constantinople. In return for their assistance, the Russians, in 1833, secured the Treaty of *Unkiar Skelessi* from Turkey, gaining for Russia lucrative political and military benefits. Palmerston in particular was furious that such an alliance had been allowed to happen. Right under Britain's nose the Russians were gaining easy access into the eastern Mediterranean.

Such political happenings in the region of the Holy Land stirred the evangelical Christian world, especially those disposed towards seeing Israel's restoration. And it was not only these Christians who were interested in Israel's restoration. John Nicolayson[20] wrote from the region in August 1831:

---

[20] John (Hans) Nicolayson, from Logumkloster in Denmark, had been sent to Jerusalem by the LJS in 1825 to work alongside Dr. George Dalton, who himself had only recently arrived there. At the time Nicolayson found it near impossible

The disposition of Jews in Europe to return to this land of their fathers seems to grow stronger as the period fixed for the appearance of their great Deliverer is approaching. They here still stick to their calculation of the term, which is now reduced to the short space of eight years ... We are told again and again that eight short years will decide the great question between us, to their triumph and our confusion.[21]

Many Jewish people both in Europe and Turkish Palestine were of the opinion that the period of the Jewish year coinciding with 1839-1840 would witness the coming of the Jewish redeemer. The question alluded to by Nicolayson would be – had this redeemer appeared before!

It was also during this same period, thanks to the Egyptians, that the LJS, and indeed evangelical Protestant Christianity, was finally able to secure a permanent presence in Jerusalem. Turkish law forbade foreigners the right to reside in the Land of Israel. The Egyptians however, in their endeavours to placate the Europeans, opened the gates. The invitation was there, if anyone wanted it. John Nicolayson of the LJS took up this offer in October 1833. Nicolayson became the first permanent Protestant resident in Jerusalem. The ground was being prepared for Michael Solomon Alexander.

Alexander's Work in London
Meanwhile Alexander was still very active back in London. In 1834 the LJS undertook a serious revision of the Hebrew New Testament. The reason is stated by the LJS to its supporters:

Your Committee have felt it their bounden duty to do all in their power to give to the Jews an accurate edition of their own Scriptures, and have therefore taken measures for the immediate revision of the stereotype plates before another impression is struck off.[22]

The revision of the Society's Hebrew Bible was entrusted to Alexander, McCaul and Reichardt and was completed in July 1836.[23] This was not the only project to which Alexander was committed. The second major project was the translation of the Book of Common Prayer into a Hebrew

---

to settle in Jerusalem, but remained in the region awaiting the opportunity to move there.

[21] *Jewish Monthly Intelligence*, (*JMI*), 1832, p. 124. The *JMI* replaced the *JE*.

[22] *LJS Report*, 1834, p. 59.

[23] See Minutes 1839, 1840 & 1842, 23 February 1836, LJS Minute Book c.14, Bodleian.

Prayer Book. Explaining this decision to its supporters, the Society stated in its 1834 Report, that the traditional Jews in particular accused the Christians of being without God. The LJS concluded:

> What better proof can be given to them of their mistake than a copy of the authorized daily prayers of our Church, in which they must discover a spirit of deep and devoted piety, and moreover a striking similarity, both in the contents and the ceremonies, to the prayers and usages of the synagogue. The very circumstance that a certain portion of the Psalms, to which all pious Jews attach such importance, is appointed for every morning and evening, must give the Jew a very different idea of Christianity ... There is a large body of Jews scattered through the world, and amongst them the most learned and the most devout who will read nothing but Hebrew, and if they are to see our Liturgy at all, it must be in a Hebrew dress ...
>
> Rabbinical Jews, who have all their lives been accustomed to a form of prayer, and that in Hebrew, feel a great want of something to supply their place when they become Christians ...
>
> ... There can be no doubt that divine service conducted in Hebrew, according to the forms of our Church, would be highly useful at Jerusalem, and other places where Hebrew is much studied. The number of Jews who understand the Hebrew prayers is much larger than is supposed by some; and it is hardly necessary to observe, that all who understand the language esteem it above all others. The very circumstance of Christian worship in Hebrew would go far to remove the prejudices against Christianity. Everyone who knows anything of the Jews, knows that a good knowledge of Hebrew is the key to a Jew's heart.[24]

This translation work was originally undertaken by Mr. M. Czerskier in Warsaw, but was then entrusted to Alexander, McCaul and Reichardt for revision.[25] By 1835 the first portions were available, and in November 1836 the full version of the Hebrew Book of Common Prayer was complete. At the November 22 meeting of the LJS Committee, Cartwright, the LJS secretary, gave copies to all members of the Committee, and it was agreed that copies would be sent to all the bishops

---

[24] *LJS Report*, 1834, pp. 61-2.

[25] According to Elizabeth Finn (McCaul) they were assisted in this task by Mr. Stanilaus Hoga, 'an accomplished Hebraist, who was a Roman Catholic converted from Judaism in Poland and who came to London.' See Finn, *Reminiscences,* p. 25.

in England and Ireland, as well as the Professors of Hebrew in the various Universities.[26]

The complete version was first used at the Episcopal Jews Chapel on 5 February 1837. The LJS wrote of this occasion:

> It is with great pleasure that your Committee are now able to report to you, that a *regular Hebrew Service* has been established in your Episcopal Chapel. After the lapse of centuries, Christian worship has again commenced in the holy language of the Hebrew nation. On Sunday, the 5th of February, at three o'clock in the afternoon, the Hebrew translation of the Liturgy of the Church of England was used, for the first time, in public. The prayers were read by Rev. A. McCaul, and a sermon was then preached in English by the Rev. M. S. Alexander, upon the appropriate words, "If by any means I may provoke to emulation them which are my flesh, and might save some of them." (Rom xi. 14). A little band of Hebrew Christians joined with Gentiles in worshipping the Redeemer of Israel, in the language and words of their forefathers. It is to be hoped that this remarkable restoration of Christian Hebrew worship may be viewed as a gracious pledge of the approaching revival of the Hebrew Church. It is, at all events, a visible sign of the union of Jew and Gentile, and a striking illustration of the apostolic declaration, that Christ "is our peace, who hath made both one, and that He hath abolished in his flesh the enmity, even the law of commandments contained in ordinances; for to make in himself of two one new man, so making peace."[27]

In the following years Alexander regularly presided at the Hebrew service, often assisting McCaul.[28] He also attended to regular mission duties, as well as travelling and speaking at the LJS centres around the country.

But his ministry wasn't always without incident. On one occasion Alexander had employed 'a policeman to remove an individual from the Mission House in New Street on account of very disorderly behaviour.' It seems that the individual involved must have then begun legal action against Alexander, as the Committee requested a Mr. Grane 'to take the necessary legal steps for the defence of Mr. Alexander.'[29] If this was the

---

[26] Minute 116, 22 November 1836, CMJ Minute Book c.14, Bodleian.

[27] *LJS Report*, 1837, p. 38.

[28] Minute 255, 28 February 1837, CMJ Minute Book L 15, Bodleian. There it was stated that McCaul was to conduct the Hebrew services and Alexander was to assist.

[29] Minute 232, 14 February 1837, CMJ Minute Book L 15, Bodleian.

first time Alexander was involved in such an action, it certainly would not be the last – he would gain considerable experience in Jerusalem!

Apart from such occasional unpleasant experiences, it would seem that Alexander was very content with his lot during this period. His family was growing and enjoying life at Palestine Place, and by all accounts Michael Solomon seemed satisfied with both of his tasks. Yet, ironically, by 1835 he again desired to relocate. He received an invitation to become British chaplain at Constanz[30] for a twelve-month period.

Both King's College and the LJS agreed to him accepting this position, if he so desired, and the LJS offered for him to return afterwards to the same task and salary as he enjoyed previously.[31]

Alexander did not accept the position, but remained at his post in London, and continued his work as before. He had numerous deputation tours: 8-16 May to Portsea and Guildford; 29-30 May to Ipswich and Colchester; 21-22 August to Dunstable; and 11 September to 25 October to various places as determined by the LJS Committee.[32]

Alexander – the Family Man

It was also during this period that the Alexanders hosted Joseph Wolff, an old acquaintance. Deborah, Alexander's daughter, recalled her early impressions of this unusual and eccentric missionary:

> He was very wild, untidy and had dirty finger nails. His black hair hung in curls and he talked very loudly. Everything he did and said was noisy. He bounced about our house, thundered at our knocker at all hours, and one very early morning I heard him in our garden, loudly calling out "Alexander, Alexander, I cannot find a barber, I want my hair cut." This was quite early.
>
> He preached at the Chapel one Sunday morning. Our pew was just under the pulpit, and I was afraid the cushions would come down on our heads, he was so excited. Two ladies in front of us got more fidgety than usual, after he had preached for an hour, so he leant down and said to them, "Ladies, you disturb me, please sit still and don't go. Your dinners will not run away". When we got home after his 1½ hour's sermon, we were at dinner, when we heard his thundering knock, and in he came. He said,

---

[30] A university city in southern Germany bordering Switzerland, and adjacent to Lake Constanz. A popular holiday spot, also for English travelers.
[31] Alexander to H. Smith, 11 May 1835, A9 1835, King's College Archive. Minute 1163, 24 March 1835, LJS Minute Book, c.14, Bodleian.
[32] Minute 116, 22 November 1836, LJS Minute Book c.14, Bodleian.

"Robert,[33] my dear, I have left my spectacles in the pulpit. Just run and fetch them." Robert put down his plate of cherry tart, and the Dr. sat him down and ate it up!

One day he and Mr. Stoddart ... came to dinner. I remember the dessert was laid out in the drawing room, and Bessie and Minnie[34] were sitting one on each side of the chimney piece ... The doctor walked in, and went straight up to the table, and put his dirty hand into a dish of Normandy pippins, spilling the juice on Mama's cherished table, and gulped it down. I couldn't bear him, especially because one day he put me up on a table. I was only 6 years old, and made me show him how he finished his sermon, as he had been told I made fun of him.[35]

In 1837 Alexander and his family enjoyed a month at Kingswalden near Luton. Deborah recalled the trip there:

We drove all the way in a glass coach and stopped half way there for luncheon and rest, at an old-fashioned wayside inn. To this day I remember that drive and our meal in a room smelling of stale beer, with sawdust on the floor. [36]

This and other happy family activities were, unfortunately, seriously affected when in the middle of 1840 the Alexander's eldest daughter, Sarah, died of inflammation of the lungs.[37] Deborah wrote:

Mama was a very long time getting over her death. Papa wrote a little memoir of her life called The Flower Fadeth.

She died in June – the month of roses. To this day, scent of faded roses reminds me of her, surrounded by a profusion of those dear flowers.[38]

Enter Shaftesbury
While Alexander was quite comfortably settled in Palestine Place and King's College events in the East began to stir once again. Unbeknown to Michael Solomon, each stirring moved him closer to his ultimate destiny.

----

[33] The second eldest child.

[34] Two of Alexander's daughters.

[35] Ransom, *ibid*, pp. 2-3.

[36] *ibid*, p. 3.

[37] Mrs. Ransom indicates it may have been 1838. See Ransom, *ibid*, p. 4a.

[38] *ibid*, p. 4. The little Memoir that Michael Solomon wrote about his daughter was entitled *Memoir of Sarah J. W. Alexander, daughter of Rev M. S. Alexander. Written by her father.* MSS 3393 [25], Alexander Papers, Lambeth.

A relative calm had prevailed in the region especially in the province of Syria during the period of the Egyptian occupation. Although the Egyptians upset many of the locals by imposing a centralized and more efficient form of government in the land, calm and security were often the result. Both European and Jewish people had benefited from this new government. The LJS consolidated its presence, especially after 1835 when the General Committee decided to establish a more permanent presence in the Land by purchasing property and building a Protestant Church in Jerusalem.[39] This matter was entrusted to the wise hands of John Nicolayson.

But in the same year another person entered the scene who would play a very prominent role in the restoration of Jerusalem, and of Alexander's future. This man was Anthony Ashley Cooper, later the 7th Earl of Shaftesbury, more commonly known as Lord Shaftesbury.

There were two people who played a significant role in shaping Shaftesbury's perspective concerning Israel, which in turn influenced the future of Alexander. One was an English evangelical, Edward Bickersteth, and the other was a Prussian named Christian Charles Bunsen.[40] In January 1834, while on a visit to Rome, Shaftesbury dined with his cousin, Philip Pusey, and sat next to Bunsen, the Prussian Minister in Rome, whom Shaftesbury described as 'a most simple, unaffected, learned man.' Several days later Shaftesbury wrote in his journal:

> Went in the evening to M. Bunsen's. I was anxious to improve my acquaintance with that excellent and enlightened man. Had some useful and pleasant conversation. He informed me that the Prussian Government had determined to establish, for the maintenance and advancement of the Protestant faith, bishops and cathedral institutions. Jan 18 ... I am really glad to have made the acquaintance, and indeed almost the friendship, of this superior man; his learning and abilities are embellished by a sound and ardent piety. Such men are an honour and comfort to their generation![41]

---

[39] *JI* 1835, pp. 1-2.

[40] Bunsen, the son of a poor soldier, lived in the town of Corbach in the principality of Waldeck. He studied classics at Gottingen University, then Oriental languages in Paris. He then visited Rome and became private secretary to the renowned historian Bartold Niebuhr. He became secretary to the Prussian Embassy at the Holy See, then its charge d'Affaires and finally the Prussian Minister from 1839-41. He was a close friend of King Frederick William IV from 1828, and both men had a keen interest in the Anglican Church.

[41] E. Hodder, *The Life and Work of the Seventh Earl of Shaftesbury* (London: Cassell & Co, 1887), p. 100.

Philip Pusey's brother Edward was prominent in the newly formed Tractarian Movement. Some within this movement desired to bring the Church of England closer to Rome, while others, like Pusey, desired to bring the Church of England back to its ancient Christian roots and to minimize the connection with Lutherans and Calvinists on the continent.

One of those sympathetic to the Roman Catholic Church was John Henry Newman (later a Cardinal in the Catholic Church), who in 1833 was in Rome. While there he too met Bunsen, whom he described as 'most hospitable and kind.' Newman wrote:

> I think I am right in saying that it had been long a desire with the Prussian Court to introduce Episcopacy into the new Evangelical Religion, which was intended in that country to embrace both the Lutheran and Calvinistic bodies. I almost think I heard of the project, when I was at Rome in 1833, at the Hotel of the Prussian Minister, M. Bunsen.[42]

The other person who influenced Shaftesbury was Edward Bickersteth.[43] According to Shaftesbury's biographer Georgina Battiscombe, Bickersteth was a Millenialist, who 'believed that Christ would return in person to establish a glorious kingdom and reign on this earth for a fixed period before the final Day of Judgment ... the sequence of supposed happenings ran as follows. First would come the fulfillment of prophecy by the return of the Jews to Palestine; not till they were established in their ancient home could the Second Coming of Christ take place.'[44]

It appears that Shaftesbury held a similar, basic belief (as did many within the LJS), that the Jewish people would return to the Land of Israel, hear of Jesus as Messiah, and Jesus would then return to Jerusalem. But Shaftesbury was also a committed and compassionate social reformer in Britain, so his natural compassion was also felt towards the Jewish people.

Following his 'conversion' to the Millenialist belief in 1835, Shaftesbury became the leading evangelical proponent in Britain of Israel's future restoration. As the LJS was then the leading restorationist platform, Shaftesbury, like Lewis Way before him, thereafter lent his

---

[42] J. H. Newman, *Apologia Pro Vita Sua*, (London, Longman Green, 1890), p. 141.

[43] Bickersteth, 1786-1850. A prominent evangelical and staunch opponent of the Tractarian movement. He was one of the secretaries of the CMS.

[44] G. Battiscombe, *Shaftesbury, A Biography of the Seventh Earl 1801-1885.*,(London: Constable, 1974), pp. 100-101.

efforts to the Society, becoming at first a vice-president, and later president. His active involvement spanned half a century from 1835 to 1885.

Shaftesbury's wide circle of connections, both ecclesiastical and political, later assisted the restorationist cause. His wife was step-daughter of the Foreign Secretary Lord Palmerston, who would greatly influence the future movements of Michael Solomon Alexander.

Progress in Jerusalem

After much trial and error, finally in 1838, Nicolayson was able to purchase property inside the walls of Jerusalem for the LJS centre. His choice of property could not have been better. Immediately opposite the Citadel or fortress of Jerusalem and adjoining the Jewish, Christian and Armenian sections of Jerusalem, it was perfectly located. There would still be problems though in obtaining the objectives of the LJS, especially the building of a Protestant church, but this was a huge step forward.

Nicolayson was able to purchase the property through the direct intervention of Shaftsbury and Sir Thomas Baring, the President of the LJS, as well as the British Consulate-General in Egypt. Palmerston was very much involved also. Ever since the 1833 Treaty of *Unkiar Skelessi* he was determined to abort Russian (and French) moves in the region, and therefore took a keen interest in any British initiative in the region.

Shaftesbury in particular was excited by this development in Jerusalem. He wrote in the *Quarterly Review Magazine*:

> … a more important undertaking has already been begun by the zeal and piety of those who entertain an interest for the Jewish nation. They have designed the establishment of a church at Jerusalem, if possible on Mount Zion itself, where the order of our service and the prayers of our Liturgy shall daily be set before the faithful in the Hebrew language …
>
> To anyone who reflects upon this event, it must appear one of the most striking that have occurred in modern days, perhaps in any days since the corruptions began in the Church of Christ. It is well known that for centuries the Greek, the Romanist, the Armenian, and the Turk have had their places of worship in the city of Jerusalem, and the latitudinarianism of Ibrahim Pasha has lately accorded that privilege to the Jews. The pure doctrines of the reformation, as embodied and professed in the Church of England, have alone been unrepresented amidst all these corruptions; and Christianity has been contemplated both by Mussulman and Jew, as a

system most hateful to the creed of each, a compound of mummery and image-worship.[45]

Shaftesbury here was clearly challenging the ecclesiastical authority in Jerusalem; the establishment of a Protestant church would confront the 'corruptions' of much of the established religious community there. Little did he, or others realize it at that stage, but the individual who would ultimately be at the forefront of this challenge was none other than Michael Solomon Alexander.

Although the Egyptians were governing Jerusalem and wished as much as possible to placate the British, Mehmet Ali realized the issue of building a new church in Jerusalem was one that could easily inflame Muslim sensitivities there. He referred the matter to the Sultan of Turkey, the custodian, or Caliph, of Islam.

---

[45] Hodder, *ibid*, pp. 239-241.

Chapter 7

Time for Israel's Restoration:
1838-1841

Palmerston and the British Consulate in Jerusalem

For several decades the British Government and LJS had been laying down a clear challenge to the established political *status quo* in Jerusalem. In the period 1823-5 the pioneer LJS missionaries in Jerusalem, Rev. William Lewis and Dr. George Dalton in particular, had written to London and informed their Society that any Protestant work in the City and indeed the Land would be fruitless unless there was a change of government, and the presence there of a British consulate.[1]

The Egyptian occupation fulfilled the first requirement, namely a change of government, while Palmerston was instrumental in answering the other.

Palmerston, no doubt influenced to some degree by Shaftesbury, decided in 1838 to establish a British vice-consulate in Jerusalem.[2] As could be expected the restorationist minded Christians of Britain were very excited by this move. Shaftesbury wrote that the vice-consul's residence 'will be fixed at Jerusalem, but his jurisdiction will extend to the whole country

---

[1] *JE,* 1824, p. 380 & 382; *JE* 1825, p.16-17. Lewis wrote on 21 June 1825: 'I hope the Committee and the friends to the general welfare and peace of Jerusalem, have determined before this to effect something, with the view of obtaining a resident consul or protector, in behalf of visitors and European settlers at Jerusalem, Jews as well as Gentiles.' *JE,* 1825, p. 427; *JE,* 1826, p. 76.

[2] Shaftsbury himself stated as much, but Professor Meir Verete in his fundamental work '*Why the British established a Consulate in Jerusalem,*' English Historical Review, LXXXV, April, 1970, p. 317ff, challenged this assumption, stating that there is no substantial evidence to support such a view. My conclusion is, that with the relationship between these two men as it was and their respective attitudes towards the Levant, there is every likelihood that Shaftsbury influenced the Foreign Secretary.

within the ancient limits of the Holy Land; he is thus accredited, as it were, to the former kingdom of David and the Twelve Tribes.'[3]

The establishment of the consulate was a sound geo-political move. It would enable the British to keep a close eye on Russian and French initiatives in the region – the Russians had a proxy group, the Greek Orthodox, through whom they could increase their political presence, while the French could do the same through the Catholics, whom they protected.[4]

The British Consulate would be possibly the most profound political act affecting the development of the Holy City. It put Jerusalem on the political map. It also proved to be a turning point for the Jewish people living in Jerusalem and Palestine. Amongst the initial instructions given to the British vice-consul, William Tanner Young, were those 'to afford protection to the Jews generally.'[5] Young himself alluded to the potential of this new political initiative, by writing to Palmerston shortly after his arrival:

> There are two parties here, who will doubtless have some voice in the future disposition of affairs – 'The one is the Jew – unto whom God originally gave this land for a possession, and the other, the Protestant Christian, his legitimate offspring. Of both these Great Britain seems the natural guardian.[6]

By stating that there was a position and future for the Jewish people and the Protestants, Young was unconsciously crossing many red lines. His comments were a direct confrontation to the established *status quo,* according to which the Muslims were at the top of the social ladder, followed by the Greek Orthodox, the Roman Catholics, the Armenians, the smaller churches, and on the bottom rung were the Jewish people. The Protestants were not even on the ladder.

The stage was being set for the biggest challenge to this established system for centuries.

---

[3] Hodder, *ibid* pp. 239-241.

[4] The legal provision for this was the Capitulations, laws enacted by the Ottoman Turks regulating foreign involvement in the Turkish Empire. France had entered into a Capitulatory Agreement with Turkey in 1535, and Russia, following defeat of Turkey in war, enacted concessions for her to provide protection to Orthodox Christians within the Turkish Empire, in 1774.

[5] Bidwell to Young, 31 January 1839, FO [Foreign Office file] 78/368 (No 2).

[6] Young to Palmerston, 14 March 1839, FO 78/368 (No 8).

Eastern Question again

Young's efforts in Jerusalem were simultaneous to further political moves in the region. Tensions between the Turkish sultan and Egypt's Mehmet Ali remained high. In 1838 Mehmet Ali announced plans to unite Egypt and Syria into a hereditary kingdom. Turkey, understandably, was perturbed. Palmerston for one wanted Egypt tamed, fearing French involvement with Egypt. He wrote: 'Egyptian civilization must come from Constantinople, and not from Paris, to be durable or consistent with British interests of a most important kind.'[7]

The Turkish sultan then unwisely sent his forces against Mehmet's Egyptian forces in Syria in June 1839 - and suffered a crippling defeat.[8] Then a week after this devastating loss the sultan died in Constantinople. In response to these catastrophes, the Turkish viziers (ministers) agreed to bestow upon Mehmet Ali permanent sovereignty over Syria, which included Palestine.

Palmerston, Prince Metternich of Austria, and other foreign ministers agreed that this would not be a satisfactory arrangement and asked the Turkish government not to agree to these Egyptian demands. Palmerston maintained that Britain's interests would not be served if Egypt (with French support) occupied Syria, especially while Russia was still bound by her treaty with Turkey.

A difficult diplomatic struggle followed. The European powers wished to solve the situation politically and have Mehmet, and his adopted son Ibrahim Pasha, quietly leave Syria. Russia, Austria and Prussia supported Palmerston in this initiative. The French however procrastinated, partly because of the strong support in France for Mehmet Ali. France was the main European supporter of Egypt, and it suited French interests to have Egypt firmly ensconced in Syria and the 'Holy Land.' Besides this, France, which had recently annexed Algeria, would benefit by having Egypt as an ally in North Africa. Thereafter the French press went into action to win over popular support for the Egyptian cause.

The French made it clear to Palmerston that they were not interested in forcing Mehmet Ali to leave Syria if he failed to do so willingly. Palmerston responded by stating that the other Powers (including Russia, Austria and Prussia) would remove him, if necessary without the French.

At this juncture in the political manoeuvering the new Turkish Sultan, Abd-ul-Mezid, issued a reform aimed at satisfying European desires for

---

[7] Jasper Ridley, *Lord Palmerston*, (New York: E.P. Dutton, 1971), p. 222, quoting Palmerston to Granville, 27 May 1839.

[8] See, Ridley, *ibid*, p. 220.

more leniency for non-Muslims in the Turkish Empire. Although quite ineffectual, the *Hatti Sherif of Gulhane*, when issued in November 1839, was nevertheless a progressive move by the Turkish regime.

The Damascus Blood Libel
In this political climate any incident in the Levant was sure to cause serious ramifications. Such an incident occurred in February 1840 in Syria.

A Capuchin monk under French protection was murdered in Damascus. A rumour quickly spread that the monk had been murdered by the Jews, who used his blood for the Passover meal. Several leading Jewish men were put into prison and tortured. A mob then fell upon the Jewish quarter murdering a number of Jewish residents.

The imprisoned men were tried by the French Consul, who, wrote Albert Hyamson 'not only found them guilty but decided that the blood of Christians was an essential of the performance of the Jewish Passover ritual.'[9] Not only did the French Consul condemn the Jews, but the authorities also placed sixty-four Jewish children in prison in order to obtain information.[10]

Palmerston was determined to assist the Damascene Jews as much as possible, and provided diplomatic support for a high level Jewish delegation that travelled to Damascus and the Isle of Rhodes (where a similar event had occurred).[11] This delegation was led by Sir Moses Montefiore, the acknowledged leader of British Jewry as well as other Jewish European representatives.

Although it is clear that Palmerston's decision to intervene in these two cases were politically motivated, namely his desire to thwart all French ambitions in the East, nevertheless there is no doubt he also felt great concern for the welfare of the persecuted Jews.[12]

Some time later Palmerston dispatched a memo to his representatives throughout the Turkish Empire, stating:

> I have accordingly to instruct you that, whenever any case is brought to your knowledge in which Jews resident within your District, shall have been subjected to oppression or injustice, you will make a diligent enquiry

---

[9] Albert Hyamson, *British Consulate in Jerusalem in relation to the Jews of Palestine 1838-1914*, (London, 1939), Vol 1, p. xxxvii.

[10] *JI*, 1840, p. 174, quoting an Arabic Bulletin.

[11] Hearing of the event in Damascus the governor of Rhodes accused the Jewish people of a similar crime, and threatened to destroy the community.

[12] See Mordechai Eliav, *Britain and the Holy Land, 1838-1914*: Selected Documents from the British Consulate of Jerusalem, (Jerusalem, Yad Ben Zvi & Magnes Press, 1997), pp. 130-131.

into the circumstance of the case and will report fully thereupon to Her Majesty's Ambassador at Constantinople ... you will, upon any suitable occasion, make known to the Local Authorities that the British Government feels an interest in the welfare of the Jews in general, and is anxious that they should be protected from oppression; and that the Porte has promised to afford them protection and will certainly attend to any representations which her Majesty's Ambassador at Constantinople may make to it on these matters.[13]

Many Europeans were horrified that such a case reminiscent of the Dark Ages could occur in an age of enlightenment. This event and the possible ramifications upon them, quite understandably, perturbed the Jews of Jerusalem. The rabbis sent a delegation to George Pieritz,[14] a Jewish believer in Jesus, and asked him to 'do what he could to rid them of this calumny; and, in fact requested him to go with one of their rabbies to Damascus for this purpose.'[15] Nicolayson dispatched Pieritz to Damascus to plead on behalf of the Jewish people there. This was such a profound move that even the rabbis offered prayers for the success of the venture.[16]

More indignant than anyone were the Jewish believers in Britain. Alexander McCaul encouraged Michael Solomon Alexander and the Jewish believers to come together over this terrible incident and some fifty-seven added their names to the following declaration:

We, the undersigned, by nation Jews, and having lived to the years of maturity in the faith and practice of modern Judaism, but now by the grace of God members of the Church of Christ, do solemnly protest that we have never directly nor indirectly heard of, much less known among the Jews, of the practice of killing Christians, or using Christian blood, and that we believe this charge, so often brought against them formerly, and now lately revived; to be a foul and satanic falsehood.

The Memo was signed by fifty seven Jewish believers in Jesus and by 'M. S. Alexander, Professor of Hebrew and Rabbinical Literature in King's

---

[13] Palmerston to Ambassador Ponsonby, 21 April 1841, FO 195/181 (No 95).

[14] George Wildon Pieritz, a German-born rabbi, had been sent to Jerusalem in 1838 to assist Nicolayson.

[15] *Nicolayson Diary*, 16 March 1840, Conrad Schick Library, Christ Church, Jerusalem. [Henceforth Schick Library].

[16] *Nicolayson Diary*, 18 March 1840, Schick Library.

College, London; Formerly officiating Rabbi in the Jewish Congregations at Norwich and Plymouth.'[17]

1840 – War and Calls for Israel's Restoration

The Damascus and Rhodes blood libel cases had barely ended when the situation in the Levant flared up again. In London on 15 July 1840 the ambassadors of Prussia, Austria and Russia signed an agreement with Britain, represented by Palmerston, calling upon Egypt to withdraw from Syria. The ultimatum was now firmly on the table.

The European powers now began devising strategies for the future of the province of Syria once the Egyptians were ousted. It provided an ideal opportunity also for British restoration minded evangelicals to present their cause. The LJS in particular was aware of the proclaimed belief amongst Jewish people that the year of their redemption was drawing near, and great things were anticipated in the Jewish year 5600 between September 1839 to September 1840. The LJS spokesman, Shaftesbury, wrote in his diary on 25 July 1840:

> Anxious about the hopes and prospects of the Jewish people. Everything seems ripe for their return to Palestine ... Could the five Powers of the West be induced to guarantee the security of life and possessions of the Hebrew race, they would now flock back in rapidly augmenting numbers. Then by the blessing of God I will prepare a document, fortify it by all the evidence I can accumulate, and, confining to the wisdom and mercy of the Almighty, lay it before the Secretary of State for Foreign Affairs.[18]

Shaftesbury's desire was for a clause to be inserted into the final treaty allowing for the restoration of the Jewish people to the Land of Israel, hopefully under British protection.[19] Several days later, on 1 August 1840, he again wrote in his diary:

> Dined with Palmerston. After dinner left alone with him. Propounded my scheme, which seemed to strike his fancy; he asked some questions, and readily promised to consider it. How singular is the order of Providence!

---

[17] *JI*, 1840, pp. 240-41.

[18] Hodder, *ibid*, p, 166.

[19] Ashley to Palmerston, 25 September 1840, quoted in Hodder, *ibid*, pp. 168-169. This situation is not all that different from that confronting Cyrus, King of Persia. Faced with a potential rival in Egypt and a vacant buffer zone between him and Egypt, perhaps strategic and economic factors may have induced him to permit the return of the Jewish people to the Land of Israel.

Singular, that is if estimated by man's ways! Palmerston has already been chosen by God to be an instrument of good to His ancient people; to do homage, as it were, to their inheritance, and to recognize their rights without believing their destiny. And it seems he will yet do more. But though the motive be kind, it is not sound. I am forced to argue politically, financially, commercially; these considerations strike him home; he weeps not like his master over Jerusalem ...[20]

Shaftesbury's proposal impressed Palmerston, who in turn then sent the following dispatch, on 11 August 1840, to his ambassador, Ponsonby, in Constantinople:

There exists at present among the Jews dispersed over Europe a strong notion that the time is approaching when their nation is to return to Palestine; and consequently their wish to go thither has become more keen, and their thoughts have been bent more intently than before upon the means of realizing that wish. It is well known that the Jews of Europe possess great wealth; and it is manifest that any country in which a considerable number of them might choose to settle, would derive great benefit from the riches which they would bring into it.[21]

It is easy to see here the outcome of Shaftesbury's words that he was forced 'to argue politically, financially, commercially' for Palmerston obviously exaggerated the readiness and capability of the Jewish people to return. Palmerston needed to arouse the interest of the sultan to the positive aspect of Israel's restoration, and if exaggeration was called for, then exaggeration there would be. This is further evidenced in the same memo:

... it would be of manifest importance to the Sultan to encourage the Jews to return to, and settle in, Palestine; because the wealth which they would bring with them would increase the resources of the Sultan's dominions; and the Jewish people, if returning under the sanction and protection and at the invitation of the Sultan, would be a check upon any future evil designs of Mehmet Ali or his successor.[22]

What Palmerston was proposing was the establishment of a buffer zone between Turkey and Egypt, in the Land of Israel, and for this buffer zone

---

[20] Hodder, *ibid*, p. 167.

[21] Palmerston to Ponsonby, 11 August 1840, FO 78/390 (No 134).

[22] Palmerston to Ponsonby, 11 August 1840, FO 78/390 (No 134).

to be occupied by the Jewish immigrants from Europe. This very idea was described in an editorial in the prestigious *Times* newspaper on 17 August, which endorsed the concept of the restoration of Israel.[23]

Shaftesbury and the restoration minded evangelicals were excited, and he wrote on 24 August: 'Palmerston tells me that he has already written to Lord Ponsonby, to direct him to open an intercourse with Reschid Pasha at Constantinople respecting protection and encouragement to the Jews. This is a prelude to the Antitype of the decree of Cyrus ...'

Shaftesbury added on 29 August: 'The newspapers teem with documents about the Jews. Many assail and many defend them.'[24] His efforts were greatly aided by Erasmus Scott Calman,[25] a Jewish believer in Jesus and member of the LJS mission in Jerusalem, who was in London at the time. Calman visited Shaftesbury, who was obviously grateful to receive a strong encouragement at this time. Israeli historian Isaiah Friedmann wrote that Calman 'was imbued with Jewish national sentiments and nourished a burning desire to see the restoration of the Jewish people to the Land of their Fathers.'[26]

Calman, at Shaftesbury's encouragement, wrote a memorandum on 3 August 1840, in which he stated that his sojourn in the Land of Israel had convinced him that Jewish people would return and till the land so long as there was security of life and possession. He wrote:

> A Proclamation like that of Cyrus would be echoed by hundreds of thousands of Jews in Poland, Russia and elsewhere, and by the rich as well as by the poor who would gladly exchange their present harassed and uncertain mode of life for the quiet and more uncertain one that would

---

[23] See, S. Lieber, *Mystics and Missionaries, The Jews in Palestine, 1799-1840*, (Salt Lake City, 1992), p. 374.

[24] Hodder, *ibid*, p. 168.

[25] Calman (1796-1890) was a Jewish believer in Jesus from Bauska, Courland, in what is now part of Latvia. He arrived in Beirut in January 1833 en route to Baghdad as a LJS worker, but instead remained to assist Nicolayson. He journeyed with Nicolayson to Jerusalem in January 1833 before leaving for Baghdad. However this venture did not succeed and Calman rejoined Nicolayson in Jerusalem in October 1834. Due to sickness he later went to Beirut. He then joined the Church of Scotland delegation of inquiry (McCheyne and Bonar), visiting Jewish communities in Eastern Europe and Prussia en route to London where he arrived in November 1839.

[26] Isaiah Friedmann, *The Question of Palestine*, (New Brunswick, 1992), p. xviii.

result from the cultivation of the soil … They would be enabled to sit under their vine and fig-tree and none should make them afraid.[27]

Calman's memorandum was added to Shaftesbury's and both were sent to Palmerston on 25 September 1840, and then in turn were forwarded to Ambassador Ponsonby on 25 November.

Outbreak of War
Meanwhile, as Shaftesbury was pushing forward his restorationist agenda, and the other powers were formulating theirs, matters took a political nose dive. French opposition to the Allied ultimatum for Egyptian withdrawal increased, and by October 1840 the French actually began increasing their Mediterranean fleet. The French king, Louis-Philippe, notified Queen Victoria of the negative mood in France towards the Allied position. There was, he stated, a strong group in France desiring a united Syria and Egypt, under French patronage (as Palmerston was looking to a Jewish presence in Palestine somehow under British patronage). King Louis-Philippe did assure Queen Victoria though that he doubted France would go to war against the Allies over this issue.[28]

Yet war was imminent, especially when Mehmet Ali adamantly refused to comply with the Allied request for him to withdraw from Syria. The campaign to oust him began in late October, and climaxed on 3 November 1840 when a predominantly British fleet[29] bombed and captured Acre, the primary seaport along the Mediterranean coast. The British commander Admiral Sir Charles Napier, then induced Mehmet Ali to surrender, and in return to accept the offer of a hereditary monarchy in Egypt.

Although temporary Turkish control was re-established over the province of Syria, a final decision on the future status of the region would now need to be determined by the European powers and Turkey. It would be at least six months though until this final decision would be reached, in London, in July 1841, with the *Treaty for the Pacification of the Levant.*

Whatever solution was found, it would surely be opposed to French designs, as they sided with Egypt. Palmerston in a letter to Queen Victoria on 11 November 1840 wrote:

---

[27] Memorandum by E.S. Calman, 3 August 1840, in Ashley to Palmerston, 25 September 1840, enclosure No 1 in Palmerston to Ponsonby, 25 November 1840, FO 195/165 (No 261).

[28] Lord Palmerston to Queen Victoria, 11 November 1840, (Connell , *Regina v Palmerston* ,pp 25-27) quoted in Ridley, *ibid*, p. 239.

[29] A small Austrian flotilla also participated which included Archduke Charles.

There is no doubt a large party among the leading politicians in France who have long contemplated the establishment of a virtually, if not actually, independent State in Egypt and Syria, under the direct protection of France, and that party feel great disappointment and resentment at finding their schemes in this respect baffled.[30]

British Reactions to Victory

All parties now had an opportunity of presenting their various ideas and agendas for the future of the Holy Land. British evangelical Christians again led the way, from both sides of the border. The Commission of the General Assembly of the Church of Scotland sent a memo to the Foreign Office on 23 October 1840 in which they appealed for Israel's restoration.[31] Palmerston also forwarded this to Ponsonby on 24 November, strengthening his case as previously presented by Shaftesbury who represented the English restorationist movement. In his letter to Ponsonby, Palmerston added:

> ... that the matters to which it relates excite a very deep interest in the minds of a large number of Persons in the United Kingdom, and the Sultan would enlist in his favour the good opinion of numerous and powerful classes in this country if he were immediately to issue some formal edict or declaration granting and assuring to such Jews as may choose to fix themselves in any part of the Turkish Dominions, but more especially in Syria, full security for their Persons and Property, and free liberty to go and come and it [would] probably contribute much to give confidence to such Jews as might determine to settle in Palestine, in consequence of such an Edict ...[32]

The LJS wrote in an editorial in its mouthpiece the *Jewish Intelligence*:

> The course of events, of late, in Syria, has been attentively watched by all those who are anxiously looking for the restoration of Israel, and awaiting the fulfillment of the sure word of prophecy ... It is true, that the Jewish nation were in no degree involved in the cause of contention, and formed

---

[30] Palmerston to Queen Victoria, 11 November 1840, (Connell, *Regina v Palmerston*, pp. 25-7), quoted in J. Ridley, *ibid*, p. 239.

[31] 'Acting Committee of the General Assembly of the Church of Scotland for Promoting Christianity among the Jews' to Viscount Palmerston, 23 October 1840, quoted in *JI*, 1840, p. 35. *JI* replaced *JMI*.

[32] Palmerston to Ponsonby, 24 November 1840, FO 78/391 (no 248).

no part of the elements in collision; but who shall say what is the hidden meaning and intention of the array of emphatic events which has lately passed before our eyes in the East? ...

The way, therefore, seems to be opening remarkably for the restoration of the Jews ...[33]

To encourage Palmerston in his thinking about making serious proposals for the future of the Holy Land, Consul Young who had temporarily vacated Jerusalem during the war, wrote to the Foreign Secretary soon after returning:

It is perfectly clear my Lord that without the aid of the British Forces the Turks could not have regained possession of Syria – and I would respectfully submit to Your Lordship my humble opinion, that without the continued aid of the British Government to advise, and assist in enforcing measures for the general good and tranquility of the Country – the Turks cannot govern Syria.[34]

Meanwhile, in January 1841 the LJS recalled Nicolayson from Jerusalem (where he had remained during the war), in order to determine future operations in Palestine in view of the expected influx of Jews. It was the desire of the LJS to consolidate and expand their work in Jerusalem. The LJS Committee made numerous resolutions and recorded the following to substantiate such a move:

That the strong feeling known to exist amongst the Jews now scattered and dispersed over the habitable Globe to their beloved City Jerusalem, and their expectations so prominently entertained by them at this time of a speedy return to their promised land, together with the equally anxious desire manifested on the part of the Christian community to do good to Zion, constitute the objects contemplated in the foregoing Resolutions ...[35]

Those resolutions amounted to various initiatives to be put into effect in Jerusalem in order to be ready for the expected influx of Jewish people, and hence a greater increase in ministry opportunities amongst them.

Such anticipation however was not based upon any definite reality from within the Jewish world. It is true that for some years a number of rabbis

---

[33] *JI*, 1841, p. 34.
[34] Young to Palmerston, 25 January 1841, p. 160, FO 78/444.
[35] Minute 1334, 10 April 1841, LJS Minute Book M, Bodleian.

were anticipating great redemptive events for the period 1839-1840.[36] However it would appear that these indicators were insufficient grounds for the LJS to have made such far reaching decisions and resolutions.

European Plans for Jerusalem and the Land of Israel

The anticipated restoration of Israel was affecting more than just the LJS and the evangelical Christian world. The secular press also got excited about the prospects. The correspondent of the *Times* wrote:

> Let the four Allied Powers now publish to the four quarters of the world their determination to restore the Jews from all nations to the Holy Land, and to assist them in rebuilding the walls and temple of Jerusalem; and assuredly, the multitudinous descendants of Abraham, already restless with the anxiety of desire, and excited by the anticipated fulfillment of this regeneration, would arise to the summons as one man. The extremest time fixed by their rabbies for the coming of Christ is passed – the close of last month quenched their expectations of the advent, and they are, in consequence, just now unusually shaken. Let, I repeat, the Quadruple Alliance take advantage of this conjuncture, and issue a manifesto for the restoration and independence of the Hebrew tribes, and by next spring the banks of the Euphrates would be once more thronged, and the long line of the European and African coasts be crowded by the gathering hosts of Israel. From the different ports on these shores they could be readily shipped, and, convoyed by the fleets that now cruise in the Mediterranean, be triumphantly landed on the strand of their long-lost Palestine – a more befitting occupation this, than the waging of a petty war to the hazard of all Europe's peace.[37]

While the British were pushing the Jewish cause, the other powers had their agendas for the future of the 'Holy Land.'

The French Plan.   The French led the way with their new foreign minister, Francois Guizot. Guizot was French ambassador to London for the first eight months of 1840. When Egypt lost the war of 1840, the French Government fell, and Guizot was recalled to become French

---

[36] Rabbi Yehudah Alkalai was one of these.   Alkalai, from his study of the Cabbalah (a Jewish book of mysticism) concluded that great events would occur in the Jewish year 5600. He, like others, were influenced by the blood libels of 1840, and believed the Jewish people had to take care of themselves. A return to the Land of Israel became the major platform of his beliefs and writings.

[37] Quoted in *JI,* 1841, p. 35.

Foreign Minister. If any Frenchman was aware of British interests in the Land of Israel and especially of the strong evangelical agenda calling for Israel's restoration, then it was Guizot.

He was determined in his new position, therefore to increase French interests, with or without Egypt as a proxy. In this, he was influenced by Alphonse de Lamartine[38] who also stated that France must use the Catholics of the Levant in order to advance their own imperial ambitions.[39] Guizot's proposal was for something like a Christian Jerusalem (guaranteed by the powers) and separate from the remainder of the *pashalik* (province), or even a Christian entity in the entire *pashalik* of the area of southern Syria, or Palestine. However, there was opposition to this proposal from King Louis Philippe.

Guizot summed up his feelings in a letter to the French ambassador in Russia, Brugiere de Barante, on 31 December 1840:

> The Christian powers have rendered a great service to the Sultan. It is necessary that the Christianity of the East gain some benefit from this [service]. It is just. It will prove of advantage not only in the East but also in the West. The Governments ought to set an example of respect, of interest, of real and active interest for the cause of the great ethical faiths of the nations and of everything connected with them … the days of the Crusaders are past, but there always is a Jerusalem, and it is always the object of veneration, of affection to many millions of people, French, English, German, Russian. If the Christian Governments are in a position, by means of negotiations and peaceful intervention, to obtain something for the security and the dignity of Jerusalem, it is their duty to make the attempt …
>
> … We are still influential in Syria, the most influential of all [the powers]. The latest events have by no means destroyed the old preference which the eastern Catholics have always had for us. We shall cultivate it in those very places. Our conduct and language in the West ought to be in harmony with our position and our deeds in the East.'[40]

---

[38] Alphonse de Lamartine, 1790-1869 was a French writer and politician.

[39] Mayir Verete, *A Plan for the Internationalization of Jerusalem,* in Norman Rose, editor 'From Palmerston to Balfour: Collected Essays of Mayir Verete,' (London, Frank Cass, 1992), p. 147. There are two ways to spell his name, Mayir and Meir.

[40] Brugiere de Barante, *Souvenirs,* Vol 6, pp. 558-60, quoted in Verete, *ibid,* pp. 142-3.

Guizot was very careful to keep his plan hidden from the British. The French idea was to adopt a joint strategy with Russia and in the process squeeze Britain out. This was logical as Russia was the only other power except France that had a sizeable proxy population in the Levant.

Palmerston heard of Guizot's proposal from his ambassador in Paris, Lord Granville, who had heard it from the Russian ambassador Petrovich Pahlen. Palmerston wrote to Granville that Guizot's Jerusalem Plan:

> ... is only a subtle plan tending to the same end which the French have steadily had in view – to weaken the Sultan as much as possible, and to obtain for France every possible opening for the exercise of domineering influence in the Levant. We cannot listen to such a plan. We want to set up the Turkish Empire and not to pull it down ... [41]

Guizot obviously contacted others about his plan, including Prince Metternich of Austria.[42] The King of Naples was interested in co-operating with the French on this Jerusalem Plan. In fact he even recommended his brother, the Prince of Capia, to be the King of Jerusalem. [43] Verete stated: 'Guizot and the French Foreign Office may perhaps also have intended to thwart proposals and schemes then current in England ... for the restoration of the Jews to Palestine.'[44]

Ultimately though it appeared there was just not the support for a Christian Jerusalem Plan. Guizot then approached Prince Metternich with a modified joint Catholic proposal. Here again he encountered problems, for Metternich was determined, like Palmerston, to stabilize not destabilize the Turkish Empire. It seemed to him that Guizot's proposal was apt to destabilize the Turkish Empire. Metternich also seemed to think that Austria would be under represented by such a scheme.

The Austrian Plan. Prince Metternich also was aware of Muslim sensitivities in this issue, as the sultan was the Caliph of Islam, and would never release one of the holy Islamic cities. The Turks, he believed, would never consent to Jerusalem becoming a free and Christian city, and most certainly not a Jewish dominated one!

---

[41] Palmerston to Granville, 7 January 1841, PRO/GD 29, box 425, quoted in Verete, *ibid*, p. 144.
[42] Prince Klemens von Metternich, 1773-1859, played a leading role in the Congress of Vienna and end of Napoleonic Wars, and dominated European politics from 1814-1848.
[43] See Verete, *ibid*, pp. 146-7.
[44] *ibid*, pp. 150-1.

Metternich thought of setting up a 'Turkish Commissioner in the Holy Land' for the protection of Christian pilgrims. But the Russians opposed this idea, as Nesselrode,[45] the Russian Foreign Minister stated that the proposal 'did not appear to him a necessary or desirable measure, and that the Consuls in Syria were adequate to protect the Europeans whom commerce, piety, or curiosity might attract to that country.'[46]

The Russian Plan. It seems that the Russians never agreed to any of the other plans, as they had their own. At this point they also seemed desirous of fostering good relations with Britain, and thereby weren't eager to endorse any French plan.

But Nesselrode did propose that the area of Palestine be made a separate *pashalik*, with independence for Jerusalem, which would be governed separately directly from Constantinople. Russian proposals were later enhanced by their representative at the London Conference, D.P. Tatitschew. These various proposals also proved unacceptable.

The Prussian Plan. Prussia, which joined the Allied forces so as not to be left out, also had an agenda.[47] In 1840 a new king, Frederick William IV, came to the throne, and it was he in particular who wanted to enhance Prussian interests in the East.

The Prussians envisaged a treaty between Turkey and the Europeans, guaranteeing control and direction by the Christians over the predominately Christian areas of Jerusalem, Bethlehem and Nazareth. Under this arrangement, Russia would appoint the Orthodox representative, the French and Austrians would appoint the Roman Catholic representative, and the British and Prussians would appoint the Protestant representative.[48] A covering letter to this proposal, which was addressed to the British Government, stated the need for gaining property near the Church of the Holy Sepulchre.[49]

---

[45] Count Karl Nesselrode, 1780–1862, was a Russian statesman of German descent.

[46] Verete, *ibid,* p. 151.

[47] Ridley, *ibid,* p. 226.

[48] Lucien Wolf, *Notes on the Diplomatic History of the Jewish Question,* (London, 1919), p. 105.

[49] R. W. Greaves, 'The Jerusalem Bishopric 1841' in *English Historical Review,* 64, 1948, p. 336.

Later, in early 1841, Helmuth von Moltke, the Prussian military attaché in Constantinople, proposed creating Palestine as a buffer zone between Turkey and Egypt, and placing it under Prussian protection.[50]

All of these Prussian proposals came to naught. They sought too much and were opposed by the Turks who had no desire to grant Christian sovereignty over part of her territory. Equally, they were bound to elicit opposition from both the Russians who protected the Orthodox and the French who protected the Catholics.

On 30 March 1841 the Prussian king dictated to Joseph Radowitz,[51] his close associate, the address he wanted delivered to the Heads of State at the forthcoming Peace Conference. This revealed the king's intentions of taking advantage of the unprecedented opportunity offered by the present situation. William Hechler[52] in his profound work entitled *The Jerusalem Bishopric* wrote that the king himself stated that his idea 'was capable of general extension, not merely as a Prussian, but a German question; and again, not merely as a German, but a general Protestant question, when viewed in its connection with the entire Protestant Church.'[53] This *Memoire,* was presented in French.[54]

Soon, though, the real world caught up with the idealistic new king. There were so few Protestants and even fewer Germans in the Holy Land, that the practicality of establishing a purely German entity there were negligible. The king needed a starting point, and where better than Jerusalem, the historic centre of both Judaism and Christianity.[55] And the king knew of the LJS presence there.

The period leading up to July 1841 was full of interest and activity. And it wasn't just confined to an interest in Israel's restoration. Many saw this as an ideal opportunity to enforce the stipulations of the *Hatti Sherif* and to confirm the protection of Christians in the East. The Earl of Chichester, the President of CMS, wrote to Foreign Secretary Palmerston on 25 March

---

[50] M. Eliav, *Eretz Israel and its Yishuv in the Nineteenth century (1777-1917),* (Jerusalem, 1978) [Hebrew], p. 48.

[51] Joseph Maria von Radowitz (1797-1853) was a Prussian general and statesman.

[52] William Hechler, (1845-1931) whose father was a LJS staff member, wrote a history of the Bishopric in 1883. Hechler was at one time tutor for the children of the Grand Duke of Baden and knew members of the German royal family. He was later chaplain of the British Embassy in Vienna, and was instrumental in introducing Theodore Herzl's Zionist programme to the German Kaiser.

[53] William Hechler, *The Jerusalem Bishopric,* (London, 1883), pp. 26-27.

[54] Bunsen, *ibid,* volume 1, quoted in Skinner, James, *The Three Anglican Bishops in Jerusalem,* in Church Quarterly Review, July 1884, p. 328.

[55] See Hechler, *ibid,* p. 27.

1841 expressing the view 'that British Christians should have the same protection and religious liberty in the Ottoman Empire as other Christian Churches.' He proposed there be 'ecclesiastical authority' directing 'the Clergy of the Church of England in those parts.'[56]

Meanwhile there was activity on the ground. Consul Young in Jerusalem was keeping a close eye on new developments. He wrote an alarming dispatch to Palmerston on 4 June 1841, stating that the Greeks were constructing two new buildings for use by Russians and 'to be at the disposal of Russia.'[57] Similar observations were made concerning French aspirations and activities through the Catholics.

All Plans Rejected

All of these proposals for the future status of Jerusalem and Palestine came to nothing. There was just too much suspicion of one party and nation against another. Each had a separate agenda.

Meanwhile, British Admiral Napier had concluded an agreement with Mehmet Ali at the close of 1840, whereby in exchange for surrendering the Turkish fleet (which Egypt had previously captured) and accepting the terms of the 1840 Treaty of London, Napier would ship out the remaining Egyptian soldiers before they were massacred by the locals.

He also promised that the Sultan would confer a hereditary *pashalik* upon Mehmet Ali in Egypt. Napier's superiors were furious about this move made without their agreement. Nevertheless this was finally agreed to on 13 February 1841, although the Egyptians had still to accept the sovereignty of the Sultan over Egypt.

The final terms for the future of the province of Syria and other issues from the War of 1840 were still to be resolved at a meeting scheduled for 15 July 1841 in London. Yet numerous issues were resolved already – none of the European powers would gain any advantage in the region over another. Not even Britain, whose navy did the most to oust the Egyptians from the Land of Israel, gained any advantage. But many Britons, politicians and restoration minded Christians alike, remembered the debt that Turkey owed Britain.

---

[56] Stephen Orchard, *English Evangelical Eschatology 1790-1850*, unpublished PhD thesis, University of Cambridge, 1968, incomplete copy in author's possession p. 205, quoting CMS letter book G/AC1, p. 405 letter of 20 March 1841.

[57] Young to Palmerston, 4 June 1841, FO 78/444.

Chapter 8

The Protestant Bishopric: 1841

The New Prussian Proposal

In April 1841 the Prussian King summoned Christian Carl Josias Bunsen,[1] his envoy in Switzerland and confidant, to the Sans Souci Palace at Potsdam. Bunsen, on 24 April 1841, wrote to his wife from Naumburg:

> Early in the morning, the thought was clear and living before my soul, that the King had called me with a view to do something in the Holy Land; and that it might be the will of the Lord, and probably would be that of the King, that in Jerusalem the two principal Protestant Churches of Europe should, across the grave of the Redeemer, reach to each other the right hand of fellowship.[2]

Bunsen also wrote to his wife: 'The centre of the thoughts of all hearts is the Holy Land; and many assured me, that with prayer and with true affection they look to Frederick William IV.'[3]

Bunsen was no stranger to the affairs of the Land of Israel, as he knew Shaftesbury and the work in Jerusalem of the LJS. Bunsen and Shaftesbury, as previously related, became acquainted in 1834 when Bunsen was a Prussian minister at Rome, and Shaftesbury had 'formed a very high estimate of the excellence of his character.'[4] According to a letter Bunsen wrote to his wife, both he and Shaftesbury had together

---

[1] Bunsen had just received a commission as Prussian minister at Berne when he was summoned by the King of Prussia in 1841. Later he was the Prussian representative in London from 1841-1853. His son Ernest remained in England, and Ernest's son, Sir Maurice de Bunsen, chaired the important *De Bunsen Committee* in 1915 which provided the platform for the Balfour Declaration.

[2] F. Bunsen, *Memoirs*, I, (London, 1868), p. 594, Bunsen to his wife, 26 April 1841, quoted in Greaves, *ibid*, p. 335.

[3] Bunsen to his wife, 26 April, 1841, quoted in W.H.Hechler, *The Jerusalem Bishopric*, (London, 1883), p. 26.

[4] Hodder, *ibid*, p. 199.

worked on a plan, called 'the Jerusalem Plan', as early as 10 December 1838.[5] It was this 'Plan' that the King was about to discuss.

Through the spring of 1841 the King and Bunsen worked at Sans Souci Palace over the 'Plan' for establishing German Protestantism in Jerusalem, in partnership with the British. Bunsen recalls that the King told him: 'Go to England, and in my name offer the hand of brotherhood and of brotherly co-operation to the Church of England over the tomb of our common Saviour.'[6]

Geo-politically the King wanted to introduce Prussia into the orbit of the East. Having being rebuffed concerning his purely Prussian plans, he saw his only chance was to attach himself to the British concerns in Jerusalem, which were almost synonymous with the LJS. P. J. Welch commented:

> Frederick William was intelligent enough to see that political and economic facts ruled out an exclusively Prussian episcopate in the Holy Land: it was a shrewd move to attach German congregations to a bishopric closely associated with the Church of England.[7]

Yet the King had other more local ambitions also for the Jerusalem Plan, as Robert Blake suggests:

> He was also anxious to bring about a union between the Protestant churches. Episcopacy was a serious difficulty…But, although no Lutheran bishops actually existed, bishops were not incompatible with Lutheranism. The King and Bunsen hoped – and their opponents feared – that the Jerusalem Bishopric would lead to episcopacy in Prussia. Protestant unity, alleviation of the Christian condition in Jerusalem, and an increased diplomatic leverage in Turkey combined to encourage the project Baron Bunsen put forward to the British Government in June 1841.[8]

Two reasons made it imperative that the King of Prussia move quickly to present his 'Plan' to the British. Firstly in June 1841 the British Government passed the *Colonial Bishoprics Act*, whereby it was decided

---

[5] Bunsen to his wife, no date, quoted in Bishop Wilberforce, *Life,* vol. I, p. 608, quoted in James Skinner, *ibid,* p. 329.
[6] Message given at LJS AGM, May 1842, in *JI,* 1842, p. 191.
[7] P.J. Welch, *Anglican Churchmen and the establishment of the Jerusalem Bishopric,* in Journal of Ecclesiastical History, Vol. 8, No 2, 1957, p. 193.
[8] Robert Blake, *The Origins of the Jerusalem Bishopric,* p. 90, in *Church State and Society in the 19th Century,* (Munchen: 1984), pp. 87-95.

to establish overseas bishoprics, the first to be in New Zealand, and the second in the Mediterranean, either at Malta or Gibraltar. If the King wanted to 'use' Britain as a stepping stone to the East, (that is, Jerusalem), he needed to act before any decision was firmly made concerning either of these other Mediterranean locations.

The second reason was that on 5 June 1841, the Whig Government of Melbourne and Palmerston was defeated in the House of Commons. If the Prussians were to have a sympathetic hearing in England, it was essential they moved before the Tories could establish a new Government.

Finally, by 8 June all seemed in place for Bunsen to travel to England, a country not unfamiliar to him. He had worked there before and he was married to an English woman, formerly Frances Waddington. Bunsen was also on good terms with C. J. Blomfield, the Bishop of London, and had contact with a future leader in church affairs, Samuel Wilberforce, and future prime minister, William Gladstone.[9]

Bunsen carried with him three proposals, two of which were to be attached to the Memorandum for the 15 July London Conference, for the *Treaty for the Pacification of the Levant.* One of these was for the Turks to issue a new land settlement law, permitting in particular Protestant Christians the right to own land. The second proposal called for the setting up of a Protestant corporation so that 'members of the two national churches of England and Prussia' could capitalize upon the benefits guaranteed under the *Hatti Sherif.* The third Prussian proposal, separate from the two attached to the Peace Conference and for direct discussion with the British Government and Church, pertained to the establishment of a *Protestant Bishopric* in Jerusalem. The King's instructions were for Bunsen to ascertain and propose:

In how far the English National Church, already in possession of a parsonage on the Mount Zion, and having commenced there the building of a church, would be inclined to accord to the Evangelical National Church of Prussia a sisterly position in the Holy Land.

THAT THE ENGLISH CHURCH ERECT A BISHOPRIC OF IT'S OWN[10] at Jerusalem, the King's Majesty regards as first condition and beginning of combined operations. The foundation appears already laid, as it were, by a special Providence. The first-fruits of the mission in Jerusalem warrant the fairest hopes. Its suspension and present

---

[9] Welch, *ibid*, p. 193.

[10] Capitals in original.

melancholy condition seem to render an Episcopal arrangement in that place advisable and of urgent necessity. Nothing but Episcopal superintendence and decision on the spot can be of any use: the subjection of the mission to a see at Malta would not appear to his Majesty either a satisfactory or a truly apostolic arrangement.

The Bishopric to be erected at Jerusalem would, therefore, connect itself with the foundation and buildings already begun on the Mount Zion, and comprehend all evangelical Christians willing to take part in it ... His Majesty is willing and disposed, when a bishopric of this kind is founded, to allow one or more clergy and missionaries of his subjects, for the sake of the Jewish converts who speak German, and for the benefit of the evangelical Christians of the German language, to join this Episcopal arrangement. As a manifestation of his sentiments, his Majesty will readily allow such persons to obtain ordination from the English Church. His Majesty specially desires to see this place in Jerusalem itself. [11]

The King obviously also wanted some political advantage for Prussia. But it appears he also entertained ecclesiastical changes in the structure of the German Church, and thought Jerusalem would be a good place to experiment. Samuel Wilberforce wrote:

The King of Prussia's hope is, by degrees, to get ... his future bishops ordained in Palestine, in order to co-operate with us. Of course, a stubborn old-grown Lutheran would kick. [12]

Bunsen in England
Bunsen arrived in London on 18 June, and several days later, on 24 June, he met with Shaftesbury, who wrote: 'My friend Bunsen has just called, and has brought me a most honourable and gratifying message from the King of Prussia ... The mission of Bunsen is a wonder; God grant that its issue may be a wonder.'[13] Of this meeting Bunsen wrote to his wife:

It is to me an indescribable delight to be enabled to-day to read to that excellent Lord Ashley the "Instruction" and my further statements; for he

---

[11] *The Jerusalem Bishopric*, (London, Hatchard & Son, 1856), p. 4.
[12] Bishop Samuel Wilberforce, *Life,* Vol. 1, p. 201, quoted in James Skinner, *ibid*, p. 331.
[13] Hodder, *ibid,* p. 199.

was the man who took up our plan for both in the night of December 10, 1838 ...[14]

Although Prussia had been part of the Quadruple Alliance which defeated Egypt in 1840, (though they had played only a minor role in the campaign), the Prussian King knew he would need the full diplomatic assistance and co-operation of Britain, the other major Protestant power, and the Anglican Church, to carry through his various schemes.

Following Bunsen's initial meeting with Shaftesbury matters progressed very quickly. He wrote to Palmerston on 3 July 1841 that these new proposals were 'so entirely and so essentially different from the former proposals.'[15] Bunsen then met with Palmerston on 4 July[16] and several days later with Queen Victoria. He also held other high profile meetings: with Howley, the Archbishop of Canterbury; Blomfield, the Bishop of London; Kaye the Bishop of Lincoln; and Dr. Vernon Harcourt, the Archbishop of York. And there were further meetings with Shaftesbury, of whom he wrote to his wife on 13 July: '... he was the man who took up our cause, and set the Jerusalem bishopric a-going.'[17]

The Treaty for the Pacification of the Levant – 15 July 1841.

Two days after penning this letter the *Treaty for the Pacification of the Levant*[18] was ratified in London. None of the proposals of the Allies for the future status of the Holy Land were accepted – not the British plan for Israel's restoration, nor the King of Prussia's initial grandiose plans for Protestant expansion. Palestine would return to Turkish control. Henceforth, it would appear, Britain's restorationist hopes, and Prussia's pan-Protestant ambitions, would need to be channeled through other means - namely the LJS and the Bishopric 'Plan.'

Palmerston did have one triumph though – the 1833 *Treaty of Unkiar Skelessi* was revoked. Henceforth the Bosphorus Straits, Sea of Marmara

---

[14] Bunsen to his wife, no date, Bishop Wilberforce *Life ,*vol I, p. 608, quoted in James Skinner, p. 329.

[15] Bunsen to Palmerston, 3 July 1841, FO 64/235, quoted in R.W Greaves, 'The Jerusalem Bishopric 1841' in *English Historical Review,* 64, 1948, p. 335. Former proposals referring to those of late 1840 and early 1841.

[16] Bunsen to Palmerston, 3 July 1841, FO 64/235, quoted in Greaves, *ibid,* p. 335.

[17] Bunsen to his wife, 13 July 1841, quoted in Bishop Wilberforce, *Life,* vol I, p. 608, quoted in James Skinner, p. 329.

[18] Also known as the *Straits Convention.*

and Dardanelles would be closed to foreign warships as long as Turkey was at peace.

The Protestant Bishopric – The British Position

The issue of a Protestant bishopric in the Mediterranean was part of a larger issue confronting the Anglican Church. Following the American War of Independence, the Anglican Church was forced to pass legislation to provide episcopal supervision for the Anglicans remaining in America. With this as a precedent evangelical Anglicans later promoted the establishment of a bishopric in Calcutta, India, in 1812.[19]

As the British Empire continued to expand, especially eastward, the need was seen for the establishment of further bishoprics. So in 1840 the *Colonial Bishopric Fund* was established, in order to finance bishoprics in the British Colonies, including New Zealand. The Bishop of London had responsibility for such entities. These cases were quite clear cut, as the United States of America was once a British colony, and New Zealand a present one.

A new situation, however, began arising from 1815 onwards as the LJS and Church Missionary Society (CMS) in particular, began entering into the Mediterranean region, an area not part of the British Empire. Some believed it sufficient to place these men under the episcopal authority of the Roman Catholic Church, but these were very much a minority. Others were leaning towards the covering of the Greek Orthodox Church.

Many evangelical Christians however were not inclined towards either of these historic churches, believing them to be part of an 'anti-Christ' religious system. Many, and in particular the CMS, favoured the establishment of their own Anglican bishopric, on the British held territory of Malta.[20] From 1837 the CMS was involved in establishing a chapel on Malta, so this seemed the logical location. Even the American missionary Eli Smith urged the appointment of a bishop perhaps at Malta to protect the Protestants of the East.[21]

Smith's suggestion was endorsed by the Earl of Chichester, the President of CMS, who wrote to Foreign Secretary Palmerston on 25 March 1841 expressing the view: '... that British Christians should have the same protection and religious liberty in the Ottoman Empire as other Christian

---

[19] Orchard, *ibid,* p. 202.

[20] *ibid,* pp. 203-4 and footnotes 4 and 5.

[21] Meeting of 22 December 1840, considering a letter of Eli Smith dated 4 July 1840, CMS Minutes Vol XIX, G/CI, p. 295, quoted in Orchard, *ibid,* in footnote 8.

Churches.' He proposed there be 'ecclesiastical authority' directing 'the Clergy of the Church of England in those parts.'[22]

Coincidentally, in October 1838 Shaftesbury had also written of the possibility of establishing a Protestant bishopric in Jerusalem, not Malta:

> Could we not erect a Protestant Bishopric at Jerusalem, and give him jurisdiction over all the Levant, Malta, and whatever chaplaincies there might be on the coast of Africa.[23]

This obviously was the essence of the 'Jerusalem Plan' that Shaftesbury would discuss with Bunsen on 10 December 1838. It appears that Shaftesbury already had the idea prior to his discussion with Bunsen.

By the middle of 1841 there was momentum for an Anglican bishop somewhere in the eastern Mediterranean, with the CMS bidding for a bishopric at Valetta in Malta. Simultaneously the LJS was seeking to further its operations in Jerusalem, in preparation for an expected large scale Jewish restoration. Despite Shaftesbury's diary entry of 1838, there doesn't seem to be evidence that the bishopric in Jerusalem was high on the list of priorities for the LJS. That changed with Bunsen's arrival in London.

The Bishopric Proposal Accepted in Principle

Naturally Shaftesbury and the LJS were enthusiastic about the Jerusalem bishopric proposal, coming on the heels as it did of the failed attempt to restore Israel. Here was an opportunity to achieve similar goals – but through a different channel.

The major problem at that juncture was timing. The sympathetic Whig Government of Peel and Palmerston was on its way out, soon to be replaced by the less enthusiastic (as far as the Jewish question was concerned) government of Melbourne and Aberdeen. It was imperative therefore that Shaftesbury do all he could to get the 'Plan' accepted in principle as quickly as possible.

By 19 July 1841 Palmerston was in agreement. Now there was the minor issue of attaining the best candidate for the post. The obvious choice was none other than the renowned gentile 'rabbi' – Dr Alexander McCaul. McCaul's daughter Elizabeth Anne, recalls, that 'on a July afternoon' she noticed a distinguished carriage outside her father's door. It was none

---

[22] Chichester to Palmerston, 20 March 1841, CMS Letter book G/ACI, p. 405, quoted in Orchard, *ibid*, p. 205.
[23] Hodder, *ibid*, p. 125.

other than Bunsen, come to convey the King's wish for him to become the first bishop. 'My father's reply to the King,' wrote Elizabeth, 'after thanking him, was that he considered that the Bishop of Jerusalem ought to be of Hebrew descent, and as he had not this honour, he asked leave to recommend his friend, the Rev. Mr. Alexander.'[24]

There is also good reason to believe that Shaftesbury himself proposed Alexander to be the new bishop. Perhaps Shaftesbury had proposed two candidates, McCaul and Alexander, indicating that if McCaul refused Alexander might agree. Although there doesn't seem to be any available evidence, it could be that Bunsen merely went next door and saw Alexander, or visited him on another occasion. Alexander accepted the invitation, prompting Bunsen to record in his diary on 19 July 1841:

> So the beginning is made, please God, for the restoration of Israel. When I read, with the warm-hearted, clear-headed Lord Ashley, the translation of the Minute, he exclaimed, 'Since the days of David, no king has ever spoken such words!' It was his fortunate idea that directed the choice of the future Bishop.[25]

Although the scheme had now been accepted in principle by both the ecclesiastical and government bodies, it still had to be approved by both Houses of Parliament and by Queen Victoria. It would be expected that the Queen would be positive towards a scheme associated with Germany, considering her own Germanic family connections.

Palmerston wrote to Queen Victoria on 21 July 1841 stating, that as 'the Plan now proposed by the King of Prussia seems practicable' that he recommends that the Queen authorize 'to send out immediately Instructions to Lord Ponsonby to concur with the Prussian Minister at Constantinople the best means of endeavouring to carry this Plan into effect.'[26] The Queen recorded in her diary for 23 July 1841:

> '... saw Ld. Palmerston to whom I said I quite agreed & approved that we should consent to Bunsen's proposals, & Ld. Palmerston said they wished to send out a Protestant Bishop to Jerusalem, & that there was a man of the

---

[24] Elizabeth Anne Finn, *Reminiscence of Mrs. Finn,* (Marshall, Morgan & Scott, London & Edinburgh), pp. 33-34. See also W. T. Gidney, *The History of the London Society for Promoting Christianity Amongst the Jews,* (London, 1908), p. 207 and Corey, *ibid,* p. 52.

[25] Hodder, *ibid,* quoting Bunsen's Diary, p. 200.

[26] Palmerston to Queen Victoria, 21 July 1841, A10/72, RA [Royal Archives], Windsor Palace.

name of Alexander, who is at Cambridge, & who seems to unite all the qualities required.   He is a Doctor of Divinity, a converted Jew, & a Prussian subject by birth ...'[27]

The initial *Bunsen Memorandum* worked on by Bunsen, Shaftesbury and others, and entitled 'The Church at Jerusalem,'[28] was completed and submitted to Palmerston on 25 July 1841.   It adapted to this new twist concerning the Jewish nominee.   Obviously there was no initial stipulation for sending out a bishop of Jewish descent otherwise McCaul would not have been approached.   Now, however, it seems that matters changed somewhat in orientation.   In Bunsen's *Memorandum* Article I, it was stated 'that it must "appear in the highest order desirable" that the Bishop of Jerusalem should, in addition to the ordinary essentials of a bishop, possess the following qualification:
1.   Jewish descent
2.   Learning
3.   Membership of the ministry of the English Church.'[29]

The Ambassadors in Constantinople Informed.
When informed of the 'Plan', neither the British nor the Prussian ambassadors at Constantinople were overly excited with the project. Palmerston informed Ambassador Ponsonby on 26 July 1841 that Her Majesty's Government 'adopts with great earnestness the plan proposed by the King of Prussia' and were deeply interested in the project.[30]   He also wrote:

I have to state to your Excellency that in consequence of the communications which have taken place between the Prussian and the British Governments, and between Chevalier Bunsen, Envoy of the King of Prussia, the Archbishop of Canterbury, the Bishop of London and myself, it has been decided that a Bishop of the Church of England should be sent to Jerusalem, especially consecrated for the purpose of exercising his ecclesiastical function in Palestine, over such persons whether British or Prussian subjects, or others, who being of the Protestant faith may choose to place themselves under his spiritual care.

---

[27] Queen Victoria's Journal, 23 July 1841, RA [Royal Archives].
[28] *Bunsen Memorandum*, Memo No 1, Count Plessen, 19 September 1884, FO 406/5460.
[29] Baron Plessen, Memo No 2, 19 September 1884, FO 406/5460.
[30] Palmerston to Ponsonby, 26 July 1841, FO 78/429 (No 187).

It will be necessary however, in order to invest the Crown with power to authorize the Prelates to consecrate a Bishop for this purpose that a short Act of Parliament should be passed; and the Archbishop of Canterbury is going immediately to bring into the House of Lords a bill for this end; and as soon as that bill shall have been passed into law, a bishop will be consecrated accordingly and will be sent to Jerusalem.

Her Majesty's Government conceive that no special permission for this purpose will be required from the Porte [Turkish Government]. This bishop will like any other British or Prussian subject have the right to reside in any part of the Turkish dominions, and the spiritual functions which he will exercise will in no way whatever interfere with the Mahometan subjects of the Sultan, and therefore they will be matters of which the Turkish Government will have no right to take any cognizance whatever.

I state this to your Excellency now in order that you may be aware of what is intended to be done, but you will make no communication on the subject to the Turkish Government till you receive instructions from the Secretary of State to do so. You will in fact consider this intimation as purely confidential, and intended solely for you as personal information. I have to add that the stipend for the Bishop will be defrayed by private contributions.[31]

This *Instruction* is very revealing. Palmerston was keenly aware of the potential Turkish suspicion and opposition to the scheme, following so soon as it did after previous British and Prussian plans for post war Palestine. No doubt the British and Prussian ambassadors were aware of how it would be perceived in Constantinople – by both the Turkish authorities, the ministers (*viziers*) and religious leaders (*ulema*) and the ambassadors of the other powers resident there.

The 'Plan' Ratified

With formalities concluded and the 'Plan' agreed to in principle, it was now time for the prelates and diplomats to work on the basics of the Agreement. They met together at Addington Lodge near Croydon, the official property of the Archbishop of Canterbury, where they completed some adjustments and modifications known as the *Addington Articles*, by 5 August 1841. The Archbishop then summoned a meeting with the Bishops to explain to them what was happening. Apparently few responded.[32]

---

[31] Palmerston to Ponsonby, 27 September, 1841, FO 78/429.
[32] Welch, *ibid*, p. 196.

According to the arrangement thus concluded the British Crown would be asked to authorize the consecration of a bishop in Jerusalem. As Bunsen later wrote in his Report to the Prussian King, on 22 August 1841, there was also provision for independent Prussian expansion in the future:

> The Bishops consider it just that so long as your majesty has no Bishopric of your own in the Holy Land, that now founded should hereafter have alternately a Prussian or an English Bishop; or, more accurately, one proposed to the Primate alternately by your Majesty and by the Crown of England. For your majesty might propose an Englishman, instead of one of your subjects. In any case, the Primate would consecrate him according to the English form of consecration, just in the same way as the possible Bishop of Bethlehem. In a word, your majesty will get in Jerusalem that which you wished for in Bethlehem, until the foundation of a Bishopric at the last-named place is possible.[33]

There were some legal and financial complications. The Jerusalem Bishopric did not fall into the category of the *Colonial Bishopric Fund (Act),* as Jerusalem was not a Crown Colony.

The Queen's advocate thereupon produced a bill in twenty-four hours. The *Foreign Bishoprics Act* (sometimes referred to as the *Jerusalem Bishopric Act*)[34] was introduced into the House of Lords on 30 August. It passed, and then also passed through the House of Commons, almost in silence.[35] Despite this, the new Prime Minister, Robert Peel remained apprehensive of the whole venture, especially when Shaftesbury requested a British warship to transport the bishop and his family to Jerusalem.

The second obstacle, financial, was solved in two ways. To prove his personal interest in the project, the King of Prussia signed the Royal Prussian Deed of Endowment on 6 September 1841, promising the capital

---

[33] Bunsen to King Frederick William IV, 22 August 1841, in Memo No 2 Baron Plessen, 19 Sept 1884, *ibid.*

[34] Also officially known as the Foreigners Consecration Act Amendment Bill [see Welch, *ibid*, p. 195].

[35] Greaves, *ibid*, p. 344. The Act amended the previous Act 26 George III, c. 84, which allowed for foreign subjects to minister to Anglicans outside the king's dominions, for example Americans to minister to Anglicans in America. The new Act was thus named Act 5 Vic. C 6, and stated it was 'to amend an act of 26 Geo III to empower the archbishop of Canterbury or York ... to consecrate ... persons being subjects or citizens outside His Majesty's dominions.'

of 15,000 pounds, with the annual interest of 600 pounds going towards the Prussian contribution[36] for the bishop's stipend, paid yearly in advance.

The remainder, some 20,000 pounds was raised by general subscription in Britain, the interest from this, another 600 pounds, supplying the balance of the bishop's yearly stipend. The LJS gave 3,000 pounds towards the subscription, and the Archbishop of Canterbury and Bishop of London each gave 200 pounds towards it.[37] The two Archbishops and the Bishop of London would be the trustees of the fund.

Nominations for the bishop would alternate between the British and Prussian Governments, but the Archbishop of Canterbury would have the veto over the Prussian nomination. 'This arrangement' wrote Greaves, 'was to continue until a purely Prussian bishopric was set up at Bethlehem, when the Jerusalem see would become wholly English. Finally, by a clause which was apparently kept secret at first,' Greaves continued, 'it was agreed that until the "restoration" of a Christian Jewish church, but not afterwards, the Archbishop of Canterbury should be the metropolitan of the new see.'[38]

The bishop-elect, even when named by Prussia, had to be consecrated according to the Anglican rite, and had to conform to the Thirty-Nine Articles of the Anglican Confession of faith, which practically excluded members of the Evangelical German Church from being nominated.

Political Opposition

Following the summer recession of Parliament, Shaftesbury and Bunsen had to contend with growing opposition to the scheme. This opposition was two-fold: firstly from various sections of the English church who resented the concept of a Protestant Bishopric in Jerusalem, which they viewed as interfering in the jurisdiction of the ancient churches. And, secondly, from the new Government, that took office at the end of August. This is evident in the outcome of an interview Bunsen had with Aberdeen, the new Foreign Secretary, who highlighted the dangers of the bishopric:

---

[36] For full account, see W. H. Hechler, *The Jerusalem Bishopric*, Documents section p. 46.

[37] Minute 2063, LJS General Committee Minutes, Vol. M, Bodleian; and Hechler, *ibid*, pp. 37-39, 179-181. The English fund was made formal in a deed dated 15 November 1841.

[38] Bunsen to Palmerston, 5 August 1841, FO 64/235, quoted in Greaves, *ibid*, pp. 342-343; Count Munster to Earl Granville, 17 July 1882, FO 406/5460.

We shall excite the jealousy of Russia, Austria, France; they will demand more of the Porte and so shall we; and thus we shall accelerate the downfall of the Turkish kingdom – it may ... have been a good plan for the Conversion of the Jews, but I do not see that it would have answered for anything else ...[39]

Ponsonby, in response to Palmerston's earlier directive, (which came not to Palmerston incidentally, but to his successor Aberdeen) was not in agreement with the 'Plan', stating that there was now a new regime in Constantinople[40] and that such a far-reaching plan stood to endanger other specific British plans in the region, and especially the permission to build the LJS church in Jerusalem.[41] The Prussian ambassador, Count de Koenigsmark, too, was not favourable, believing that the Porte (Turkish Government) was suspicious of concealed ambitions by the British for gaining influence in the Levant.[42]

Once news of the impending bishopric became public, opposition to it increased. It seems that the Austrians issued a formal protest at Constantinople.[43] Despite this wariness, especially from the British Government, Bunsen stood firm on Britain's international obligation to Prussia.

Ecclesiastical Opposition

On 5 October Shaftesbury attended the first meeting of the *Ecclesiastical Commission*, and recorded:

Spoke to the Archbishop: found him almost totally changed ... must take time to consider the propriety of a Jew for a Bishop; it would not, he was told, suit the Greek Christians; the Christian in the East would never acknowledge a Jew; the hatred of them was indelible, - that all these things should be considered.'[44]

Bishop Blomfield of London, received a terse letter from Pusey, leader of the Tractarian movement, a strong opponent, who stated 'it is now for the

---

[39] Ashley Diary, 23 September 1841, quoted in Orchard, *ibid,* pp. 224-5.

[40] The sympathetic Reschid fell from power in March 1841.

[41] Ponsonby to Aberdeen, no. 4, 29 September 1841; no. 9, 6 October 1841; no 11, 7 October 1841, FO 78/437, quoted in Greaves, *ibid*, p. 339.

[42] Koenigsmark's report no 53, 6 October 1841, and forwarded by Bunsen to Aberdeen, 17 January 1842, in FO 64/241.

[43] J. Finn, *Stirring Times,* (London, 1878) Volume I, p. 138.

[44] Ashley Diary, 5 October 1841, Orchard, *ibid*, p. 226.

first time that the Church of England holds communion with those that are "without the Church"[45]

Members of the Tractarian movement now returning from summer break, were opposed to the concept of an evangelical bishopric associated with the non-episcopal German Church, established in an ancient see which belonged to the historic churches. Pusey wrote to his cousin Shaftesbury:

> No one objects to the Bishopric of Jerusalem for what I imagine you value it – the sake of the Jews – but on account of the 'experimental church' (as it has been called) which they are going to make of Prussians, one knows not when. Our Church was never brought into contact with the foreign reformation without suffering from it; and certainly that Reformation is not in a state now to do us less harm than heretofore, besides the grave injury of countenancing heresy ...[46]

It was believed by Pusey and others that the episcopal Anglican Church was incompatible with the non-episcopal German Church. One prominent Tractarian John Henry Newman later declared that it was this issue, the Protestant bishopric, which 'was the third blow, which finally shattered my faith in the Anglican Church.'[47] He wrote of this bishopric experiment:

> Jerusalem, it would seem was considered a safe place for the experiment; it was too far from Prussia to awaken the susceptibilities of any party at home; if the project failed, it failed without harm to anyone; and if it succeeded, it gave Protestantism a *status* in the East, which, in association with the Monophysite or Jacobin and the Nestorian bodies, formed a political instrument for England, parallel to that which Russia had in the Greek Church, and France in the Latin.[48]

He wrote again on 12 October 1841:

> We have not a single Anglican in Jerusalem; so we are sending a bishop to *make* a communion; not to govern our own people. Next, the excuse is, that there are converted Anglican Jews there who require a Bishop; I am told there are not a half-a-dozen. But for *them* the Bishop is sent out, and for them he is a Bishop of the *circumcision* ... against the Epistle of the

---

[45] Ashley Diary 12 October 1841, quoted in Orchard, *ibid*, p. 228.
[46] Quoted in Tibawi, *ibid*, p. 47.
[47] Newman, *ibid*, p. 143.
[48] *ibid*, p. 141.

Galatians pretty nearly. Thirdly, for the sake of Prussia, he is to take under him all the foreign Protestants who will come; and the political advantages will be so great, from the influence of England, that there is no doubt they *will* come. They are to sign the Confession of Augsburg, and there is nothing to show that they hold the doctrine of Baptismal Regeneration.[49]

To officially register his opposition Newman wrote to the Archbishop, stating, that 'Lutheranism and Calvinism are heresies, repugnant to Scripture, springing up three centuries since, and anathematized by East as well as West.'[50]

One prominent opponent, Lord John Manners wrote to William Gladstone:

> I don't at all like ... the bishopric in the Holy Land ... A spirit of insanity is abroad ... The Jerusalem Bishopric is the sorest point of all; the Russian papers and the French Dissenters all look upon it as a flag of alliance held out to Zurich and Geneva from Lambeth; and have they not good reasons for so regarding it?

These opponents were basically concerned that the Church of England was allying herself, for the sake of a broader union of sorts, with Protestantism rather than with Rome. The Anglican Church by its essence was the *via media*, the middle way between both continental Protestantism and the Roman Church. Any movement by the Archbishop and hierarchy to be deemed one way or the other, would attract opposition. There were those, especially evangelicals, whose leanings were more towards a union with continental Protestantism, for whom a union with Rome was anathema. And likewise, there were those, primarily of the Anglo-Catholic or High Church persuasion (the Tractarians), whose allegiance was more towards Rome, for whom a union with continental Protestantism was anathema.

There was some reason for stalwart Anglicans to be concerned by the whole venture. The Anglican Church holds to the doctrine of Apostolic Succession, as does the Roman Church, while the Lutheran and Calvinist Churches basically do not. On this issue alone there was a much closer link with Rome rather than continental Protestantism. However not all

---

[49] Newman, *ibid*, p. 143.
[50] Newman to Archbishop Howley, 11 November 1841, quoted in Newman, *ibid*, p. 145.

Anglicans held to this doctrine to the same degree. Blomfield, for instance was not strongly in favour.[51]

What was on offer here, although not completely clear in 1841, was the possibility of a common Protestant centre of reference in Jerusalem, instead of Canterbury (Anglicanism), Augsburg (Lutheranism) or Geneva (Reformed Christianity). For the Roman Catholics there was Rome, and for universal Protestantism, potentially, a restored Jerusalem.

In an effort to appease the opposition from the High Church and Tractarian party, the Archbishop appointed Rev. George Williams as Alexander's chaplain. Williams, a man of High Church tendencies, was instructed to give attention to the Eastern Churches.[52]

The Archbishop also sent with Alexander a '*Letter Commendatory from the Most Reverend the Lord Archbishop of Canterbury to the Patriarch of the Greek Orthodox Church.*' This letter, written in both English and Greek, informed the Orthodox Patriarch that it was sent 'in order to prevent any misunderstanding of this our purpose, we think it right to make known to you that we have charged the said Bishop, our brother, not to intermeddle in any way with the jurisdiction of the Prelates or other ecclesiastical Dignitaries bearing rule in the East.'[53]

There was also opposition to the 'Plan' in Prussia, especially from those opposed to any form of episcopacy. Blake wrote of these opponents: 'They saw in Frederick William's action a covert plan to introduce Lutheran bishops into Prussian and perhaps other German states. Many Lutherans took an unfavourable view of any step in the direction of uniting them with a church as riven with dissension and as packed with antique abuses as the Church of England ... Strict Lutherans regarded the united Church of England and Ireland with doubt and distrust, but they were a minority. In general Prussian opinion was relatively indifferent.'[54]

Influence upon permission for a Protestant Church in Jerusalem

While en route to Jerusalem in August Nicolayson visited Constantinople where he made inquiries for gaining the necessary permits in order to build a church and expand the LJS work. The British ambassador, Lord Ponsonby, took up the cause most enthusiastically, especially concerning the official permit or *firman* to build the church.

---

[51] Welch, *ibid*, pp. 200-201.
[52] Greaves, *ibid*, p. 348. It seems that Williams was an adherent of Pusey. See Greaves, *ibid*, footnote No. 6.
[53] Quoted in *JI*, 1842, pp. 24-26.
[54] Robert Blake, *ibid*, p. 93.

But he encountered numerous obstacles. Ponsonby learned from the Turkish authorities that they could not permit the building of a new church in Jerusalem. 'The Porte' he told Nicolayson 'will not violate the Law.' Ponsonby proposed that Nicolayson 'procure the site of an ancient Church and erect the new Building thereon.' Nicolayson in turn approved of this plan, and assured Ponsonby that the area he purchased several years previously, had been a Chapel belonging to the Convent of Jacobius.

All seemed to be going well. Ponsonby then learned that the Porte permits new churches to be built on the site of existing ones, but those churches had to be either Catholic or Orthodox or of a recognized Christian sect. He wrote to Palmerston, that, 'if the Porte could now be induced to grant to the Protestant Christians similar privileges, the Porte would have to contend against the opposition of the Clergy of the Catholick (sic) and Greek Churches whose influence will probably be exerted to the utmost to prevent the establishment in this Country of a Church considered by them to be a dangerous rival.'[55]

Ponsonby stated it again two weeks later to Palmerston after further exertions had been made:

> With respect to the affairs of the Protestant Church to be erected in Jerusalem, the Porte positively refused a Firman as being contrary to ancient practise and rights, the real motive is probably the fear of bringing on the clamour of other sects ... This plan will certainly be furiously opposed by the priests, Catholicks (sic) and Greeks, and I think it better to obtain from the Sublime Porte, if possible, distinct acknowledgement of the Rights of England to have a Church dedicated to her National Worship in this country.
>
> I propose to say that when the churches for the Catholicks (sic) were allowed, the Protestant Church of England was not established and it is now established over a vast portion of the world, and belongs to the most powerful nation; the close Ally of the Sublime Porte; that England has a strong claim perhaps the right to demand that the Porte shall not exclude Her Church from the benefits the Porte permits other Churches to enjoy.[56]

While Ponsonby took upon himself the seemingly impossible task of obtaining a *firman*, Nicolayson returned to Jerusalem to obtain further documentation which he thought would assist with the task. Palmerston meanwhile sent a very blunt letter to Ponsonby on 28 August, stating:

---

[55] Ponsonby to Palmerston, 18 August 1841, FO 78/437 (No 270, p. 62).
[56] Ponsonby to Palmerston, 2 September 1841, FO 78/437 (No. 280, p. 161).

I have accordingly to instruct your Excellency to apply earnestly for such a Firman. It cannot be supposed that at a moment when the whole of Syria has so lately been restored to the Sultan by the powerful intervention of Great Britain, so small a favour as this [permission to build a church - ed] could be refused to the British Government upon grounds of a pedantic adherence to Mohammedan doctrine.[57]

Then in September 1841, Ponsonby was able to gleefully write to Palmerston: 'I expect to succeed in obtaining a Firman to authorize the erection of a Protestant Church at Jerusalem.' But in the same letter he acknowledges Palmerston's letter of 4 August 1841 that mentioned the King of Prussia's interest in the proposed church. Ponsonby sounded a warning to Palmerston, by stating that he had thus far negotiated the matter himself and doesn't really need Prussian interference.[58]

Ponsonby's apprehension that Prussian involvement in British affairs in Constantinople would be detrimental proved to be well founded. As instructed, he met his Prussian counterpart, Count de Koenigsmark, in mid September concerning the establishment of 'Protestant Churches in this Country.' In a communiqué to Palmerston on 15 September, Ponsonby reported about a recent meeting he had at the Porte. Although he wrote of progress and optimism, he also sounded a warning against asking too much of the Turks. He wrote:

Since the above mentioned interview took place I have learned from those who I employed to further the measure that nothing more will be obtained than an unavowed permission from the Ottoman Ministers for us to build an English Church at Jerusalem, and a promise that they (the Ministers) will order the Turkish Authorities (including the Cadi at Jerusalem) not to oppose our erecting it; but a condition that the Fabrick shall be modest and unostentatious in appearance and dimensions and not calculated to attract attention. I hope to have this promise in writing. The Porte will not, I fear, grant any Firman.

If we do obtain these things I am certain we shall, ere long, be enabled thereby to do all we can reasonably desire as to the establishment of Protestant Churches generally.

I presume Her Majesty's Government would not attempt to force the Will of the Porte on a matter connected with the religious feelings of the Turks. It would be mischievous, and I think unsuccessful and therefore it is better to be contented to obtain a footing now which will secure our

---

[57] Palmerston to Ponsonby, 28 August 1841, FO 78/429.
[58] Ponsonby to Palmerston, 8 September 1841, FO 78/437 (No 284, p. 187).

ultimate success, than to risk a total failure by grasping at too much. Persons unacquainted with this country may imagine that it is easy to carry such points, it is far otherwise and I assure your Lordship that this measure would have totally failed but for the aid I was fortunately enabled to secure.[59]

Although stating that no *firman* would be issued, a tacit permission to build the church was a major breakthrough. Word of this 'promise' made its way to London, and from London to Jerusalem.

Unfortunately subsequent communiqués showed a deterioration in the situation – resulting, it would appear, from Prussian interference. Ponsonby wrote on 15 September to Palmerston: 'The difficulties about the Protestant Church at Jerusalem, which were before so great, have been increased by the demands made by the Prussian envoy.' The Prussian ambassador, stated Ponsonby, had sent an official note, which, he stated 'has excited great alarm by the extent of its demands.' He continued:

The building of a Church is opposed in the Divan by the Ulema[60] who have seats there and bring matter connected with religious opinions, as they are commonly received by the mass of the Turks, it may be difficult for the Ottoman Ministers to overcome the Zealots.
If we do gain this point it will be mainly owing to the learning of Mr. Frederick Pisani[61] who has carried on controversial discussions with an ability and zeal that may at last be successful ...

Ponsonby concluded this statement by stating that Pisani's success had now been jeopardized by 'injudicious Measures.'[62] And again Ponsonby wrote on 6 October 1841:

The affair of the Church at J'salem having been violently opposed by some members of the Council of Justice upon the ground of religious opinions, I considered it my duty to proceed in it with great caution and to avoid if possible, either wounding the feelings of honest men on such a subject, or of enabling men of another description to accuse me of endeavouring to obtain privileges mischevious to the national religion. I hoped to gain the

---

[59] Ponsonby to Palmerston, 15 September 1841, FO 78/437 (No 288).
[60] The Muslim jurists and legal scholars, who are experts in the *Sharia,* the Islamic Law.
[61] Pisani was the dragoman or interpreter, who accomplished valuable work on behalf of the British Embassy.
[62] Ponsonby to Aberdeen, 29 September 1841, FO 78/437 (No 4).

point without having recourse to positive demand ... I think I should have succeeded by the means I wished to use, if the Prussian Minister had not been ordered to make proposition to the Porte which gave strength to the prejudices relied upon by our adversaries for support, but finding that I could not carry the measure in the way I desired, I wrote enclosed official Note in which I asserted Right of Her Majesty's Government to insist upon the consent of the Sublime Porte to the building of a Church at Jerusalem for the performance of the rites of the Anglican Church.

This Note was given on the 3rd to Rifaat Pasha who will immediately commit it to the Council. His Excellencies (sic) language on that day was to the following effect, referring to the opinion of the Council before that he, Rifaat Pasha, had received my official Note. His Excellency said:

'The Council refuses to grant permission for the erection of the Church because it is contrary to the religious law of the Turks.

'Because the Porte is not bound by any Treaty to grant that permission

'Because the franks[63] cannot possess any landed property in Turkey

'Because the present is not the proper time to grant such permission owing to the state of minds in Syria

'Because the Patriarch[64] will oppose the erection of a Protestant Church

'Because the law of this Country being contrary to the demand, no foreign Government can find fault with the refusal given by the Sublime Porte ...

Ponsonby also stated that Rifaat Pasha had said that Count de Koenigsmark had asked for permission for Prussians to 'perform the rites of their religion in Turkey like other Nations, and Rifaat Pasha says that the Porte refuses to give such a Note.'[65] By October therefore, as the final touches were being put to the Bishopric Plan in London, the environment was becoming noticeably uncomfortable in Constantinople for British designs in Jerusalem.

An official from the British Embassy, Mr. Bankhead, had met with Sarim Effendi at the Porte on 12 November 1841 and discussed Bishop Alexander. It was only too obvious that the Turks were very wary about this new British initiative.[66] In a subsequent communiqué to the Foreign Office, Ponsonby reiterated that the Turks were concerned about granting

---

[63] Franks was a general term applied to all Europeans within the Turkish Empire.

[64] Refers to the Greek Orthodox Patriarch, either of Constantinople or of Jerusalem, who for the most part did not reside in Jerusalem.

[65] Ponsonby to Palmerston , 6 October 1841, FO 78/437 (No 9, p. 284).

[66] Ponsonby to Aberdeen, 22 January 1842, FO 78/473.

special privileges for Bishop Alexander.[67] Then in response, Aberdeen, the new foreign secretary, mentioned that he had sent to Constantinople the letter from Bunsen, showing that the idea of the Bishopric came from Prussia, and not from England!

This reveals an interesting bit of political jockeying. It appears that to take the heat off the British Embassy, and Ponsonby's endeavours to secure permission for the building of the church at Jerusalem, Aberdeen wanted to show that Britain was not solely responsible for both issues – the church in Jerusalem, and the Protestant Bishopric, but wanted some of the pressure to be transferred to the Prussians.[68]

Widespread Support for the Bishopric.
Many evangelicals, especially within the LJS, were ecstatic about Alexander's appointment, and were seemingly unaffected by the intrigues and prospective complications in Constantinople. The LJS wrote: 'The appointment of a son of Abraham as Bishop of the United Church of England and Ireland at Jerusalem, forms a new era in the history of the missionary labours among the Jews.'[69] Shaftesbury recorded that there were 'Twenty-four sermons on one Sunday in our behalf in Liverpool alone.'[70] Welch states that: 'Ashley and the Evangelical party saw in the Anglo-Prussian venture the blessed beginning of a restoration of Israel...'[71]

On 15 October 1841 there was a dinner at the 'Star and Garter' in Richmond, to mark the occasion of the birthday of the Prussian king. Bunsen recorded of this event:

Dr. Alexander gave the King's health in an enthusiastic speech ... I returned thanks, and gave the health of the Queen and afterwards of the Queen Dowager; whereupon we sang (in a chorus), 'Heil! Friedrich Wilhelm, heil!'... Then I rose, and proposed 'The Church of England, and the venerable Prelates at her head,' and spoke as I felt. McCaul returned thanks, speaking of Jerusalem which led to Gladstone's toast, 'Prosperity of the Church of St. James at Jerusalem, and to her first Bishop.'

Never was heard a more exquisite speech; it flowed like a gentle and translucent stream. And in the second portion he addressed Alexander directly, representing the greatness and difficulty of the charge confided to

---

[67] Ponsonby to Aberdeen, 24 February 1842, FO. 78/473 (No 19).
[68] Aberdeen to Ponsonby, 24 March 1842, FO 78/473 (No 27).
[69] *JI*, 1842, p. 3.
[70] Ashley Diary 28 September 1841, quoted in Orchard, *ibid* p. 225.
[71] Welch, *ibid*, p. 195.

him, the latter at first covered his face from emotion, but then rose, and returned thanks with dignity as well as feeling.' [72]

One Christian magazine, the *Christian Observer*, wrote in their November 1841 edition, that the establishment of the Protestant Bishopric would check the advancements of 'all-encroaching Popery' as the real battle was with Rome.[73]

Bunsen held his own personal opinions of this great venture, and wrote to a friend on 12 October 1841:

> This appearance of unity is only possible by forming a connection with an establishment already there, that of the English Jewish Missionary Society.
>
> The matter to be accomplished was the converting of this private establishment into a national and universal Christian foundation; and this could only be effected by the foundation of a Bishopric by the Church of England.
>
> To the Turks we must display unity; among ourselves we must maintain a brotherly understanding.
>
> Germany must assume an honourable and independent position in such a connection with the English establishment. We must acknowledge that establishment, and therefore also Episcopal authority.
>
> The English, on the other hand, must acknowledge our *Augsburg Confession*, and our German order of worship.[74]

Foreign Bishoprics Act (Jerusalem Bishopric Act)

The final political act was obtaining the Royal Assent, which the Queen gave on 5 October 1841, to what was commonly known as the *Jerusalem Bishopric Act*. Now all was accomplished, save the consecration of the new bishop, and his departure to his new See.

However Alexander could not be consecrated until the Queen had given a license, which she did on 6 November 1841 at Buckingham Palace. Queen Victoria authorized the Archbishop of Canterbury to consecrate Rev. Michael Solomon Alexander to be bishop over 'Syria, Chaldea, Egypt, and Abyssinia, as the limit within which the said Michael Solomon Alexander may exercise spiritual jurisdiction pursuant to the said Act,

---

[72] Hechler, *The Jerusalem Bishopric,* pp. 41-2.

[73] *Christian Observer,* November 1841, New Series, xlvii, p. 703, quoted in Welch, *ibid,* p. 197.

[74] Bunsen to Frederick Perthes, 12 October 1841, quoted in Hechler, *ibid,* p. 30.

subject nevertheless to such alterations in the said limit as we from time to time may be pleased to assign.'[75]

The scene was now being set for the future. The LJS, many other evangelicals and restorationists, and even a large portion of the British public was excited and enthusiastic about the Bishopric Plan. Conversely a new and less enthusiastic British Government administration had now come into office, and, despite headway having been made in Constantinople over the building of the Protestant Church in Jerusalem, it would appear that the Bishopric was potentially going to adversely affect that endeavour.

By this stage the 'Bishopric Plan' had gone too far to be pulled back – far too much had by now been invested in it. It was now time for the next stage of the outworking of this 'Plan' – the consecration of the future Jewish Bishop for Jerusalem.

---

[75] Queens' license for Consecration, see Hechler, *ibid*, Documents section, p. 60.

Chapter 9

A Jewish Bishop for Jerusalem: 1841

'BISHOPRIC OF THE CHURCH OF ST. JAMES AT JERUSALEM'
The full extent of the LJS's commitment to Alexander's task is revealed in a most profound statement written by the General Committee, and expounded in the November edition of their mouthpiece, the *Jewish Intelligence*. They wrote, under the title BISHOPRIC OF THE CHURCH OF ST. JAMES AT JERUSALEM:

> The friends of Israel have for some years desired that, amidst the various hostile parties at Jerusalem professing the religion of Christ, the Church of England should also have a representative, who might appear as a messenger of peace, and exhibit to the Jews the pure and simple Christianity of the Gospel. Some earnestly desired, in addition to a sacred edifice and clergy for the celebration of Divine worship, the residence of a Jewish Bishop, as being indispensably necessary for the spiritual prosperity of the Mission to the Jews, and the adequate representation of the Church of England as a branch of the Catholic Church. They saw that without a bishop, friendly and edifying intercourse with the Eastern Churches was hopeless, and the revival of the Church of the circumcision impossible. The object, however, of their pious desires appeared only as a lovely vision, or a feeble ray of glory on the horizon of a remote futurity. But what they scarcely ventured to hope, God in his providence has been pleased to realize. The King of Prussia, with a zeal becoming a Christian monarch, looking with compassion on the state of Protestants in the Turkish dominions, desired to secure to them the same privileges and the same protection enjoyed by the Greek, the Oriental, and Latin Churches; and for this purpose sent a special Envoy ... in the person of the Chevalier Bunsen, to propose to Her Majesty's Government an united effort at the Porte for the attainment of this desirable object. The Chevalier Bunsen was also authorized to request the co-operation of the Church of England in placing a Bishop as the visible representative of the Protestant Church in the Holy City. It must be deeply gratifying to the friends of the London Society to know, that the whole of the glorious and all-important plan was

suggested by the efforts which they have made to erect a church upon Mount Zion.

Lord Palmerston, with a sagacity that does him honour, immediately perceived the advantages, political and religious, that would accrue from the execution of that plan, and its incalculable importance in reference to the civilization of the east. He therefore undertook the negotiation with his usual ability and vigour, and by God's blessing, his Lordship's exertions have been so far crowned with success, that the principle has been acknowledged by the Turkish Government. Permission for the building and establishment of the Church at Jerusalem is guaranteed; and, if Lord Palmerston's efforts be followed up with suitable energy, the complete attainment of the object may be regarded as certain. It is a subject of still greater thankfulness that the prelates intrusted with the government of the Church, have heartily concurred in the proposed measures. The Rev. Professor Alexander, himself a brother of St. James, both after the flesh and after the Spirit, has been nominated as BISHOP OF THE CHURCH OF ST. JAMES AT JERUSALEM; and Sunday, the 7th of November, is the day fixed for his consecration ... It is unnecessary to urge the powerfully beneficial effect which an Anglican Bishop at Jerusalem may exercise over the Churches of the East, and how, without any intrusion, by example, by love, by meekness, he may do much towards the healing of the unhappy divisions, towards the correction of ancient errors, and the diffusion of the pure light of the Gospel. The friend of Israel need scarcely be told of the influence to be exercised by a Jewish Bishop over his brethren scattered through the world. In him the Church of the circumcision, 1700 years ago, rudely expelled from its holy habitation by heathen intolerance, will again find a centre of life and unity; in him the people of Israel may again behold a symbol of national resuscitation. In this most wonderful event, the mediator upon prophecy must recognize a sign that the time, the set time, to favour Zion is come ... [1]

This official memo from the LJS Committee made their position very clear. And as they had made a financial commitment to this venture they now needed financial partners. The memo continued:

The providence of God has moved, in a marvellous manner, the hearts of the monarchs, statesmen, and prelates, to help forward the great work of the conversion of Israel. He has removed the prejudices of Mahometanism. Under such circumstances, is it possible for the individual

---

[1] BISHOPRIC OF THE CHURCH OF ST. JAMES AT JERUSALEM, *JI*, 1841, pp. 383-384.

Christian to withhold his hand, or to give grudgingly? Never, since the days that Cyrus called upon his people to help the exiles of Israel "with silver and with gold, beside a freewill offering for the house of God that is at Jerusalem" – never was such a call made upon the liberality of God's believing people. God grant that it may not be in vain![2]

Consecration of Alexander

In the midst of all this support and opposition, Michael Solomon Alexander was consecrated Bishop in Jerusalem on 7 November 1841 at Lambeth Palace. Among those officiating were Archbishop Howley, Bishop Blomfield, Bishop Murray of Rochester, and the recently consecrated bishop of New Zealand, George Selwyn, who read from Acts 20:22; 'Now, behold, I go bound in the spirit unto Jerusalem, not knowing the things that shall befall me there.' Considering that New Zealand is the furthermost point on earth from Jerusalem, it seemed appropriate that Bishop Selwyn would participate.

Also present were: Shaftesbury; Mr. W.E. Gladstone (future Prime Minister of Britain); Bunsen; Sir George Rose (former British ambassador to Berlin, and whose son would soon meet Alexander in Beirut); Herr Abeken (Under-Secretary of Foreign Affairs at the King of Prussia's Court); Baron Schleinitz, the Prussian Charge d'Affaires; the Prussian Consul-General Hebeler; Sir Robert Inglis; Sir Thomas Baring (President of the LJS); Arthur Guinness from Dublin; Sir Stratford Canning (British ambassador designate to Constantinople) and others.[3] Alexander's daughter Deborah, wrote that: 'After the Service, Lady Stratford Canning embraced Fanny so warmly that she broke Fanny's watch glass.'[4]

The sermon was preached by Alexander McCaul, from Isaiah 52:7:

> How beautiful on the mountains are the feet of those who bring good news,
> Who proclaim peace, who bring good tidings, who proclaim salvation,
> who say to Zion, "Your God reigns!"

McCaul concentrated upon prophecy, and the prophetic nature of the bishopric, bringing in other relevant Scripture verses, including Isaiah 60:1-3 and Romans 11:15. Speaking of the restoration of Jerusalem, and it's role in the future McCaul spoke from Isaiah 52:9-10:

---

[2] BISHOPRIC, *ibid,* p. 384.
[3] Ransom, *ibid,* p. 7.
[4] *ibi*d, p. 7.

"Break forth into joy, sing together, ye waste places of Jerusalem, for the Lord hath comforted his people. He hath redeemed Jerusalem. The Lord hath made bare his holy arm in the sight of all nations; and all the ends of the world shall see the salvation of our God." At the time of the redemption vouchsafed by Cyrus, the Lord did not make bare his holy arm in the sight of all nations. There was nothing miraculous in that deliverance; and, from that hour to this, it never has been true that all the ends of the earth have seen the salvation of our God. The prophecy must, therefore, refer to that glorious period yet to come, when the conversion of the world is to result from the restoration of Jerusalem. For to believe that such is the will and purpose of God seems most agreeable to the declarations of Scripture.[5]

In emphasizing the importance of Jerusalem as the centre for the vital mission to the Jewish people, McCaul added:

The prophets all point to Jerusalem as the hope of the nations, and St. Paul expressly declares that the receiving of the Jews is to be as life from the dead to the rest of the world.[6]

McCaul, as the LJS representative, left no doubt as to his, and the LJS's position, that the bishopric was bound up with the restoration of Israel. Perhaps not everyone though would have agreed with this emphasis.

Bishop Alexander preached his farewell sermon at the Episcopal Jews Chapel on 8 November 1841, taking Acts 20:22-23 as his text:

And now, behold, I go bound in the Spirit unto Jerusalem, not knowing the things that shall befall me there: save that the Holy Ghost witnesseth in every city, saying, that bonds and afflictions abide me. But none of these things move me, neither count I my life dear unto myself, so that I may finish my course with joy, and the ministry that I have received of the Lord Jesus, to testify the Gospel of the grace of God ...

Had it been said but a short time ago, that ere long this pulpit would be occupied by a humble member of the despised race of Israel, raised and consecrated to be the Bishop of the United Church of England and Ireland in Jerusalem, it would have been rejected as absurd, visionary, and altogether impossible; yet, brethren, here I stand a monument of the Divine

---

[5] Alexander McCaul, *A Sermon preached in the chapel of Lambeth Palace at the Consecration of the Lord Bishop of the United Church of England and Ireland in Jerusalem on Sunday, November 7, 1841,* (London, 1841), p. 18.
[6] *ibid,* pp. 18-19.

sovereignty and power, a proof that nothing is too hard for the Lord, that with him all things are possible, and that his thoughts and ways are not ours ... Surely, no one will now venture to doubt the possibility of the literal fulfillment of God's promises to Israel.[7]

Alexander then spoke of the early life of Paul, as well as the period of the beginning of the church. Paul, he stated:

... knew the awful judgments which the Saviour himself had denounced upon that devoted city and her people; we are privileged to go as repairers of the breach, in obedience to the call of the prophet, "Comfort ye, comfort ye my people, saith your God. Speak ye comfortably to Jerusalem, and cry unto her, that her warfare is accomplished, that her iniquity is pardoned: for she hath received of the Lord's hand double for all her sins." For though Jerusalem has been and still is trodden down of the Gentiles, yet we know it was only to be for a time, until the time of the Gentiles be fulfilled, and whilst we must confess that it is not easy to determine the precise period meant by that expression, we must also admit that there are strong indications in our day of God's returning mercies to Israel, and that "the set time to favour Zion is come, yea, even the set time;" and brethren, the very occasion on which we are assembled proves more than ever, even to a demonstration that the servants of God, the rulers both of Church and State, "take pleasure in the stones of Zion, and favour the dust thereof;" and whenever that is the case, we are plainly told by the inspired Psalmist [Ps 102:13,14] "That the time to favour Zion is come.".... We might enlarge upon this delightful subject, and bring forward some of those striking passages of Scripture which plainly predict the universal kingdom of Christ, and the restoration of Israel in particular.

Alexander then revealed how the Apostle's journey to Jerusalem was a duty laid upon him, and that there was a parallel with his own situation: "'Behold, I go bound in the Spirit unto Jerusalem." This was the declaration of the Apostle; and this, brethren, I can truly say, is the language of my heart.'[8]

He continued:

---

[7] Farewell Sermon of Michael Solomon Alexander, (Wertheim, London, 1841), p. 5, found in Alexander Papers, DS.3.a5, St. Anthony's.
[8] *ibid*, p. 10.

The Christian course is one of great difficulty; it is indeed a warfare between light and darkness, a fighting against principalities and powers ...

And now brethren what shall I say respecting that ministry which I also have received of the Lord Jesus? "Behold, I also am bound in the Spirit to go to Jerusalem, there to testify of the Gospel to the grace of God; to preach to both Jews and Gentiles repentance towards God, and faith towards our Lord Jesus Christ." In the wonderful and mysterious providence of God, who first called me by his grace from a state of darkness to the marvelous light of the Gospel, and afterwards put me into the ministry, I am now set apart for one of the highest offices in the Church, destined to go to the land of my forefathers. I know not what shall befall me there, save that trials and afflictions abide me; but shall I thereby be discouraged from following the call of my Lord and master, who has done so much for me? God forbid! In holy confidence and in humble reliance on the mighty arm of the God of Jacob, I would say with the apostle, "I am persuaded that neither life, nor death, nor angels, nor principalities, nor powers, nor things present, nor things to come, nor height, nor depth, nor any other creature, shall be able to separate me from the love of God which is in Christ Jesus my Lord."[9]

Alexander then addressed the members of the LJS, exhorting them to persevere, and that there were, he emphasized, promising signs, 'surely there are not wanting many indications of encouragement, that the time to favour Zion is at hand; that he who scattered Israel will gather him, and keep him as a shepherd doth his flock. You are God's chosen instruments to be the bearers of glad tidings unto Zion.'[10]

He then likened the LJS to a collective body that had been 'bound in the Spirit, like the Apostle, to go to Jerusalem. You knew not what would befall you there' he continued 'save that mountains of difficulties were in your way. You have' he added, 'by the grace of God, persevered hitherto; you have seen many of those mountains removed ... You have yet many, many difficulties to encounter; but let the language of the apostle be also yours: "None of these things move me;" and be assured, brethren, that the God of Israel will be faithful to his promise, "I will bless them that bless thee."'[11]

Alexander concluded his message by beseeching his brethren to strive together with him in prayer, that he would be delivered 'from them that do

---

[9] *ibid*, pp. 15-16.
[10] *ibid*, p. 17.
[11] *ibid*, p. 18.

not believe in Judea, and that my service which I have for Jerusalem may be accepted of the saints.'[12]

Shortly afterwards the LJS wrote their final tribute to Alexander:

> ... the consecration of a Jewish Christian to be a shepherd unto Israel is an event unheard of since the day that Jerusalem was delivered to be trodden down by the Gentiles, and forms an era in the history both of the Jewish nation and the Christian Church ... What the friends of Israel longed and prayed and laboured for was not simply the conversion of a few individuals, but the resuscitation of the Jewish people and the resurrection of the Jewish Church.[13]

English Deed of Endowment and Prussian Announcement

On 14 November the Prussian Minister of Spiritual Affairs, Eichhorn,[14] released a circular to inform the German populace of the bishopric, stating:

> The result of the negotiations carried on by Prussia, for the purpose of obtaining for Evangelical Christians of the German Nation, the same privileges in the Turkish empire, and especially in Syria and Palestine, now enjoyed there by the adherents of the Latin and Greek Churches, excites universal interest ...
>
> The harmony existing between the great powers of Europe, to which the Turkish empire owes its independent existence, and the world its peace, presented an opportunity of essentially ameliorating the lot of German Evangelical Christians in the east. To avail itself of this opportunity in a manner becoming the dignity of its political position, Prussia felt it to be a sacred duty ... that the great impetus given to the commercial and industrial intercourse of the nations will also increase the connexion (sic) of German Protestants with the East, and possibly on their part give rise to settlements in those countries ...
>
> The Porte knows Prussia only as a great power of Europe, which, by its harmony with the other great powers, guarantees its security. Different is the relation in which Great Britain stands to the Porte. England possesses by her fleet and her commerce a preponderating influence. An union, therefore, with England, *whose Church, in origin and doctrine, is intimately related to the German Evangelical Church,* presents itself as the most certain means of attaining this most important object.

---

[12] *ibid*, p. 19.

[13] *JI, 1*841, pp. 390-1.

[14] Karl Friedrich Eichhorn, 1781- 1854.

The negotiations to be entered into for this purpose were dependent upon a previous question, whether Great Britain was inclined to give to the independence and national honour of the German Evangelical Church their due consideration, and, in a full understanding with Prussia, to treat this matter on the fixed principle, that *Evangelical Christians should, under the advocacy of England and Prussia, present themselves to the Turkish Government as an unity, and thus receive from it all the privileges of a legal recognition.*

The steps taken for the adjustment of the previous question were attended with the most satisfactory results. Not only the Government of Great Britain exhibited the utmost readiness and willingness to engage in the matter on the basis proposed, but the heads of the English church entered into the proposal with a warm interest ...

By a cordial co-operation ... a particular Bishopric has now been founded in Jerusalem, in which, in all dealings with the Turkish Government, and wherever else mediation on their behalf as a Church-unity may be necessary, all Evangelical Christians may find a common stay and centre of union, but at the same time, the German Protestants, especially, may assert the independence of their Church in respect of their own particular Confession and Liturgy ...

Thus the ecclesiastical necessities of the new Bishopric may be considered as provided for. But, inasmuch as a Church community cannot have a growth rich in blessing, except in connexion (sic) with the instruction of youth, and the care of the sick, a still larger contribution is to be expected from the pious interest and beneficence of Evangelical Christians of Prussia and other German lands.

Particularly important is the foundation of an Hospitum in which travellers, whom scientific research, ecclesiastical interest, or even other purposes, will probably bring to Jerusalem in increased numbers, may find a reception in case of need.[15]

Attached to this general letter was another circular calling for a special collection on a Sunday yet to be announced in order to raise funds for the establishment of such a hospice for travelers. For the sake of national pride, the circular did exaggerate, continuing:

The King's majesty has taken advantage of the opportunity afforded by his participation in the preservation of peace in the East, to procure for the Evangelical Church, for all future times, the same legal recognition in

---

[15] Circular from Karl Eichhorn, Prussian Minister of Spiritual Affairs, Berlin, 14 November 1841, quoted in Hechler, *The Jerusalem Bishopric,* pp. 62-74.

Turkey, which the Greek and Latin Churches have long since enjoyed in those countries ... In a very short time a Church for German Protestants will lift up its head in Jerusalem, and be opened for their worship according to their Confession and Liturgy ...

On 15 November 1841 the English Deed of Endowment for the Jerusalem Bishopric was signed and sealed. The Trustees for the Deed of Endowment were Lord Shaftesbury, Sir George Rose, Sir Thomas Baring, Sir Robert Inglis and John Labouchere.

A week later, on 23 November 1841 the LJS Committee met, and resolved that 'as the Bishop of Jerusalem is by virtue of his Lordship's office, ecclesiastical head of all the English clergy & the English Church at Jerusalem, so this Committee request his Lordship to take upon himself the direction and Governance of the Mission in the Holy Land & in the Province included in his Diocese.'[16]

There was a further resolution requiring Nicolayson, Rev. F. C. Ewald and Dr. Edward Macgowan, both of whom were to accompany Alexander as LJS workers, to submit to the ecclesiastical authority of Alexander.

In summary then, the bishop's role, as far as the British were concerned revolved around the LJS and involvement with the Jewish people. But on 16 November the *Prussian State Gazette* wrote, as the goals of the bishopric, the need for securing legal recognition for Protestants in the east, to counter-balance in some form the political aspirations of Russia, which protected the Orthodox, and France, which protected the Roman Catholics. Prussia could only do this by joining with Britain. [17]

On the eve of the bishop's departure the dual expectations of his task, the British and Prussian, were out in the open. The die had been cast and there was now no turning back. The Jewish bishop was on his way to Jerusalem. And upon his shoulders he was carrying the expectations, diverse goals and aspirations of two nations, and two ecclesiastical bodies. Would it all be too heavy a burden for one man to carry?

---

[16] Letter from W. Ayerst to J. Nicolayson, 25 November 1842, in *Letters from Jerusalem 1834-1842*, p. 222, Schick Library.

[17] *Prussian State Gazette,* 16 November 1841, quoted in F.D. Maurice, *Three Letters to the Rev. W. Palmer,* (London, 1842), pp. 45-6.

Schönlanker Marktplatz mit evangelischer Kirche

Marketplace in Schonlanke, Prussian Posen (above) with evangelical Lutheran Church in the foreground and arrow pointing to the Synagogue (below). Photographs from 'Muzeum Ziemi Nadnoteckiej im. Wiktora Stachowiaka w Trziance' in Trzcianka, Poland.

Innenansicht der Synagoge

Above: The Synagogue at Plymouth (foreground) and St. Andrews Church in the background.
Below: St. Anne's Church in Dublin.

THE PREDICTIONS AND PROMISES OF GOD
RESPECTING ISRAEL.

A

SERMON

PREACHED

On Wednesday, June 22nd, 1825,

IN THE

Parish Church of St. Andrew's,

PLYMOUTH,

ON THE BAPTISM OF

MR. MICHAEL SOLOMON ALEXANDER,

Late Reader in the Jewish Synagogue.

WITH AN APPENDIX.

BY THE

REV. JOHN HATCHARD, A. M.

VICAR OF ST. ANDREW'S, PLYMOUTH.

PLYMOUTH:

PRINTED AND PUBLISHED BY ROWES, WHIMPLE-STREET;

SOLD ALSO BY NETTLETON, PLYMOUTH;

AND J. HATCHARD AND SON, PICCADILLY,
LONDON.

1825.

Price One Shilling and Sixpence.

Cover of pamphlet of sermon by Rev. Hatchard at the
baptism of Alexander.

INTRODUCTORY LECTURE,

DELIVERED PUBLICLY IN

KING'S COLLEGE, LONDON,

NOVEMBER 17, 1832.

———◆———

BY THE

REV. M. S. ALEXANDER,

Professor of Hebrew & Rabbinical Literature in the College.

LONDON:

B. FELLOWES, BOOKSELLER & PUBLISHER TO THE COLLEGE,
39, LUDGATE STREET ;
HATCHARD AND SON, PICCADILLY ; AND W. CURRY,
SACKVILLE STREET, DUBLIN.

M DCCC XXXII.

Cover of booklet containing Alexander's introductory lecture at King's College, London, 1832.

A Jewish Bishop in Jerusalem

Above: Palestine Place, Centre of the LJS in London.
Below: Rev. Dr. Alexander McCaul.

A Jewish Bishop in Jerusalem

The architects of the Jerusalem Protestant Bishopric: Lord Shaftesbury (above) and King Frederick William IV of Prussia (below – from painting by Franz Kruger in 1845, located in Julius H. Schoeps, *Preussen*, Berlin, 2000, p. 126).

A Jewish Bishop in Jerusalem

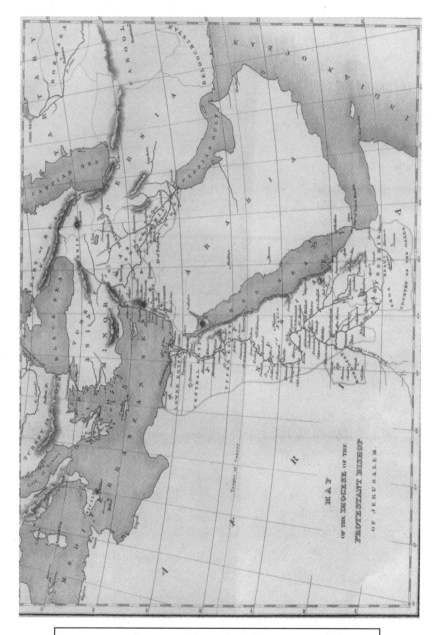

Map of the Protestant-Anglican Diocese of Jerusalem.

A Jewish Bishop in Jerusalem

Alexander's two close and trusted colleagues:
Above, Rev. John Nicolayson.
Below, Dr. Edward Macgowan.

Chapter 10

A Jewish Bishop in Jerusalem: 1842

Departure for Jerusalem
Much of the work involved in preparing for the move to Jerusalem fell
onto Mrs. Alexander's shoulders, as her daughter Deborah testifies:

> She superintended everything before we left England, received many
> visitors, accompanied Papa to numerous dinners, and Receptions. She
> engaged two ladies as our Governesses, two maids, a butler, bought outfits
> for Papa, herself, and us children, and for Robert, who was to remain in
> England. She selected China, Glass, Linen, Furniture, Plate, saddlery, a
> Medicine Chest, a Harp, a Piano, Haberdashery, Mops and Brooms and
> Provisions. Nothing whatever could be bought in Jerusalem.[1]

Following the consecration, the Alexanders, minus Robert who was to
remain in England, made their way to Gosport for departure. They stayed
the night with Archdeacon Wilberforce, of Alverstoke.[2] Then on 7
December 1841 they departed aboard the ship *Devastation.* The
Admiralty had previously offered the ship *Infernal* but Alexander did not
think that appropriate for such a voyage! Of the ship, Irwin wrote: 'The
Admiralty's assistance was supplemented by Mr. Arthur Guinness, who in
the first of his firm's timely benefactions to the Anglican church had
provided without charge a supply of stout.'[3]

Those accompanying Bishop Alexander were his pregnant wife, and six
children: Fanny (13), Deborah (9), Annie (7), Bessie (5), Minnie (5),
Benny (2), Miss Gannon and Miss Pitt (cousins), Ellen and Margaret
(maids), James Sumpter (the butler), Rev. George Williams, (Alexander's

---

[1] Ransom, *ibid*, p. 7.

[2] *ibid*, p. 8.

[3] Patrick Irwin, *Bishop Alexander and the Jews of Jerusalem,* in 'Studies in
Church History,' Vol. 21: Persecution and Toleration, ed. W.J.Shields, Oxford
1984, p. 317.

chaplain), Dr. Edward Macgowan (the physician), Rev. F. C. Ewald, his wife Mary Ann, and child, and an Italian nurse named Palmeira.[4]

The first stop on the journey was Lisbon, where they stayed three days. The next port of call was Gibraltar and then Malta. In both these locations the vessel was met by a seven-gun bishop's salute. In Gibraltar Michael Solomon, Mrs. Alexander and Fanny stayed with the Governor Sir Alexander Woodford and in Malta with the Governor Sir Francis Mason.

In both locations the Governors' wives pleaded for Mrs. Alexander to remain with them for the period of her confinement. In Malta, where they were delayed some seventeen days due to the need of some repairs to the ship, Mrs. Alexander was more than pleased to enjoy the comforts of Government House rather than the slightly overcrowded *Devastation*. But she was determined to be at her husband's side when he entered the Land of Israel and Jerusalem.

In the *Holy Land*

From Malta the party finally set sail for the Holy Land, calling first at Beirut for three days. Michael Solomon recorded: 'I cannot describe our feelings on getting the first sight of the land of our forefathers.'[5] Alexander's first duty was to notify Consul-General Colonel Hugh Rose,[6] of his arrival, and shortly afterwards the consul-general came aboard.

Rose was able to assure the party concerning the political situation, in particular that the recent conflict between the Maronites[7] and Druse,[8] and ruthless actions against the Christians by Amer Pasha, had ended. In fact this conflict had been a matter of concern for the British Government. Aberdeen had informed Ambassador Ponsonby, that: 'Her Majesty's Government must hold the Porte responsible for any harm which befalls

---

[4] Ransom, *ibid*, p. 10

[5] Alexander to CMJ London, 17 January 1842, in *JI,* 1842, p. 127.

[6] Son of Sir George Rose. Hugh Rose later became Lord Strathnairne.

[7] The Maronites are a group of Christians who gathered round Maron, a priest from Antioch in the 5th century and adopted his pattern of life. They adhered to the beliefs of the Council of Chalcedon in 451 CE. Later following the massacre of 350 monks in the 6th century by the Monophysites of Antioch, the Maronites were recognized by the Roman Catholic Church and many escaped to the mountains of Lebanon.

[8] The Druse are an off-shoot of Islam. Their faith is based largely on the beliefs of Hamzah ibn Ali ibn Ahmad, a minister of the Egyptian Fatimid Caliph al-Hakim in the 11th century. The Druse at that time were found throughout the province of Syria, but primarily in the areas of modern Lebanon and Syria.

Bishop Alexander in consequence of the unwarranted proceedings of Amer Pasha.'[9]

Alexander and the party were not idle during these days. Three young Englishmen had approached Ewald and asked for confirmation. Williams then instructed them, found them to be serious candidates, and Alexander performed the ceremony at the British Consulate. Also present were officers of the *Devastation*, the captain of the war ship *Vesuvius*, Mr. Thompson (the American missionary formerly from Jerusalem), and others.[10]

For the on-going leg of the journey Consul-General Rose joined the party, with Major Doyle, and accompanied them to Jaffa, where they arrived mid-afternoon on 19 January 1842. Rose later reported concerning Alexander that he was 'surprisingly in the dark as to the state of affairs in this and other countries, and totally unacquainted with the laws and rights of Turkey.'[11]

Alexander's daughter Deborah recalled this time:

By the middle of January we arrived off Jaffa. Owing to its dangerous rocks and surf, we had to be carried ashore by Arabs, through the breakers. Mama was landed in a litter, made for her on board, of a hammock slung on two poles, and in that way she was carried to Jerusalem between 2 mules.[12]

While in Jaffa the party was welcomed initially by the British honourary consul, Yosef Jarash Matback, at whose house they were 'served with lemonade, coffee and a pipe.'[13] The Turkish governor (pasha) and Muslim *Cadi*[14] also arrived and paid respects to the bishop and consul-general.

With the exception of the Ewald family, the party began the journey to Jerusalem on the following day. Nicolayson who had anticipated meeting the party in Jaffa, did in fact meet them between Ramle and Jaffa, and escorted them back to Ramle. Here they stayed at the house of Nicolayson's friend, Abood Markos. Deborah the bishop's daughter describes their experience thus:

---

[9] Aberdeen to Ponsonby, 24 March 1842, FO [Foreign Office file] 78/473, (No 26).

[10] F. C. Ewald, *Journal of Missionary Labours in the City of Jerusalem*, (London 1846), p. 16.

[11] Rose to Aberdeen, 4 February 1843, FO 78/535, (No 11).

[12] Ransom, *ibid*, p. 11.

[13] Ewald, *ibid*, p. 18.

[14] Also spelt Kadi – religious leader.

We were the guests of the Pacha. Papa, Mr. Williams and the other gentlemen were received into the Pacha's own Palace, but Mama and we feminines were banished to the Harem. Shall I ever forget that night of misery! We had to sleep on the divans, eat our meals on the floor, and it was past midnight before the ladies of the Harem left us alone. Skinny old hags, henna painted wives – girls, and little boys of 7 years old pawing us all over – tried on our clothes, especially corsets, and chattering, like monkeys and parrots. Oh, how tired we were, how we longed for rest, but not until our hosts chose to leave us, could we show signs of weariness, so sacred was the law of courtesy in the East.[15]

The following morning, Friday 21 January, the party continued on to Jerusalem, arriving in the late afternoon. Some distance from the Holy City they were met by Mr. Johns, architect of the church, and pro-consul (*locum tenens*) in the absence of Consul Young. Also present were the American missionaries.[16] The *Times* correspondent later wrote that the Turkish pasha sent a guard 'to compliment Colonel Rose on his arrival.'[17] It must have been an interesting spectacle, especially with Mrs. Alexander and her younger children being conveyed in a *taterwan* or Oriental litter, supported before and behind by mules.

The party, which now comprised of about forty persons, then proceeded towards Jaffa Gate, arriving at the same time as the Muslims were celebrating one of their main festivals, the *'Id Al-Adha*. Then as they entered through the gates, the 'guns thundered forth the salute for the eve of Courban Bairam.'[18] Nicolayson described quite graphically this moment:

---

[15] Ransom, *ibid*, p. 13. Ewald quotes a source stating that Alexander stayed the night with the American Consul, 'the wealthiest Christian in the place' and Consul-General Rose at the Armenian Convent. See Ewald, *ibid*, p. 24. Nicolayson however states they stayed with Abood Markos, and Colonel Rose at the Latin Convent. See *JI* 1842, p. 129.

[16] Belonging to the American Board of Commissioners for Foreign Missions.

[17] *Times*, written in Jerusalem on 27 January, and printed 14 February 1842, pp. 2-5. Quoted in *JI*, 1842, pp. 131-132. Alexander later claimed that the pasha had come out to meet the party, but had been forced to return to Jerusalem about 6 o'clock due to the damp. Tibawi however contends this, claiming that the pasha would not be coming to greet Alexander, as Alexander, legally, had no official status, he was merely a British subject. See A. L. Tibawi, *British Interests in Palestine 1800-1901*, (Oxford, 1961), p. 58 and notes 3 and 4.

[18] *Times*, quoted in *JI*, 1842, p. 132. The Courban Bairam is the Muslim Feast of the Sacrifice that commemorates what Muslims believe to be Moses' sacrifice of Ishmael.

The Pasha had himself been out at the gate waiting to receive his Lordship and the Consul-General till sunset; and when we arrived, the commander of the troops, with a detachment of cavalry, was still in waiting, and escorted us in. A body of soldiers were drawn up at the gate and presented arms, another again at the door of my house, where I had the honour and pleasure to entertain the whole party.[19]

According to the correspondent of the *Times* by the time the party had arrived at the Bethlehem [Jaffa] Gate, 'The procession consisted of more than 100 persons on horseback.'[20] This very same correspondent then concluded his article with a most profound, yet unfortunately somewhat incorrect, statement, as time would reveal:

The mission is sure of the firm support of the British Government and the British Ambassador at the Porte. As regards Syria, the Consul-General has lent all the force of his official authority, personal influence, and popularity, to set the undertaking afloat, while the mild and benevolent character of the Bishop, and the sound practical sense and valuable local experience of his coadjutor, Mr. Nicolayson, are sure guarantees that caution, charity, and conciliation will preside at all their efforts.[21]

First Days in Jerusalem
The Alexanders spent the first night at the home of John Nicolayson. The following days were, naturally, both busy and bizarre for the Alexander family and the entire entourage. There was official business to be taken care of, as well as the basics of procuring food, accommodation and becoming familiar with the new and totally different environment. Nicolayson meanwhile procured the house where Consul Young had previously lived for the Alexanders, which although the best available, prompted Michael Solomon to write:

... it would be considered in England a miserable hovel. When I first came to see it, it gave me the idea of a dungeon, which seems to me here almost

---

[19] Nicolayson to LJS London, 24 January 1842, in *JI* 1842, p. 129. The *Times* added that the pasha had sent a guard of honour and his *Janissaries,* guardians, to meet Colonel Rose.
[20] *Times,* 14 February, quoted in *JI,* 1842, p. 131.
[21] *ibid,* p. 132.

universally the appearance of the houses outside. I am happy to say Mrs. Alexander is quite satisfied, and so are the rest of the party.[22]

Mrs. Alexander and the party may have been satisfied, but daughter Deborah wasn't. Many years later she wrote of her recollections:

> The house which we first inhabited, down in the Turkish Quarter was very unhealthy. It was in full view of the Pool of Hezekiah, a stagnant tank of rain water, where frogs croaked, lizards and newts abounded, also there was a very noisy Turkish coffin shop close by, from which uproarious revels, much beating of tomtoms, clapping of hands, yellings and shouting made night hideous. Nearby was a tall and slender minaret from whose 4 sided gallery, four times a day, the blind Meuzzin in a powerful voice, called the Moslems to pray. Bells are not allowed by the Turks.[23]

On 22 January Colonel Rose accompanied Alexander to a formal meeting with Tahir Pasha, the Turkish governor of Jerusalem, who must have been quite perplexed about how to meet this new resident. [24]

The following day, being Sunday, Alexander preached his first sermon,[25] from Isaiah 60:15: 'Whereas thou (alluding to Jerusalem) hast been forsaken and hated, so that no man went through thee, I will make thee an eternal excellency, a joy of many generations.' The tendency of Alexander's discourse, wrote the *Times* correspondent, was to show that, although Jerusalem had endured, and might still endure, much suffering in the fulfillment of inspired prophecy, nevertheless brighter days were at hand.'[26]

In his sermon Alexander also referred to the Turkish government in the country as 'an usurped one' – a matter that led to a rebuke by Consul-General Rose. Alexander promised never again to speak in such terms.[27] From the very outset though Alexander made it quite clear, especially to

---

[22] Alexander to LJS London, 25 January 1825, *JI,* 1842, p. 128.
[23] Ransom, *ibid*, p. 14.
[24] According to Corey, the Pasha, 'in conformity with instructions receive from Constantinople ... ordered a proclamation to be made in all the mosques to the effect that "he who touches the Anglican Bishop touches the apple of the Pasha's eye." In reality though it does seem quite unlikely that this communication would have been received from Constantinople. See Corey, *ibid*, p. 69.
[25] Probably in a small room on the LJS property where the present Christ Church Centre dining room and *Bet Nicolayson* Heritage Centre are now located.
[26] *Times*, quoted in *JI,* 1842, p. 132.
[27] Rose to Aberdeen, 15 February 1843, FO 78/535, (No 19).

Rose, just how difficult it was going to be to fulfill his duties, and remain faithful to Britain's official line towards the Turkish authorities.

Concerning the Bishop's relationship with the local inhabitants, Nicolayson recorded: 'I have just had evidence that the fact that his Lordship is nationally a member of the house of Judah, will make a strong impression on Moslems here, when it shall become generally known.'

And of the Jewish people, he added: 'The Jews are loud in proclaiming it and seem to take pride in extolling his Lordship's learning and office among them ...'[28]

Opposition to Alexander's Presence.

The *Times* correspondent also wrote of certain opponents to Alexander's coming to Jerusalem. 'It cannot be disguised' he stated 'that these individuals have a severe ordeal of groundless calumny, intrigue, jealousy, and opposition to go through. Even a few days before their arrival the Greeks and Catholics had been circulating cock-and-bull stories about the decline of English influence.' [29]

Israeli historian Yehoshuah Ben Arieh also writes that Alexander's appointment 'sparked the interest of the Roman Catholics of Central Europe who demanded a counter balance to Western Protestant and Greek Orthodox activity. On 14th January 1842 the decision was made to appoint a Roman Catholic Bishop.'[30]

Indeed there was considerable opposition to the Protestant Bishopric, which is further highlighted in a letter by W. Ayerst to Nicolayson dated 19 February 1842:

> The public papers abound with rumours of difficulty in his way. These are chiefly taken from the French and Austrian papers, and we may well suppose that they endeavour to represent things as they wish to have them, and do not fail to look out for obstacles in the way of the execution of those plans which must tend to injure Popery.[31]

Yet the bishop did not initially receive as much personal opposition in Jerusalem as could have been expected, a matter which both the *Morning*

---

[28] Nicolayson to CMJ London, 24 January 1842, in *JI*, 1842, p. 131.

[29] *Times*, quoted in *JI*, 1842, p. 132.

[30] Y. Ben Arieh, *Jerusalem in the Nineteenth Century,* (Jerusalem, 1984), Vol I, p 231. He probably means a patriarch.

[31] W. Ayerst to John Nicolayson, 19 February 1842, in *Letters from Jerusalem, 1834-1842*, No 20, p. 224, Schick Library.

Herald and the *Times* papers commented upon.[32] In fact, some very distorted stories were circulating in Europe, stating that the bishop had been stoned while preaching in the open air, and more. Alexander was able to repudiate all such stories.

Personal Trials & Official Duties
One of Alexander's first duties was to institute, in a more formal way, the daily Hebrew meeting at seven o'clock in the morning, and evening prayers in English. Nicolayson had been holding Hebrew prayers since 1839. Alexander wrote: 'We have now regular daily services in the temporary chapel: at seven in the morning in Hebrew, and at sunset in English; and though we are but a small band, yet I feel it peculiarly delightful thus daily to worship on Mount Zion.'[33]

In early February, Mrs. Alexander bore a daughter, Louisa, the first that Bishop Alexander baptized. This was obviously a high point, both for the Alexander family, and the small Hebrew Christian - Protestant community. Yet Alexander had to write on 26 February: '... it has pleased God to cause death to enter into our dwelling, by taking from us our dear infant on February 13, when just a fortnight old. This has been an unexpected additional severe trial to us, but our God is gracious, and enables us by his grace to acknowledge his fatherly hand in all things.'[34] This was to be the first of many difficulties for the Alexander family during their stay in Jerusalem.

Further deaths consumed the bishop's time and energy. About 10 March, some two weeks before Easter 1842, seven British sailors from the war ship *Hatchet,* were drowned near Jaffa. Alexander proceeded there and purchased land for a burial ground for them.[35]

Such set-backs were partly compensated by ministry opportunities. In the same week that Louisa Alexander died, two German missionaries associated with the CMS arrived from Egypt to receive ordination. Although encouraged, Alexander had to confess: 'I should have been glad if Jewish missionaries of our Society had been the first to receive ordination from the first Hebrew Bishop of the Anglican Church in Jerusalem.'[36]

[32] Articles from *Morning Herald* and *Times* quoted in *JI*, 1842, pp. 233-4.
[33] Alexander to LJS London, 26 February 1842, in *JI*, 1842, p. 161.
[34] *ibid,* p. 161.
[35] *JI*, 1842, p. 192. Ewald, *ibid,* p. 82. This site is now located on land adjacent to the former CMS Mission-house and Tabeetha School in Jaffa.
[36] Alexander to LJS London, 26 February 1842, in *JI*, 1842, p. 161.

Laying Foundations for the Physical Church

On 28 February Bishop Alexander placed the first stone under ground upon the foundations of the new Protestant Church. Altogether eight stones were laid, one by Alexander, and one by each of the seven mission workers. Such an act so soon after arrival was a major challenge to the Turkish governor and Muslim authorities, as the building of a new church was a challenge to Islamic Law, the *Sharia*, which forbade the building of new churches.

The foundation-laying event was of great significance for the small Protestant community and in particular for Alexander, for whom the issue of completing the building of the first Protestant church in the Ottoman Empire, was of major importance. A bishop without a church was incongruous to the local inhabitants.

Nicolayson and Alexander were oblivious to the intense battles then ensuing in Constantinople between the Turkish religious leaders, the *ulema*, and the British (and Prussian) ambassadors. Alexander and Nicolayson based their authority to build upon the information provided by Palmerston to Shaftesbury in October 1841 which stated that Ambassador Ponsonby in Constantinople 'had obtained a positive promise' that instructions 'should be forthwith sent' to the governor of Jerusalem granting permission for the church to be built.[37]

In a letter to Chevalier Bunsen in April, Alexander stated that no obstacle had been placed before them concerning the building of the church. He had feared that the governor-general of Syria, Mustapha Pasha, would have been opposed. But following a visit by Mustapha Pasha in April, Alexander wrote that he: 'has done or said nothing to impede our progress, as was generally feared, from the general impression, that he is not friendly disposed towards us, but from a circumstance which has transpired, it became evident that he took it for granted that we have a right to build the church.' [38]

Alexander mentioned here that Mustapha Pasha 'took it for granted that we have a right to build the church.' The problem remained however that there was still no official permit, or *firman*, to build the church.

So for the time being Alexander and Nicolayson continued on with their plans, despite the perennial Jerusalem problem, which Alexander terms the 'general natural tardiness of the people.' [39] On 7 August a master stonemason and several labourers left Malta en-route for Jerusalem to

---

[37] Tibawi, *ibid,* pp. 60-61.

[38] Alexander to Chevalier Bunsen, Easter Monday 1842, in *JI* 1842, p. 192.

[39] Alexander to LJS London, 16 April 1842, in *JI*, 1842, p. 248.

speed up construction on the church.[40] All being well, the church should have been finished within the year.

... and for the Spiritual Church

On 17 March Alexander ordained Mr. John Muhleisen of the CMS into deacon's orders. Muhleisen was destined for service in Abyssinia. The service was joined by a number of visitors, including members of the Greek Church. The same afternoon the newly ordained deacon read prayers at the German service.[41]

There was certainly no shortage of work for Alexander and his assistants during this initial period. Macgowan was busy trying to re-establish the medical work with Melville Peter Bergheim, while Ewald was busy attempting to establish contacts with the Jewish people, although some contacts had previously been made by Nicolayson, Pieritz and Calman.

The obstacles that Ewald, and indeed Alexander, faced, are summarized by the comment made by several Jewish men to Ewald: 'We know that all of you have turned Christians for money; it is money that has induced you to forsake the faith of your fathers. It is often very difficult under such circumstances,' wrote Ewald, 'to keep one's temper.'[42]

These attitudes were often countered by positive responses. At this time three rabbis, whom Mr. Pieritz, a former LJS worker had previously befriended, were showing considerable interest in the message of the missionaries. Ewald in particular was involved with them. Also a Jewish family, Mr. A. L. Ducat and his wife Rose, had recently arrived in Jerusalem and were serious inquirers about Jesus. On 21 March, the family of John Meshullam arrived from Malta, boosting the numbers of the small believing community.[43] In fact Ewald was able to write on 25 March:

> Our small congregation of believing Jews on Mount Zion, consists at present of twenty-five souls. May the Lord soon add many, many more! Zion, with its small number of believing Jews, will still become a place of attraction to many sons of Abraham.[44]

---

[40] *JI*, 1842, p. 353.

[41] Ewald, *ibid*, p. 72.

[42] Ewald, *ibid*, p. 89.

[43] Ewald, *ibid*, p. 90. Ewald had befriended this family in Tunis, and they had later gone to Malta where they were baptized by Rev. Samuel Gobat of the CMS.

[44] Ewald, *ibid*, p. 92.

Unfortunately, tragedy struck the young Meshullam family shortly after their arrival. One of the young children died of small-pox (an annual occurrence in filthy Jerusalem). While this child was being buried, news came that another of the small Meshullam children had also succumbed to the same illness.[45]

First Visit – to Bethlehem

It took several months before Alexander was able to leave the confines of Jerusalem and visit the land. On 4 May he, Mrs. Alexander, some of their children, Ewald and several English travellers set out for Bethlehem. Here they were received by the local Greek Bishop. While in the Church of the Nativity, Miss Anna Alexander read the nativity story. Then, following Alexander's insistence, the Greek Bishop did the same in Greek.[46] Later they dined with the Greek Bishop – and all were of the opinion that the Alexanders needed a spacious house in Jerusalem such as the Greek Bishop had in Bethlehem.

On this visit Ewald keenly observed that very few Muslims lived in Bethlehem – and that: 'No Jew is permitted to live at Bethlehem, nor even to visit the place.'[47]

Shortly afterwards Alexander received an interesting letter from Methodius, Greek Patriarch of Antioch, acknowledging various materials sent to him by Alexander, including a letter from the Archbishop of Canterbury and a copy of the Book of Common Prayer. Methodius stated that the Book of Common Prayer is discordant with the doctrines of the Greek Orthodox Church in the East, and added that although he desires peace, he hopes that nothing of a disturbing nature would be propagated amongst the local Greek clergy.[48]

Encouragements in England

Following the initial reports of Alexander's successful entry into Jerusalem and subsequent achievements, the supporters in England and Prussia became more enthusiastic. Not surprisingly, the issue of the bishopric was one of the main matters at the LJS Annual General Meeting (AGM), held on 6 May 1842, in London.

---

[45] Ewald, *ibid*, p.105.

[46] *ibid*, p. 96.

[47] *ibid*, p. 98.

[48] Methodius to Bishop Alexander, 23 May 1842, Alexander Papers, MSS 3393, Lambeth. Methodius presumably received these materials via the Russian consul at Beirut, Constantine Basily, to whom Alexander gave them on his arrival there.

Lord Shaftesbury's statement emphasized again the grand expectations now placed upon the broad shoulders of Bishop Alexander. Shaftesbury stated:

> ... the first Hebrew that for 1700 years was raised to the dignity of the Christian episcopate; was borne on one of her majesty's vessels, under the safeguard of the British flag ... and escorted by our gallant sailors ... to aid in the fulfillment of that august command, "Bring my sons from afar, and my daughters from the ends of the earth." But while we give our most humble and hearty thanks to God for the past, we feel that we have equal reason to thank him for the prospects of the future. At no time has the horizon been so bright for the Jewish people. At no time has that prophecy seemed so near its fulfillment, "Kings shall be thy nursing-fathers, and queens thy nursing-mothers." A great and wise Prince now offers us his alliance in this cause; his people ... have answered his appeal, and have shown, by their voices and their contributions, that the cause is common, the duty universal, and the benefit everlasting. After many years of estrangement, the sister Churches of Protestant England and Protestant Prussia have now entered on the path of reconciliation, and in the person of our Hebrew Bishop, have given each other "the right hand of fellowship."... over the tomb of our common Saviour;" thereby adding to the ties of political interest or political necessity the stouter and holier bonds of religious union, and of sympathy for the conversion and welfare of the whole body of the Jewish people. It is a noble and a heart-stirring thing to see two great Protestant nations, bringing as it were into a common stock whatever they have of temporal power or spiritual privilege, and combining for the purpose of relieving and exalting the oppressed, the despised, and the destitute of the earth ... we ourselves, perhaps, but certainly our children, may be blessed with the sight of that great and ultimate consummation when the usurped supremacy of Rome shall sink forever ... into the dust before the lawful supremacy of Jerusalem ...[49]

The anti-Catholic sentiment was also echoed by Rev. Edward Bickersteth, who stated of Alexander's activities: 'I do not wonder that the enemy was alarmed, that the hatred of the Romanist should be developed.' [50] This was followed by an even more profoundly anti-Catholic speech by another strong restorationist, Rev. Hugh Stowell. Stowell stated:

---

[49] Speech of Lord Shaftesbury, LJS AGM, 6 May 1842, in *JI*, 1842, pp. 178-179.
[50] Speech of Rev. E Bickersteth, LJS AGM, 6 May 1842, in *JI,* 1842, p. 180.

We do not marvel at Rome, and those who sympathize with her, being jealous of the appointment of a bishop to Jerusalem, for now who is the lawful Metropolitan of the Universal Church? Dr. Alexander, the Bishop of Jerusalem, where the first Christian Church was formed upon earth, and which the Saviour himself graced with his presence ... If, then, there be a Metropolitan Church on earth, that Church is the Church of Jerusalem; if there can be a Metropolitan on earth over the Universal Church, it is Bishop Alexander ... Therefore we cannot marvel that Rome is filled with jealousy, and mistrust, and apprehension, when she hears of a Bishop of Jerusalem.[51]

Stowell in turn was followed by one whose heart was firmly linked to restorationism and Alexander – Rev. Alexander McCaul. McCaul stated of the Bishopric that it was a matter to be extremely thankful for, but, he continued, 'it is no wonder, as it has been remarked already, that this should excite the indignation of Rome and all who think with her.' And McCaul, being the great restorationist he was, also alluded to the restorationist nature of the bishopric. He stated:

I would earnestly impress upon all the friends of the Jews one great truth, which is frequently lost sight of - that is, that before the general conversion of the Jews, there is to be a select Church, a remnant according to the election of grace, to be restored and acknowledged as the first-fruits of the nation ... from Scripture it is clear that previous to the restoration of the Jews we are to have restoration of a remnant ... It is also necessary to remind you that the restoration of the Jews is in great part to be accomplished by human agency ... you will find in prophecy that human agency is to be employed.[52]

McCaul was followed to the rostrum by Alexander's old-time friend, Rev. William Marsh. While alluding to Queen Victoria's habit of daily reading Scripture, Marsh remarked, 'for no one can read the sacred Scriptures with understanding and faith, and dependence upon God's Spirit, and be indifferent to the cause of Israel. There is not a passage in favour of that people which is not pregnant also with a blessing on those who bless the descendents of Abraham, Isaac and Jacob. Let Church and State show kindness to the Jews, and Church and State will receive a blessing.'[53]

---

[51] Speech of Rev. H. Stowell, LJS AGM, 6 May 1842, in *JI*, 1842, pp. 182-183.
[52] Speech of Rev. A. McCaul, LJS AGM, 6 May 1842, in *JI*, 1842, pp. 185-187.
[53] Speech of Rev. William Marsh, LJS AGM, 6 May 1842, in *JI*, 1842, pp. 187-190.

Marsh stressed the connection between Alexander's mission and passages in the book of Romans pertaining to the full restoration of Israel.

In June, the Archbishop of Canterbury, sent a letter to the King of Prussia, informing him of the relation between future German Protestant congregations in the Holy Land, and the Anglican bishop. This letter was intended to clarify some ambiguities which some parties, especially in Prussia, had about the bishopric.

Hectic Schedule & Armenian Visit

The month of May was as active as any since Alexander arrived. On the fifteenth day of the month the vibrant little community was able to observe the baptism of Mr. Ducat and his wife – the first Jewish people to come to faith in Jesus as messiah since Alexander arrived in the City. Later, on the twenty-fourth, Alexander welcomed visitors to his home to celebrate the Queen's birthday. Amongst those present were some Greeks and Armenians – as well as one of the chief rabbis.[54]

On 27 May, Alexander, Williams, a Mr. Rowlands, Johns and Ewald were invited to meet the Armenian Patriarch – an event which Ewald states was very cordial. In fact it seems that the Armenians from the beginning received Alexander respectfully, and Ewald stated: 'His Lordship, and our whole party were delighted with the open, frank, and hospitable manner in which we were treated by the venerable Patriarch.'[55]

Deborah Alexander recalled a slightly humorous side of this visit:

Papa was very friendly with the Armenian Patriarch, and he with us all. On returning the Patriarch's first visit, Papa – by special request, took some of us children with him. Fanny and I, respectively aged 13 and 9. It was a visit of ceremony and I well remember how the venerable Patriarch received Papa and Mama with every cordiality placing them by his side, while the rest of our party were ranged on divans down the side of the lofty room. Sherbet, coffee and sweetmeats were handed round by deacons on silver trays and in filagree silver cups and to everyone was handed a richly embroidered towel where with to rub our hand. I could not drink the coffee because it was so strong and thick with grounds and without sugar. The dear Patriarch discovered my trouble, though I was quite at the far end of the room. He clapped his hands and upon a deacon going to him for orders, the man was sent to a high and very dusty shelf. He took down a dirty screw of paper, opened it, and bit a piece off a lump of sugar candy,

---

[54] Ewald, *ibid*, pp. 98-99.
[55] *ibid*, pp. 99-101.

and then dropped it into my cup. Poor little me, and I had to drink the coffee.[56]

Shortly afterwards Alexander and daughter Deborah, succumbed to serious illness. Macgowan recorded that Alexander:

> ... was attacked ... with symptoms of fever and congestion of the head, which for some days gave cause for anxiety on his account; but the application of prompt and active remedies was followed by decided relief, and after an illness of ten days, I am happy to state that he is restored to health ... The effect of climate, and a more sedentary life than his Lordship has been accustomed to in England, were probably the causes of this attack. I have strongly recommended daily regular exercise, both on foot and horseback, which I trust will be conducive to his general health and prevent similar attacks in future.[57]

Despite sickness, the bishop was always on call for sundry matters. One area of ministry that Alexander seemed to enjoy and appreciate was entertaining the constant flow of overseas visitors. Amongst these were, in July, Lord Castlereagh, accompanied by his physician, Dr. George Fisk and Rev. H. M. Erskine. Fisk wrote that on Sunday 19th July he was invited by Alexander to read the prayers at the morning service. The service, he wrote 'was conducted in a small temporary chapel – "upper room", in which some of the early efforts of Mr. Nicolayson were made. There was an air of primitive simplicity about it, according well with the position which we at present occupy in Jerusalem. It overlooks the site on which the new church is in process of erection. The congregation consisted of about thirty persons.'[58]

Fisk also related that Alexander invited him to attend the evening service at his own home, where it was conducted. He recalled: 'The windows of the room in which we assembled looked over the city, towards the Mount of Olives, on which the setting sun was shedding his last beams as we prepared for the service.'[59]

Often times there was much merriment at these evening meetings. Music would be played and songs sung. Alexander seems to have relished

---

[56] Ransom, *ibid*, p. 29.
[57] Macgowan to CMJ London, 1 July 1842, in *JI*, 1842, pp. 321-322.
[58] *JI*, 1844, p. 6.
[59] *ibid*, p. 6. Also Ewald, *ibid*, pp. 106-107. Ewald wrote that the service took place in June.

these opportunities to sing praises to the Lord. Daughter Deborah recorded: 'At our evening receptions, we always had much music. Papa kept open house on that day, as we could not hold service in the Church after sun down at that time. On one occasion we had 13 nationalities present.'[60] Of her father's music abilities, Deborah also wrote:

> Of all music Hebrew melodies are the most mournful. There is a touching pathos in the Jewish voice. Papa had a fine tenor voice and at such times as he would consent, and the occasions were very rare, to chant in Hebrew the Lamentations of Jeremiah, it was truly thrilling and would draw tears in some cases.[61]

In June another visitor came to Jerusalem, a Jewish doctor, Dr. Anton Kiel, who soon afterwards came to faith in Jesus as Messiah. Then a little later Alexander conferred priest's orders upon Mr. Muhleisen, who left immediately for Abyssinia.[62]

Sickness and 'settlement' at Jifna

Michael Solomon became sick again in July, but this time his entire family also succumbed. This was such a trying time that Alexander was forced to leave his house, and on 2 August moved with his family to the Georgian Monastery of the Cross about two kilometers west of Jerusalem.[63]

Unfortunately the bishop was not able to fully recover at this location. Macgowan and for a time Bergheim, who had both also succumbed to sickness, had retired to the village of Giffna (Jifna) to the north of Jerusalem. Macgowan invited the Alexanders to enjoy this healthier site with him. Macgowan wrote:

> I wish that our friends in England could have had a peep at us in our encampment, living, like the patriarchs of old, in tents, surrounded by the richest plantations of olives and vines, pomegranates and fig-trees, laden with fruit; around were the beautiful hills covered with luxuriant vegetation, and above, the deep and cloudless serenity of the deep blue sky. We all enjoyed ourselves extremely, especially the children, who

---

[60] Ransom, *ibid*, p. 21.

[61] *ibid*, p. 31.

[62] Nicolayson to LJS London, 27 July (appendix of 1 August) 1842, in *JI*, 1842, p. 348.

[63] Alexander to LJS London, 1 August 1842, in *JI*, 1842, p. 345.

were quite delighted with the freedom and novelty of this new mode of life.

But our enjoyment was soon interrupted by the illness of Miss Alexander, his Lordship's eldest daughter, who, previously to her coming to Giffna, had been observed to be indisposed. She was seized with a very serious attack of fever, and for some days was alarmingly ill. It was necessary to have recourse to very active measures for her relief, which, through God's blessing, have been successful, and she is now, I am happy to say, convalescent, after an illness of fifteen days.[64]

Macgowan may have painted an idyllic biblical picture of the camp at Jifna, but this was not how the Greek Church, and it's protector, Russia, saw their presence there. They viewed the whole thing as a British settlement – in Orthodox Christian territory. It would seem that whatever Alexander was apt to do he was going to fall foul of one community or another.

Return to work in Jerusalem

The bishop did manage to recover from his bout of fever,[65] and in September, the Alexander family returned to their house in Jerusalem. Soon afterwards Alexander was able to write (rather excitedly) that they would soon be moving to the house belonging to Joseph Amzalak[66] in which the American missionaries Mr. and Mrs. Whiting had been living. The Whitings were moving to Lebanon. His daughter Deborah wrote of this move:

The best house in Jerusalem was at that time occupied by ... Mr. and Mrs. Whiting ... and very nice people they were. They approached Papa on the subject of their house, offering it at once to him, stating that theirs was a Pioneer Mission, and they always went to work where others had not broken ground. Accordingly, in due course of time, they departed to Beyrout, after handing into Papa's charge, some of their young converts. One of them was a sweet girl, Salome by name. She afterward married a handsome young Gregory Waterbet, a dragoman. Thus it came about that we occupied our nice house on Mount Zion, opposite the Castle of David,

[64] Macgowan to LJS London, 31 August 1842, in *JI*, 1842, p. 379.

[65] Alexander to Rev. William Wynne Willson, 28 September 1842, MSS 3393, [No f.61], Lambeth.

[66] Amzalak was a British subject, originally from Gibraltar. He was quite special in that being Jewish, he had considerable contact with the British mission, and in particular with Nicolayson.

and near the Zion Gate. Our landlord was Rabbi Amstek [sic], a splendid specimen of a Jew, with flowing beard, keen eye, and fine bearing.[67]

On 12 August Mr. E. M. Tarkover arrived from England, with mail and goods from their friends there. Tarkover was to be trained for ordination. Then in early October eight Hebrew Christians and one gentile Christian were confirmed. This occasion was indeed a high point of Alexander's first year, and prompted Nicolayson to write:

> Such was the depth of feeling with which he performed this truly affecting service, that when he began to lay his hands on the head of each candidate, and came to his own daughter, he was so completely overcome, that at first he could not proceed at all, and only gradually recovered firmness enough to go on.
> ... Our little chapel was quite crowded on this occasion, there being upwards of forty persons present, a large party having just come up from the Vesuvius steamer at Jaffa.[68]

Then the following week Alexander performed the marriage of two Jewish believers, Peter Bergheim, the medical missionary, and Dorothy Rosenthal, a member of the Rosenthal family whom Nicolayson had baptized in 1839.

Alexander was not just interested in developing the work amongst the Jewish people. He also endeavoured to foster good relations with the other ecclesiastical heads as well. He visited the Syrian Bishop on 15 October, and found himself in the midst of a very interesting debate. The Syrian Bishop had read that the Church of England labelled the Syrian Church, alongside the Armenians, Copts and Ethiopians, with the Eutychian heresy.[69]

Alexander, Nicolayson and a visitor, Mr. Rowlands, were able to argue that this was in fact not true. Nicolayson concluded: 'This affords, by the

---

[67] Ransom, *ibid*, p. 15. Deborah also mentions that later when Holman Hunt lived in Jerusalem he used Amzalak as one of his model Jewish men around Christ in his paintings, 'The Scapegoat' and 'The Finding of Christ in the Temple.'

[68] Nicolayson to LJS London, 1 November 1842, in *JI*, 1843, p. 16.

[69] A doctrine taught by Eutyches about the nature of Jesus - one divine person being both God and man. The Church Council at Chalcedon in 451 declared this a heresy, and provided the Church with the creedal statement of Christology that affirmed the doctrine of two natures in Christ, divine and human. It gave to the Church the creedal statement on Christology which has stood the test of the centuries.

way, an interesting illustration of the importance of personal intercourse with these Churches to remove prejudices and misunderstandings.'[70]

Several days after this visit, the Greek Bishop from Bethlehem visited Alexander, returning Alexander's visit to Bethlehem several months previously. Nicolayson noted: 'It is remarkable, that the ecclesiastics here always inquire after our Bishop's young family, and seem particularly pleased when the little ones make their appearance.'[71]

Development of General Missionary Work

Due to his varied responsibilities Alexander, was not always able to carry on general missionary duties. These were often left in the capable hands of Nicolayson and Ewald, for whom there was no shortage of opportunity. Ewald made numerous efforts to make contact with the Jewish people. In early March he met one of the three rabbis who had first heard about Jesus from Mr. Pieritz and Nicolayson, but who had then been compelled to leave Jerusalem.

Ewald also re-established contact with the other rabbis. He asked them why they would not come out openly and confess faith in Jesus as Messiah, to which they replied that their wives and children would leave them. [72] This indeed was the reality facing many within the Jewish community. They were so dependent upon the rabbis, and the money they received from the *halukah*[73] distribution, that they dare not invoke the wrath of their leaders.

On another occasion Ewald relates the struggles that the secret Jewish believers had to encounter:

> *June 4* – To-day I met outside the gate some of the believing Jews, who were sitting together in a lonely place reading the New Testament; they dare not take it to their houses for fear of the Jews and their own households; so they hide it in the rocks, and go as often as they can to read it together in secret and undisturbed by unbelieving Jews.[74]

---

[70] Nicolayson to LJS London, 1 November 1842, in *JI*, 1843, p. 18.

[71] Nicolayson to LJS London, 1 November 1842, in *JI*, 1843, p. 18-19.

[72] Ewald to LJS London, no date, in *JI*, 1842, p. 250.

[73] *Halukah* is the Hebrew word for alms distribution, and is used to describe the system then operating in the Holy Land whereby alms were collected in Europe and then distributed by the rabbis amongst their co-religionists in Jerusalem. This system was apt to be misused and abused.

[74] Ewald, *ibid,* p. 103.

Development of the Medical Work

The activities of Dr Macgowan were one of the most important adjuncts of the LJS work. Macgowan saw tremendous potential for the medical work. He set about his task immediately upon arrival in Jerusalem. And he did not have to wait long for patients. Within days both Nicolayson and Johns, as well as one of the Maltese workers at the church and Edward Jonas, (Johns' assistant), became ill. Marie Rosenthal, daughter of Simon Rosenthal, became seriously ill, and only just survived, thanks to Macgowan's intervention.

Macgowan began using the small building previously used by Bergheim, as a dispensary and consulting-room, but found it very inadequate. Nevertheless he met Jewish patients there, as well as visiting them at their homes. He sent his first report to London on 26 February, and stated that for several weeks past he had set in motion certain plans for improving the medical facilities. This report included his daily routine, which even at that early stage had a set pattern, and during which he met between twenty and thirty sick Jewish people. Macgowan listed the most common causes of illness in Jerusalem: rheumatism, ague, typhus fever, obstructions and enlargement of the abdominal viscera, dropsy, ulcerated legs, leprosy, acute and chronic affections of the eye, especially cataract. He mentioned too that the majority of these ailments were due to the dreadful living conditions of the Jewish people, and feared that many would not convalesce following treatment, as they would return to the same squalid conditions they had just come from.

Macgowan concluded by impressing upon the Committee in London: '... to lose no time in carrying into effect their plan of establishing a hospital in Jerusalem, in connexion with the mission.' He recommended: '... that a hospital establishment of twelve beds be made in the best existing building which can be procured in Jerusalem for that purpose.' In fact even by that stage he and Nicolayson had located a suitable building, which they desired to secure. Macgowan also mentioned his desire to have land on which he could grow medicinal herbs.[75]

In his next report, on 1 July, Macgowan could state that he had fixed up a suitable building for a new dispensary, where Bergheim spent much of his time, and a surgery. During this interim period, he said he had seen some 1,000 patients! There were times when so many people wanted to visit him that they sat on the steps outside. No wonder he felt he had good

---

[75] Macgowan to LJS London, 26 February 1842, in *JI*, 1842, pp. 162-165.

cause for recommending that the Society develop the medical department.[76]

Despite Macgowan's optimism in this report that the Jewish people in Jerusalem were favourably disposed towards the medical work, this was sure to stir up opposition, especially from those leaders who felt their authority undermined. Ewald reported in June on a debate primarily among the rabbis: 'There is at present a great stir among the Jews here. The question, whether it be lawful for a Jew to ask for and receive medical advice and assistance from a Christian... Several are of opinion that it is not unlawful; and one has publicly expressed this opinion in a sermon.'[77]

The LJS Committee was very favourable to Macgowan's plans for the hospital and he made preparations for leasing a suitable property. He wrote on 1 October however, that difficulties had arisen precluding him from achieving this.[78] On 1 November he was able to report that he had succeeded in procuring suitable accommodation.[79] This building was leased for eleven years, near his small dispensary, and on the edge of the Jewish Quarter. Macgowan proposed having separated wards on two floors for men and women, as well as a separate ward for tourists and pilgrims, who would be expected to pay.[80]

News of Macgowan's exertions soon filtered back to Jewish communities in Europe, and many Jewish leaders, especially Sir Moses Montefiore in England became alarmed. Montefiore then set out to find a suitable Jewish doctor to come to Jerusalem to work on behalf of the Jewish community. This move marked one of the first signs of the break-up of the established *status quo* within the Jewish community of Jerusalem. The authority of the rabbis was being challenged.

Political problems begin
Consul Young, who had gone to England in September 1841, returned to Jerusalem in May 1842. He was a changed person from the pro-active

---

[76] Macgowan to LJS London, 1 July 1842, in *JI,* 1842, p. 316ff.

[77] Ewald, *ibid*, p. 101.

[78] Macgowan to LJS London, 1 October 1842, in *JI,* 1842, p. 411.

[79] Macgowan to LJS London, 1 November 1842, in *JI,* 1843, p. 21.

[80] Macgowan was not only the pioneer of modern medicine in the Holy Land, but was also the first meteorologist there. He brought with him a barometer, thermometer and other equipment, and soon set in motion a system of weather recording in Jerusalem.

consul of pre-September 1841, and his new attitude soon became evident in his relations with Bishop Alexander.

Alexander soon realised that there was a difference between what he presumed would be positive assistance from the British consul in Jerusalem, with the less than positive official line now adopted by Young. The main reason for this ambivalence was the attitude of the new government in Britain. Aberdeen, in particular, had none of the aspirations in the eastern Mediterranean of Palmerston. Whereas Palmerston wished to interfere in matters there, Aberdeen wished to appease the local authorities, and especially the Turks, as best he could. This attitude is expressed in his fresh instructions to Young, prior to the consul's return to Jerusalem after furlough. Aberdeen wrote:

> I think it necessary on your return to Syria to resume your duties ... to furnish you with some Instructions for your guidance with reference to certain matters which may come before you.
>
> The principal of these is the appointment which has recently been made of Bishop Alexander to reside in Jerusalem as a Bishop of the United Church of England and Ireland, with authority to exercise spiritual jurisdiction in Syria, Chaldea, Egypt, and Abyssinia, over the Ministers of British Congregations of the United Church of England and Ireland, and over such other Protestant congregations as might be desirous of placing themselves under his Authority. With reference to this appointment I would wish you to bear in mind that Her Majesty's Government have asked of the Porte for Bishop Alexander, and those by whom he is accompanied, no other degree of protection than that which all other British Subjects, of whatever profession or denomination they may be, are entitled to enjoy in the Dominions of the Sultan; and that Bishop Alexander has been strictly enjoined by his ecclesiastical Superior in this Country, not to interfere with the religious concerns either of the Mahamedan, or of the Christian Subjects of the Porte; and not to attempt to make proselytes to the Church of England from either of those classes.
>
> Under the limitations thus stated, Her Majesty's Government desire that you should extend your official protection to Bishop Alexander, to the utmost of your ability; but you will carefully abstain from identifying yourself in any degree with his mission, and from assisting to promote any scheme of interference with the Jewish Subjects of the Porte, in which Bishop Alexander may possibly engage. You will clearly understand that Her Majesty's Government will not sanction, either in you or in any other servant of the Crown, any attempts, directly or indirectly, to interfere with the religious tenets of any class of the Sultan's Subjects. In accordance with this principle, you will most carefully abstain from affording to

persons who may associate themselves to Bishop Alexander's congregation any protection, as British Dependents, to which, under other circumstances, they could not properly lay claim. It is the express desire of Her Majesty's Government that the number of persons who receive British Protection shall be strictly limited to those who by birth are entitled to it, and also to those whom the capitulations to Turkey, construed in the strictest sense, permit to be withdrawn from the immediate control of the Turkish law.[81]

These instructions made it abundantly clear that, provided Consul Young abided by them, Alexander would have many difficulties in fulfilling his stated objectives in Jerusalem. It would only be a matter of time before serious conflict between the two parties would arise.

Conflict Between Church and State – the Three Rabbis

Due to the very nature of the Jerusalem bishopric, conflict was bound to occur with the other communities in Jerusalem living under the established *status quo*. What was not so quickly discerned was the potential for conflict between the British components in Jerusalem, between Church and State, as represented by the bishopric and consulate. But occur it did – and in a big way.

On 4-5 October 1842 three Jewish men, Abraham Walphen, Eliezer Loria (or Luria) and Benjamin Bynes, all rabbis who were serious about confessing faith in Jesus as Messiah, called upon Ewald. They informed him that they and their families were intent on proceeding to Jaffa, where the rabbis could freely discuss with their wives 'their conviction of the truth of Christianity.'[82]

The other Jerusalem rabbis then heard of this, and informed the wives of the inquiring rabbis that a boat would pick them up in Jaffa, take them to London, where they would all become Christians, and then the husbands would send the wives away. Upon hearing this false story the wives refused to go to Jaffa. In accordance with this Ewald asked the inquiring rabbis to remain in his house, while he informed Alexander.[83]

The following morning a large gathering soon appeared at Ewald's house, including Alexander, Scott Calman, Tarkover, and Nicolayson, who

---

[81] Aberdeen to Young, 3 May 1842, FO 78/501 (No 5).
[82] Nicolayson to LJS London, 15 October 1842, in *JI*, 1843, p. 59.
[83] Ewald, *ibid*, p. 133.

recorded: '... we found quite a number of the principal rabbies ... who seemed to be in warm discussion with "the three."'[84] Ewald adds:

> Then all the Jews left; but soon after the wives and children, and relatives of the converts came, and wept bitterly, entreating them, by all that was dear to them, to return. It was a most heart-rendering scene; but they also were obliged to go, without effecting what they desired ...
>
> A few days after this had happened, I fell seriously ill; and during my illness all three returned home to their families. [85]

The matter quickly became more complicated. The rabbis were all Russian subjects, and accordingly the Russian consular agent in Jerusalem, Rabbi Yeshayahu [also referred to as Rabbi Isaiah] Bordaki, proclaimed that these men were evading Russian consular jurisdiction, and demanded that the British mission surrender them.

Consul Young was asked to intervene, and forthwith demanded that Alexander comply and surrender the three rabbis to the Russian consular-agent. Alexander refused, stating that the lives of the rabbis were in danger, and that the matter was religious and not political in nature.

On 6 October Young informed Alexander that Rabbi Isaiah had referred the matter to the Russian consul from Jaffa, M. Marabuti, who was then visiting Jerusalem. This being the case, the matter seemingly was now taken out of the hands of Rabbi Isaiah. If this was so the fear of physical violence against the three rabbis was now removed.

In a civil sense this simplified matters. However not for the three rabbis, who, Nicolayson wrote: '... evidently felt much discouraged and disappointed at this, having fully hoped that they would have had the countenance at least and influence of the British Consul in their favour, whereas they now felt (and the Jews boasted) that it was against them.'[86]

Alexander, Nicolayson and Consul Young then met the Russian consul, on 7 October, to inform him of the peculiar nature of the case. Alexander and his colleagues claimed that the Jerusalem rabbinical authorities might bring charges against the three rabbis – in part due to the harm that news of three rabbis believing in Jesus might have upon their authority over the Jewish community.[87]

---

[84] Nicolayson to LJS London, 15 October 1842, in *JI*, 1843, p. 60.

[85] Ewald, *ibid*, pp. 133-134.

[86] Nicolayson to LJS London, 15 October 1842, in *JI*, 1843, p. 61.

[87] See Nicolayson to LJS London, 15 October 1842, in *JI*, 1843, p. 61.

Young wrote to Aberdeen on 11 October 1842 of his perspective of the affair:

> In calling your Lordship's attention to the circumstances of the case, and to the correspondence which has passed between Bishop Alexander and myself in reference to this subject, I would humbly beg leave to offer some observations of my own in connection with this event, as similar cases may again be expected to occur, where there is a Society settled in Jerusalem for the purpose of calling the attention of the Jews to the subject of Christianity.
>
> So soon as I received official intimation from the Rabbi Isaiah Bordaki, who is placed over the Russian and Austrian Jews in Palestine by these respective Governments – that 3 of his subjects had taken refuge from his Jurisdiction in the house of one of the Missionaries, and that he requested my assistance to enable him to bring the parties before him   - I immediately addressed a note to Bishop Alexander acquainting him of the circumstance, and hoping he would take such steps as he might deem requisite to avoid a compromise of Her Majesty's Government with Foreign Powers.
>
> Your Lordship will observe by the Bishop's reply that he anticipated no difficulty - in the meantime the three Jews continued to be countenanced in their refusal to appear before their consul.
>
> I then considered it my duty to address a second note to the Bishop hoping to impress upon him that his confidence was not well founded if the parties in question continued to be withheld by his interference from appearing before the tribunal of their own civil Superior.
>
> By the Bishop's reply to my second note, I began to apprehend serious difficulty might ensue.[88]

Rabbi Bordaki then sent a message to his superior Consul Marabuti. The rabbinical authorities feared that the three inquiring rabbis would be secreted off to Malta, so they placed guards at the city gates to hinder this.

Consul Young then met Alexander in person. At this meeting Alexander and Young's different perspectives became apparent, as expressed in a letter from Young to Aberdeen in which he stated that Alexander 'had been led to understand from all parties at home, that he was to have my assistance and co-operation in all of his attempts at conversion among the Jews, - at this I could not avoid expressing my surprise, as I assured the Bishop my Instructions from Your Lordship compelled me to adopt a line of conduct quite the reverse ...'

---

[88] Young to Aberdeen, 11 October 1842, FO 78/501 (7).

Young then had to inform Alexander that if the Russian consul came to take these persons by force, then he would have to remain neutral. Alexander was still obstinately holding his line – all the while placing Young in a delicate position. Young might have to act against British subjects in order to follow the instructions he was given. This possibility became more apparent when the Russian consul called upon him. Marabuti said he had detained a messenger he was sending to Beirut with an account of the affair 'in hopes' wrote Young 'that matters would yet be accommodated through my intervention – otherwise it would go onto Constantinople and thence to St. Petersburg.'[89]

Such an undertaking would have been disastrous for all parties involved. It would have strongly jeopardized Alexander's right to remain in Jerusalem as it would have substantiated and confirmed Turkish apprehensions about the inappropriateness of his presence there in the first place. It would have provided the Russians, and other enemies at the Sultan's Court, be they French, Austrian or Turkish, with all the ammunition they needed to harm British interests in the area. It would have also seriously harmed Young's authority in Jerusalem and credibility with the British Government.

Young, realizing the possible ramifications of this situation, assured Marabuti he would do his utmost to conclude the affair satisfactorily. Alexander soon afterwards seemed persuaded – provided there was a guarantee that no harm would befall the three rabbis. In exchange he agreed to hand them over to the Russian consul the following morning.

The following morning however Alexander was unsure and asked Young to arrange a meeting with the Russian consul for himself. This was facilitated, and resulted in a mutual understanding between Alexander and the Russians. A fair trial was agreed to, in the presence of several of the mission staff. So far so good. Then the unexpected happened. The three rabbis, under great duress from their families and the Jerusalem rabbinical authorities 'recanted, left the missionary's house and identified themselves with their Jewish Brethren.'[90]

And there the matter seemed to rest, at least for the short-term. Young in summarizing the affair to Aberdeen, stated, quite correctly, that: 'The Bishop seems to regard the matter in a religious, rather than in a Civil point of view. It appeared to me to be a purely Civil case.' He further stated that Alexander felt that by harbouring the rabbis in the home of the British missionaries they would be protected by the British consul – which

---

[89] Young to Aberdeen, 11 October 1842, FO 78/501 (No 7).
[90] Young to Aberdeen, 11 October 1842, FO 78/501 (No 7).

Young had stated was not to be the case. This was a difficult reality for Alexander to accept.

In conclusion Young provided a very sobering and realistic appraisal of the situation in Jerusalem:

> When a Jew in Jerusalem embraces the Christian faith many important considerations are involved. If the party is married a divorce takes place, until the wife becomes a convert also – The Children are also claimed by the Jews until they arrive at years of discretion. Their family and friends mourn for the convert as though he were dead, and the Widow and Children become dependent on the Congregation. The Rabbinical Law forbidding them to receive maintenance from a husband or father who has renounced his Faith ...
>
> If a European Jew professes himself a convert (as in the resent case) his Government might prefer that he should unite himself to the Church recognized by his own Government rather than to one in connection with a Foreign State.
>
> It has been hitherto imagined in Jerusalem, that to be accepted a member of the mission to the Jews here, is to become an Englishman and entitled to English privileges. This seems to be Bishop Alexander's impression, as far as regards converted Jews – I have had to undeceive several Natives on this point, who wanting assistance in some difficulty have come to me saying they wish to become Protestant.[91]

Young's dispatch to Aberdeen went initially to Rose in Beirut, who must have been dreading such an incident. He supported Young's stance, although he indicated that it would have been less complicated if Young had not involved Alexander in the dealings at all, as Alexander was but a private citizen with no special status. By referring to Alexander, as the head of the British mission, he was giving to Alexander an exalted status.

Rose instructed Young to read his dispatch and accompanying instructions to Alexander. Later Lord Aberdeen himself sent a message to Young on 30 December 1842, stating: 'I have much satisfaction in expressing to you my entire approval of your proceedings in this matter and I have to instruct you to continue to act in the same judicious manner in any case of the kind which may hereafter occur.'[92]

Bishop Alexander must have been perplexed. Only a year before he was being feted by the leaders and even the Queen of England herself, and

---

[91] Young to Aberdeen, 11 October 1842, FO 78/501 (No 7).
[92] Aberdeen to Young, 30 December 1842, FO 78/501 (No 5).

conveyed to the Holy Land on a British war ship. Now, it seemed, the British representative was working against him.

All the while, the three rabbis remained ambivalent. Nicolayson wrote on 16 October that Calman met the three rabbis, during which:

> They most bitterly lamented their weakness in having yielded to the Jews, and avowed their purpose to come out again whatever may be the consequence. They have had no peace of conscience since, and were particularly distressed at the rejoicings (with wine, music, dancing, revelry) of the Jews in the triumph they have thus obtained ...
>
> They now distinctly declared to him that the position taken, and the course followed by the British Consul, and the use the Jews made of this, together with their hesitation as to the efficiency of the promised protection, and not any doubt of Christianity itself, had been that which first staggered and discouraged them and ultimately terrified them into the unhappy retrograde movement which they now so deeply deplore.[93]

Although the position of Consul Young in this crisis disappointed the three rabbis, it was in fact a blessing in disguise for Alexander and the mission. In a way it helped to sort out the genuine from the not so genuine. If anyone thought that by going to the mission meant automatically receiving British consular protection and an easy ride to success, they now had to think twice. If they wanted to be a follower of Jesus – it would be without such protection and favour.

The three rabbis were soon to experience this reality themselves. In the period following the crisis of early October, they periodically met with the Protestant missionaries, especially Nicolayson (as Ewald was gravely ill). The Jewish leadership was aware of this. The crisis erupted again on 27 October. The leading rabbis pronounced a *cherem* or excommunication ban against the three in the synagogues, and the three rabbis were mistreated by their fellow Jews.

Upon hearing this, Nicolayson proceeded immediately to see Alexander. While at the bishop's residence, Nicolayson was summoned to his house, and there found two of the three rabbis, Abraham and Benjamin. Bergheim had brought them from the dispensary where he had treated them for their bruises. Alexander soon joined Nicolayson, as did Macgowan.

At Alexander's behest Macgowan and Nicolayson then went in search of the Russian consul, but finding he had returned to Jaffa, they then turned

---

[93] Nicolayson to LJS London, 16 October 1842, in *JI*, 1843, p. 64.

to Consul Young, asking if he would implore upon Rabbi Yeshayahu to guarantee the protection of the three rabbis.

Two of the three rabbis, Abraham and Benjamin stayed with Nicolayson, while the third, Eliezer remained with his family. But then on 31 October Abraham and Benjamin, this time of their own accord, returned to the Jewish community. Although they claimed to be convinced of the truth of Jesus as Messiah, the pragmatic cost of such a decision was too high. Again there were threats of excommunication against all three. The wife of Benjamin refused to live with him again, and a divorce followed. Only pressure from the rabbis compelled the wives of Abraham and Eliezer to remain with their husbands.

This episode like few before it, deeply upset the *status quo* of the Jewish community. The three rabbis were also compelled to supply the names of all secret inquirers, and the names of twenty-six were furnished to the community leaders. And, the annual *halukah* portion was threatened to be withdrawn from those having contact with the missionaries. Herein lay the real power of the religious authorities. Ewald met the leading rabbis and informed them that the British Government was presently concerned to protect the Jewish people of the Ottoman Empire – and it mattered not if the persecutors were Turks or fellow Jews![94]

Indeed the old order was being challenged. This was further revealed when on 5 November a delegation of some senior rabbis came from Tiberias, to determine if 'the report they had heard was true, viz., that fourteen rabbis of Jerusalem had embraced Christianity.'[95]

Further foundations for the physical and spiritual Church
On 30 October 1842 Alexander bestowed deacon's orders upon Tarkover,[96] a Jewish believer, and Mr. William Whitmarsh, a gentile believer. The occasion prompted Nicolayson to write, somewhat prophetically:

It is deeply interesting to observe that, by today's solemnities, the nucleus of a Hebrew Christian Church in this city is now complete in all its offices, as well as functions. There is now here a Bishop, a priest (Ewald), and a deacon also, all "Hebrew of Hebrews," a fact in the history of Jerusalem

---

[94] Ewald to LJS London, 30 November 1842, in *JI*, 1843, p. 70.
[95] Ewald, *ibid*, p. 142.
[96] Tarkover soon after began a small school, 'which' Alexander wrote 'I trust will increase, and prove a blessing.' Alexander to LJS London, 30 November, 1842, in *JI*, 1843, p. 59.

which had not been realized since its final destruction by Adrian (sic Hadrian) in the second century; and which thus completes also the chain of restored connexion between the first Hebrew church here ... and its present, distant, yet genuine off-shoot. May it grow into a great tree of life, under whose branches the dispersed of Israel shall find shelter, and whose fruits shall be the healing of the nations![97]

All of this extra activity prompted Alexander to write that 'through the instrumentality of the Society, a Hebrew-Christian congregation, in its complete form, is now established on Mount Zion![98] And before the completion of the one year we shall (d.v) have performed all the ordinances of the Church.'[99]

The timing of the above event was quite significant. For on 1 November, All Saints Day, the foundation stone above ground for the new church, was laid. This event was a red-letter day for the fledgling Hebrew Christian-Protestant community.

Mrs. Alexander was given the honour of laying the foundation stone, and as there was no silver trowel available for the occasion, the bishop offered his fish-slice. Johns the architect wrote:

> In the centre of the stone was a cavity, in which was placed a tin case, containing the inscription ... a variety of gold, silver and copper coins of Her present Majesty's reign, and, to prevent the possibility of their being extracted, the whole was filled in as one solid body, with molten solder, and some masonry immediately built over ...
>
> The ceremony being completed, the whole party proceeded to the Chapel, to the evening prayers, after which the Bishop gave an appropriate address; in the evening, at sunset, the workmen were, through the hospitality of the Bishop, entertained by the distribution of bread and wine, of the country ... drinking the health and bestowing their best wishes upon the 'Mattran' (Bishop) ... the whole of these immense foundations having been built in less than nine months.[100]

Another significant event was the arrival, on 4 November of a new Turkish governor Izzet Pasha. Alexander, Nicolayson, Tarkover and Ewald were

---

[97] Nicolayson to LJS London, 1 November 1842, in *JI,* 1843, p. 17.
[98] Despite Alexander's association of Mount Zion with the area where the LJS was located, this was not actually the location of the Mount Zion of the Bible.
[99] Alexander to LJS London, in *JI* 1842, p. 403.
[100] J. W. Johns, *The Anglican Cathedral Church of St. James Jerusalem,* (London, 1844), pp. 5-6.

introduced to him by Consul Young, and the reception, according to Ewald, 'was very satisfactory.'[101] Izzet Pasha soon afterwards set about determining the scene of his new domain. No doubt he was impressed (and concerned) by the events since Alexander's arrival and the obvious challenge to the established *status quo*. This could only have been confirmed by the visit of the Jewish delegation from Tiberias on 5 November.[102] The new pasha also took great interest in the new church being built.

Another family crisis – and visit to Jaffa

Due to further illness in the family Alexander took some of his family to Jaffa, from where he wrote to the LJS on 30 November:

> Our eldest daughter suffered as much from fever and ague, which at least assumed so serious a character, being accompanied by other alarming symptoms, that Dr. Macgowan recommended, as a last remedy, her trying sea air; and I am happy to say, the effect has been most beneficial. She has had no attack since we left Jerusalem, and is daily gaining strength, so that I hope to return again next week.[103]

Alexander also took three of his other children with him, all of whom also had suffered attacks of ague, and sore eyes, a disease, he wrote 'which I am sorry to find children are particularly subject to in Jerusalem in the autumn.' Of their visit Alexander concluded:

> Our lodging, which consists of two or three rooms, is close to the house of Simon the Tanner. There are several Jewish families residing here, with some of whom we have had conversations. If the Society had abundance of means, and men to spare, I should strongly recommend our having an agent here, it being the port of Jerusalem; and a number of Jews land here on their way to the Holy City.[104]

Daughter Deborah recalled her impressions of their stay in Jaffa:

---

[101] Ewald, *ibid*, p. 142.

[102] Ironically the following day, 6 November, Alexander baptised another Jewish adult, Mr. Michael Weinkauff, a contact of Ewald from some years previously, who had arrived in Jerusalem at the time Ewald initially hosted the three rabbis. No wonder Ewald's health failed him with all this excitement and activity!

[103] Alexander to LJS London, 30 November 1842, in *JI*, 1843, p. 59.

[104] *ibid*, p. 59.

At Jaffa, Papa hired an Orange Grove for our use, where change to the sea was required for us all. It was near the supposed site of Simon the Tanner's house. The house in our Orange Garden was more like a barn that [sic] a home, and was infested with enormous water rats. The Garden was lovely, more like an Orchard than a garden. Trees of pomegranates, citrons, oranges and lemons yielded fruit and blossom, their roots were copiously watered by water from an ancient well ... The rush of the water, the fragrance of the orange blossom, and the scarlet flowers of the pomegranates gave us all great delight after the oppressive inland air of Jerusalem.[105]

End of the first calendar year

On 12 December Alexander, Nicolayson, Macgowan and Ewald joined Consul Young and rode about half an hour's ride from Jerusalem in order to meet the new Prussian Consul-General von Wildenbruch, visiting from Beirut.

At the end of the year eight Jewish people had been baptised. This was a matter Alexander was truly grateful for. Also in December the Jewish community of Jerusalem was affected by the death of the great Rabbi Hirschell of London[106] – a man who previously played a significant role in shaping Alexander's early life.

A high point for the small community was Christmas Day of which Ewald wrote:

> Our Church had been embellished the previous day by Mrs. Alexander and the young ladies of the house. The communion was administered; and there were five clergymen present besides the Bishop. The Rev. Mr. Blackburn preached from Isaiah 60:1 'Arise, shine; for thy light is come, and the glory of the Lord is risen upon thee.' In the afternoon I preached in German. It was a most happy day ...[107]

Alexander ended the year by stating in his first Circular letter from Jerusalem, that:

> Although the enemies have endeavoured, by every means, to oppose the establishment of the Jerusalem Bishopric in the first instance, and have subsequently even gone so far as to endeavour to ridicule it, by abominable

---

[105] Ransom, *ibid*, pp. 12-13.
[106] Ewald, *ibid*, p. 149.
[107] *ibid*, p. 153.

and absurd inventions, I am happy to be able to state, that we have never been molested or disturbed in the least.

After stating the dangers and challenges confronting him and his work, Alexander concluded: 'But as it respects the future glory of Jerusalem, the restoration of the children, and the establishment of the Redeemer's kingdom, whilst these are sure to take place, according to the Divine promise, we must ever bear in mind, that the Lord has said, "For all this will I be enquired of." I beseech you therefore, brethren, for the Lord Jesus Christ's sake ... that ye strive together with me in your prayers to God for me, that my service which I have for Jerusalem may be accepted of him and be abundantly blessed."[108]

Indeed despite many trials and tribulations during the year, including the loss of a baby, Alexander did have much to be thankful for. He had every reason to suppose that abundant blessings awaited him in the coming year.

---

[108] Letter from the Bishop of Jerusalem, 31 October 1842, in *JI*, 1843, p. 2.

Chapter 11

The Sultan Intervenes: 1843

Visit to Bethlehem and Hebron

Alexander began the New Year by taking his wife, some of the children, Ewald and several others, to Bethlehem on 5 January to celebrate the Greek Orthodox Christmas Eve. The following day, the weather having become rather nasty, Mrs. Alexander returned to Jerusalem. The remainder of the party continued onwards, stopping firstly at Solomon's Pools, en-route to Hebron.

A senior rabbi of Hebron had invited Alexander to visit the city, so the bishop and his entourage found the house of a friend of the man who had given the invitation. The following day, being the Sabbath, Alexander and his friends attended in turn the three synagogues of the ancient city. Where possible he entered into conversation with some of the Jewish people. After the service at the German Synagogue Alexander and his friends were among the guests invited to attend the housewarming party of Rabbi N____.[1] All the while the bishop was entering into conversation with any Jewish person willing to interact with him.[2]

The following day Alexander proposed they hold divine service on the Plain of Mamre, near the famous Oak of Mamre, the traditional tree of Abraham. 'It was' he wrote, 'most affecting to us to have a service under that tree under such peculiar circumstances, a Hebrew Christian Bishop with three clergymen one of whom was likewise of the house of Israel.' [3]

The party returned to Hebron and remained for several more days, visiting the Cave of the Machpelah, the burial site of the Patriarchs. Alexander and Ewald in particular had more social interaction with the Jewish people.

---

[1] Alexander obviously wanted the rabbi to remain anonymous.
[2] Ewald, *ibid*, pp. 164-67.
[3] Bishop Alexander to Sir Richard Steele, 28 February 1843, Alexander Papers, St. Anthony's.

Alexander was quite moved by his visit to Hebron, and wrote that the Jewish people there were 'depending entirely upon the charity of their brethren, especially of Sir Moses Montefiore, whose visit to them in this country seems quite to have revived them. They make public mention of him in their prayers in the synagogue ... Indeed I have since had several calling upon me, expressing their great wish to see me amongst them again.'[4]

Church Construction Stopped

Shortly after arriving back in Jerusalem Alexander received the news that Rabbis Eleazer and Benjamin were soon to rejoin Nicolayson, (which they subsequently did on 15 January), followed soon after by Rabbi Abraham.[5] The final break had been made. Ewald wrote: 'I went into the Jewish quarter. There was again a great excitement amongst the Jews ... no one is permitted to speak to them, and they are given up by the Jews as lost.'[6]

This was a high point for the infant Hebrew Christian community. It was followed by an immediate low. On 14 January 1843 the Turkish Governor, Izzet Pasha, sent his *dragoman* (interpreter) to Nicolayson 'stating that His Excellency having applied first to the British Consul regarding the Church in building here and been told by the Consul that he knows nothing about it and has no orders on the subject either from his own Government or from Constantinople, His Excellency must desire the building to be stopped till orders shall have been obtained from Constantinople.' Nicolayson then asked the pasha to issue this decision in writing, which was declined, and then insisted upon seeing the pasha, a meeting that was not permitted initially.[7]

Nicolayson immediately dispatched a letter to Young, concluding: 'As this affects British property and the rights of British Subjects, I beg to ask your advice in this case.'[8] Young responded the same day, stating he has no authority to interfere, but insists he will refer the matter to London, Constantinople and to the Consul-General in Beirut.[9] Alexander

---

[4] Bishop Alexander to Sir Richard Steele, 28 February 1843, St. Anthony's.
[5] LJS Local Committee, 17 January 1843, Minute 104, in *Journal 1842- 1867*, [henceforth *Journal*], p. 37, Schick Library.
[6] Journal of Ewald, in *JI*, 1843, p. 168.
[7] *Journal 1842 - 1867, ibid*, p. 34.
[8] Nicolayson to Young, 14 January 1843, *Journal,* p. 35.
[9] Young to Nicolayson, 14 January 1843, *ibid*, p. 36.

meanwhile wrote a letter immediately to Ambassador Stratford Canning in Constantinople.[10]

Ironically, the following day, 15 January, the two men who had been sent out from London to construct the church, Matthew Habershon and R. Bates Critchlow, arrived in Jerusalem.

Nicolayson met with the pasha on 16 January and explained their situation, and also requested permission to continue until the necessary confirmation arrived from Constantinople, which, he stated 'had been promised by the Porte to Lord Ponsonby.' The governor however insisted that as neither he, nor Young, had received direct orders 'he must require us to desist till orders be procured from Constantinople, and that he had accordingly prohibited all native workmen from continuing in our employ.'[11]

Bishop Alexander then proposed to the LJS Local Committee that he, accompanied by Nicolayson, proceed to Constantinople, which the Committee enthusiastically endorsed.[12] At the same meeting, Nicolayson mentioned that the three rabbis, the likely cause of the over exposure of the Mission and subsequent stoppage of the church construction, had declared they would 'disconnect themselves entirely from the Jews and rejoin the Christian Church here.'[13]

Trip to Beirut
Alexander left for Constantinople via Beirut on 20 January. The recently appointed Prussian consul, Mr. Ernest Gustav Schultz, arrived in Jerusalem about the same time, proof of the King of Prussia's plan to further German interests in the Land of Israel upon the LJS-Anglican foundation on 'Mount Zion.'[14]

While in Jaffa, Alexander sent a letter forward to Consul-General Rose proposing steps for resuming construction of the church building. Once they arrived in Beirut, the bishop, the consul-general and Nicolayson could then begin discussions in earnest. This exercise was to be a reality lesson for Alexander.

At their subsequent meeting in Beirut Rose produced materials just received from Jerusalem, a letter from Young of January 20 and one from

---

[10] Alexander to Stratford Canning, 14 January 1843, MSS 3393, [No f.66], Lambeth.
[11] Report of Visit 17 January 1843, in *Journal, ibid*, p. 36.
[12] LJS Local Committee, 17 January 1843, Minute 105, *ibid*, p. 37.
[13] *ibid*, Minute 108, p. 37.
[14] Ewald, *ibid*, p. 149.

the Prussian Consul-General, von Wildenbruch,[15] who refers to a letter he had received from his new consul in Jerusalem, Mr. Schultz, dated 23 January. Young stated in his letter: 'I learnt today that there is a Firman[16] from Constantinople to the Pasha on the subject of the building of the Church.' The Prussian Consul stated that he had just been informed by Young, that the pasha 'acted in compliance with the Firman from Constantinople, which declares the ground on which the Church had been erected 'Wakef,'[17] Mosque Property, and claims it as such.'[18]

Consul-General Rose stated in correspondence to Foreign Secretary Aberdeen that Alexander and Nicolayson continued to state they were justified in building the church due to the tacit permission or positive information passed on from Ponsonby to Palmerston to Shaftesbury to Nicolayson in 1841. Rose informed Alexander and Nicolayson though, that this was no guarantee of government assistance, as Young himself had informed Nicolayson that the Turkish Government 'would not sanction the continuance of the building of the Church without a Firman.' Rose also stated that Nicolayson 'does not reply to this observation.'[19]

Despite the obvious non-compliance of Nicolayson and Alexander with the request of Young, Rose nevertheless was concerned that the Turkish authorities were dealing with this matter in an unfair manner. He informed Aberdeen that if indeed the Turks were claiming this land as '*Wakf*' he would instruct Young to apply Article 24 of the Capitulations[20] 'inasmuch as the ground is held in the name of the Rev. Mr. Nicolayson.' But, he added, such a proceeding would then be referred to Constantinople, a reference he suggested 'which would probably never take place.' In other words this approach would get buried in Turkish bureaucracy.[21]

Rose was now taking matters seriously, and asked Alexander not to proceed to Constantinople where his presence would be a great embarrassment for the British.[22] Alexander agreed, and then wrote to Bunsen on 30 January describing the difficulties with the building and

---

[15] Ludwig von Wildenbruch, 1803 – 1874.
[16] Imperial edict from the Sultan.
[17] Also spelt *Wakf* – Muslim religious property.
[18] Rose to Aberdeen, 26 January 1843, FO 78/535 (No 9).
[19] Rose to Aberdeen, 26 January 1843, FO 78/535 (No 9).
[20] Which, according to Aberdeen, provided Britain with certain extra-territorial rights.
[21] Rose to Aberdeen, 26 January 1843, FO 78/535 (No 9).
[22] Rose to Aberdeen, 15 February 1843 FO 78/535 (No 193).

asking him to use his influence with the British Government on behalf of the project.[23]

Rose tried to assure Alexander that the British Government was not working against him. He also informed Aberdeen of the peculiar nature of the situation in the East, where the suspension of the 'British' church 'is considered as a slight, or proof of mistrust' of Britain.[24] Rose and von Wildenbruch then visited the Governor-General of Syria, Assad Pasha, asking him that while the issue is being discussed in Constantinople, the *status-quo* remain as before, and he permit the building to continue. They impressed upon Assad Pasha that the previous Governor of Jerusalem had permitted the building to continue unimpeded, and they shared that 'excitement and erroneous impressions had been caused,' by the disruption 'which had best have been avoided.'[25]

Assad Pasha then related to Rose false information from an individual about Rose's own involvement in this project, that the Seraskier[26] had demanded the cessation of the building, while he, Rose had urged its continuation. Assad stated 'that the Seraskier was right, as the Law of Empire forbids the erection of Foreign Churches.' Rose assured the pasha that 'the statement of the person was entirely destitute of truth.' As the British and Prussian consuls–general departed from this meeting, von Wildenbruch said to Rose: 'It is a Russian intrigue.'

At the end of this discussion Rose concluded that Assad Pasha would not change the decision of Izzet Pasha, the Governor of Jerusalem, and concluded, as von Wildenbruch had already done, that the work of the British in Jerusalem had the effect of causing 'jealousy and alarm' for the Russian Government, who 'would have wished that the Jews her subjects should have become Greeks, not Protestants.'[27]

Rose had also asked Alexander to accept the Turkish decision to stop construction of the church, to return immediately to Jerusalem (which Alexander did on 3 February), and to abide by the stipulations of the British Government.[28] In return Rose and his Prussian counterpart agreed to assist as best they could to gain the permit or *firman* to continue the

---

[23] Alexander to Bunsen, 30 January 1843, MSS 3393, Lambeth.

[24] Rose to Aberdeen, 4 February 1843 FO 78/535 (No 11).

[25] Rose to Aberdeen, 4 February 1843, FO 78/535 (No 11).

[26] A Turkish general, and in particular the commander-in-chief or Minister of War. In this context it would seem it was the latter, and an important part of the Ottoman Government.

[27] Rose to Aberdeen, 4 February 1843, FO 78.535 (No 11).

[28] Rose to Aberdeen, 15 February 1843, FO 78/535 (No 19).

building.   Alexander assured Rose that he would do his utmost in the future 'to make the wishes of Her Majesty's Government the Rule of his conduct.'[29]

Prior to leaving Beirut Alexander and Nicolayson did finally admit that it had been wrong for the Russian rabbis to seek protection in the home of a British subject. In this context Rose wrote:

> I then stated confidentially that I must previous to Bishop Alexander's departure relieve myself of responsibility by earnestly cautioning him, that if the Mission continued to adopt proceedings which could not be countenanced by Her Majesty's Servants and, which therefore must prove to the World that the members of it were deprived of that powerful aid, consequences might ensue, which would not only prejudice the cause of the Mission, but endanger the personal safety of those who composed it.
>
> I drew the attention of Bishop Alexander to the fact that the inhabitants of Jerusalem consisted of a variety of Sects, each remarkable for its blind attachment to its own creed, and aversion to those of its neighbours ... that the proceedings of the Mission had indisposed the inhabitants of Jerusalem towards them, and awakened their watchful bigotry and caused suspicion, perhaps alarm to the Local Authorities.
>
> Finally the Porte would be too happy perhaps to urge that the presence of Bishop Alexander had produced disorder.[30]

This was indeed a sobering reprimand for Alexander. But Rose, in order to reveal the delicate position in which he found himself, of trying to allay Turkish suspicion and opposition on the one hand, and upholding British interests on the other, wrote this important statement to Aberdeen on 4 February:

> In conclusion I have the honor to represent with the greatest respect to Your Lordship, that if matters continue in their present state at Jerusalem, the influence of Her Majesty's Government in this Country, particularly in that City, will be materially hurt, and that unless a Firman, or permission, be obtained to resume the building of the Church, the position of Bishop Alexander will be anomalous, and the source of perpetual embarrassment to Her Majesty's Government and to himself.[31]

---

[29] Rose to Aberdeen, 4 February 1843, FO 78/535 (No 11).

[30] Rose to Aberdeen, 6 February 1843, FO 78/535 (No 13).

[31] Rose to Aberdeen, 4 February 1843, FO 78/535 (No 11).

Prior to returning to Jerusalem, Alexander wrote to the Archbishop of Canterbury, admitting:

> This is an important Crisis in our Mission, and I cannot but hope that it will ultimately tend to good. In the meantime I hope we shall be permitted to continue our Services as usual as the interruption has only reference to the <u>building</u> of the Church which according to the custom of the country cannot be done without a firman. From a letter of Lord Aberdeen to the Consul at Jerusalem it appears that the negotiating with the Porte on the part of HM Government is proceeding, we may therefore hope that the answer will give a fresh impetus to renew them ...

Alexander then described other relevant issues in Jerusalem:

> During this Month I received a most friendly and interesting letter from the Coptic Patriarch at Cairo, requesting me to undertake the Superintendence and Direction of his community in Jerusalem. They are a small body, but they have two spacious convents ... But I feel under existing circumstances that it would not be prudent in me to comply with His holiness's request, as it would excite great jealousy on the part of the other existing Churches in the Holy City. But the fact is deeply interesting, proving how much some of them feel drawn towards us. Amongst the Jews likewise there is a great stir; on the very day on which the building of the Church was stopped the three rabbies (sic), of whom your Grace may have heard, have again come out from among the Jews, determined to become Christians at all hazards. Numbers of others are said to be equally on the point of coming out and I trust ere long we shall be able to give British protection to all who wish to join our Church.[32]

He also wrote to Sir Richard Steele in a manner that hinted of a degree of self-justification:

> It is needful for me to tell you that the British Government made an application, through Lord Ponsonby, the late Ambassador at Constantinople, for such a firman, but the Porte refused on the ground, that it was against the Turkish Law to give a firman for the building of a new <u>Christian</u> Church in Jerusalem. A promise however was made to Lord Ponsonby that the building of the Church should not be interfered with, upon which promise we have proceeded hitherto, and no obstacle was

---

[32] Alexander to Archbishop of Canterbury, 27 February 1842, pp.1-3, St. Anthony's.

placed in our way on the part of the Authorities. It is the general opinion, that the present hindrance has been brought about by intrigue on the part of many parties, to whom the raising of the Standard of Truth in its pure scriptural form, cannot but be obnoxious.[33]

On the return to Jerusalem via Alexandria, Bishop Michael Solomon Alexander had time to contemplate all these events. This entire episode, beginning with the controversy with the three rabbis, and subsequent political ramifications, then the halt to construction of the church building, and the resultant trip to Beirut, brought him closer to an understanding of real world of politics in the Levant, and the influence of Islamic Law.

The Palmerston administration that had installed him was no longer in power. The Aberdeen administration was much less sympathetic to his cause. And despite the power and prestige of Britain, and its involvement in helping Turkey regain control over the Holy Land in 1840, the importance of Empire and the Law of Islam were all-powerful considerations. It would seem that this episode had a sobering and maturing effect upon the young Protestant-Jewish Bishop.

Regular Activities
In his letter to the Archbishop from Beirut, Alexander also stated that he has no choice but to sever the connection with his chaplain, Rev. George Williams. From the outset Williams and Alexander represented different degrees of Anglicanism. Alexander represented the evangelical party with strong sympathies to continental Protestantism, while Williams tended to be more inclined towards the High Church party and was less inclined towards evangelical Protestantism. It became progressively more difficult for Alexander to work closely alongside Williams. Upon his return then to Jerusalem on 7 February he had to begin the search for a successor for this position. Williams left in May 1843.

Five days after returning, on 12 February, Alexander preached his anniversary message in the small chapel. Using as his text Isaiah 63:7, Alexander also spoke from numerous prophecies in the book of Jeremiah,[34] and concluded: 'From these and many similar passages, we may gather, that the blessings which are yet in store for the people of Israel, will far exceed all the loving kindness and mercies which the Lord has bestowed upon them in past ages.'

Reflecting upon his first year in office, Alexander commented:

---

[33] Alexander to Sir Richard Steele, 28 February 1843, St. Anthony's.
[34] Jeremiah 31:28; 31:36; 32:42; 32:37-41; 33:6-8.

In the origin, progress, and final arrangement of this bishopric, brought about under such remarkably providential circumstances, there is, undoubtedly, great good bestowed on the house of Israel. Not many years ago it might literally have been said, "This is Zion whom no man seeketh after;" but now, some of the chief rulers of the earth are beginning to think of her low estate, and, in the best sense of the word, to seek her welfare.[35]

Alexander's official duties also involved maintaining spiritual discipline within the community. This was not an altogether easy task considering the variety of personalities and backgrounds of his congregants. Earlier in January he had several resolutions passed through the local committee resolving: '... that all members of the Hebrew nation connected with the Mission be requested to attend the daily services.'[36] It was also agreed 'that it be made a condition of their engagement that all Protestants employed for the Mission shall attend the Sunday Services in those languages which they understand.'[37]

Prussian Activities

Unbeknown to Alexander, but during this stressful period he was being remembered throughout Prussia, and indeed in many German provinces. The entrance of the Bishop into Jerusalem on 21 January 1842 was being recalled. The King of Prussia had issued an Edict 'making known the Royal permission to all clergy and congregations whose hearts moved them to remember Jerusalem, but leaving it perfectly free to others to abstain.'[38]

Due to inclement weather several different dates were available for the clergy to commemorate this occasion, and it seems that in Prussia alone, only sixteen clergy declined to observe it, while some 9,000 parishes did observe it. The same occurred in the provinces of Posen, Silesia, Pomerania, Saxony, Westphalia and the Rhine.

The LJS wrote (rather optimistically) of this event:

In Prussia, 9,000 Protestant parishes, not one of which is Episcopalian, unite as one man to invoke blessings upon a Bishop and an Episcopal Mission, because, however they may differ in their views of Episcopacy,

---

[35] Sermon by Bishop Alexander, 12 February, 1843, in *JI, 1843,* pp. 237-242.
[36] LJS Local Committee, 3 January 1843, Minute 94, *ibid.*
[37] LJS Local Committee, 3 January 1843, Minute 95, *ibid.*
[38] Editorial Note, *JI*, 1843, p. 270.

they are persuaded that the cause of Protestantism and the good of the Jewish people are at stake, and that in Jerusalem the first great step has been taken to unite the Protestant Churches of Europe, and to exhibit the purity of Protestant doctrine to the Churches of the East.[39]

Difficulties and Complexities

In his letter to the Archbishop on 27 February Alexander stated:

> Oh, my dear Lord, when I look for a moment to the numerous and various elements, the even and uneven difficulties by which I am surrounded, I cannot but exclaim with the Apostle "Who is sufficient for these things!" But by the Grace of God, I am still able to trust and not be afraid, and to say likewise with the same Apostle "None of these things move me." The work in which we are privileged to be engaged is great and glorious, and if it is to be accomplished we know that "Greater is he that is for us, than all who are against us."[40]

The difficulties alluded to by Alexander again surfaced concerning the three rabbis affair. In January they had returned and were living once again in Nicolayson's house, firmly resolved to follow Jesus and suffer the consequences. Tarkover, himself suffering from a serious eye complaint, had the task of teaching them English, while they were also preparing for baptism.

Their presence again with the English created further difficulties, especially at the time when Constantine Basily, the Russian consul-general in Beirut, was due to visit in March. The Jewish religious authorities were insisting that the rabbis (or at least two of them) divorce their wives and transfer the dowries to them.

The confessing rabbis appeared before the Russian consul-general, in Nicolayson's presence, and there Basily laid down a *dictum* – either divorce their wives, repay the dowries – or return and live with their wives – which also meant returning to the orthodox fold. One of the two immediately complied. The other remained steadfast.

At this point Nicolayson was implicated in assisting the rabbis and defying the Russian consul-general. Alexander then called upon Young to discuss the situation and he supported his colleague's stance. Young felt on this occasion to seek the advice of his Prussian colleague, Consul

---

[39] Editorial Note, *JI*, 1843, p. 274.
[40] Alexander to Archbishop, 27 February 1843, St. Anthony's.

Schultz.   Following this meeting, it appears that Alexander was in agreement to the *dictum* laid down by the Russian consul-general.[41]

Macgowan reported that Rabbi Eleazer was so affected by these events that he became quite ill, and wrote:

> Evil reports of the most cruel and unfounded nature have been raised against him, and in consequence of an appeal to the Russian Consul ... a successful attempt has been made to force him to divorce his wife, to whom he was much attached. The mental suffering produced by these distressing circumstances have weighed heavily on his spirits, and brought on an attack of illness ...[42]

The situation finally seemed to be resolved, and Young reported that Consul-General Basily was satisfied with the final outcome – and that the Russian consul-general himself gave them 500 piastres 'towards liquidating the claim on them for the payment of the dowery.'

These two rabbis, Eleazer (hereafter Christian Lazarus Luria) and Benjamin (hereafter John Benjamin Goldberg), were baptised on 21 May 1843, Young reporting: 'They were Baptised yesterday morning by Bishop Alexander, during the performance of the Early Service of the Church of England, in the Hebrew Language.' It was ironical that Alexander actually asked Young to stand as sponsor to the two rabbis, which he refused. But, Young wrote, 'as the parties were to be publicly admitted members of the Church of England, I was present at the Ceremony.'[43]

Two other 'Adult Israelites' Isaac Hirsch (hereafter Isaac Paul Herschon) and Simon Frankel (not to be confused with the Jewish doctor) were also baptized on that occasion. Alexander addressed the congregation in English, briefly explaining the history of the rabbis in particular. He then addressed the candidates in German, and then, wrote Nicolayson, 'the Bishop proceeded in his peculiarly solemn manner to administer to these four Israelites the sacrament of baptism in the holy tongue.'[44] Alexander on this occasion was able to conduct the proceedings in three languages – English, German and Hebrew. [45]

---

[41] Young to Aberdeen, 31 March 1843, FO 78/540 (No 21).

[42] Macgowan to LJS London, April 1843, in *JI,* 1843, p. 261.

[43] Young to Aberdeen, 22 May 1843, FO 78/540 (No 26).

[44] Nicolayson to LJS London, 27 May 1843, in *JI,* 1843, p. 281.

[45] Ewald, *ibid*, p. 191.

There was no doubt that Alexander and his colleagues in Jerusalem saw this event as a 'victory' in their 'battle' with the Jewish religious authorities in Jerusalem. In summary Nicolayson stated:

> It is not a small thing, that the apparently impenetrable phalanx of rabbinism at Jerusalem has thus actually been broken into; and two Jerusalem rabbies (sic) been incorporated into the restored Hebrew Christian Church on Mount Zion. How sore the Jews felt on this occasion you can easily conceive. They were, in fact, after all, taken by surprise, and felt sadly disappointed in having to yield up at last any lingering hope they might have had of their return.[46]

New Stations in Alexander's Diocese

At the Local Committee meeting held on 7 March, letters were read from London pertaining to the establishment of new stations at Hebron, Beirut and Safed. London had chosen to dispatch Rev. C. Shwartz from Constantinople to Hebron, Mr. Henry Winbolt and Mr. A. Davis to Beirut, and Mr. Paul Sternchuss and Mr. Alexander Behrens to Safed.[47]

Hebron and Safed were two of the four Jewish holy cities, the others being Jerusalem and Tiberias. Except for a few small communities elsewhere, most of the Jewish population lived in these four cities. It would only be right to consider extending the LJS operations to include these locations as well. Tiberias was the fourth of the Holy Cities – and at this stage was outside the scope of operations.

Beirut offered a different challenge. Although there was a small resident Jewish population there, Beirut's importance was also because it was a transit port for Jewish people travelling from Europe to the Land of Israel, or for others coming from Antioch, Tripoli, Sidon, Aleppo and Damascus.

Alexander was to supervise the establishment of all these new Centres. All of these men, except Schwartz, arrived in Jerusalem on 15 April,[48] and entered a period of orientation under the seasoned Nicolayson, and Alexander.

Tarkover occupied the post at Beirut for a season until Winbolt was sufficiently prepared. Then when Tarkover was ordained priest by Alexander on 18 June, he soon afterward departed for Konigsberg in east Prussia.[49] Shortly afterwards Winbolt took up this key position. Winbolt

---

[46] Nicolayson to LJS London, 27 May 1843, in *JI*, 1843, p. 281.

[47] LJS Local Committee, 7 March 1843, Minute 127, 7 March 1843, *ibid*, p. 41.

[48] LJS Local Committee, 19 April 1843, Minute 147, *ibid*, p. 48.

[49] Ewald, *ibid*, pp. 194-95.

quickly instituted daily Hebrew morning and afternoon English services, a Hebrew Saturday service and Sunday English service.

Responses to Alexander's Circular Letter

Alexander's circular letter (see conclusion of previous chapter) marking the first anniversary of his entrance into Jerusalem generated considerable interest in Britain, Germany and elsewhere. In response the LJS dedicated three pages of commentary under the enlightening title *Restoration of the Churches of Jerusalem and Judea.* There is no better summary of the expectations put upon Alexander's shoulders from his support base in Britain:

> The restoration of the Jewish Church and Nation has long been an object of faith, and therefore, to the believer, as certain as if the predictions had been accomplished. The letter of a Jewish Bishop, dated from the Holy City, and informing us that there is on the Mount Zion, besides a Jewish bishop, a Jewish priest, a Jewish deacon, and a congregation, though small, of Jewish believers, amongst whom the Gospel of Christ is faithfully preached, and all the rites of the Church administered in the last year, leads us to ask, whether the restoration of a Jewish Church is not now an object of sight and whether the glorious dawn of accomplishment has not begun to chase away the obscurity of prophecy unfulfilled. It leads us, at all events, to ask, if the Churches of Jerusalem and Judea be not already restored, what hinders their immediate restoration?... The living Church in the Holy City appears small, and the other cities of Judea are still desolate, but Safet, Tiberias and Hebron will soon possess the elements of Christian congregations. The means of making them numerous and flourishing, exist abundantly in Europe, not now to speak of those who search after the truth in Palestine itself, and on other parts of Asia and Africa ... in short, there is a great multitude of Jewish believers, who, if collected into churches, especially if reunited in their own holy land, would astonish the world by their numbers and convince the Rabbinist that they are not the only Jews in the world ...
>
> What then is the difficulty? What is there to hinder the reunion of the true Israelites in the land of their fathers? On what does this happy consummation depend? So far as man is concerned, it depends on two things: first, the will of the Israelites themselves; and secondly, upon that of their friends.
>
> In the first place, believing Jews, scattered through England, Germany, etc, must remember their nation, their country, their promises, and their duty to God and the world, and love them better than worldly ease and comfort ... But let those who have faith seek what God has promised, and

where he has promised it, in the glory of all lands. Any considerable return of converted Israelites to the land of their fathers would infallibly draw a proportional number of their Talmudic brethren; for though Talmudism itself has not sufficient life to lay hold on even the national promises of God, it has such a jealousy of Christianity ... that it will imitate what it has not power to originate ... The re-appearance of the Hebrew Churches of Jerusalem and Judea would be still more powerful in exciting attention and in drawing crowds of Jews to Judea, where they may find not only the material inheritance but the faith of Abraham...

The most efficient means, indeed, the only means, for the national conversion of any people, is the rise of a visible Church of natives. All people are suspicious of a foreign religion and foreign teachers – the Jews peculiarly so ... By the visibility of a national Church alone can this be removed; and where can the national Church of Israel command more attention, or find a more genial soil, than on the holy hill which 'is beautiful for situation, and the joy of the whole earth?" And be it remembered that this is no longer a mere vision or a theory. An infant Jewish Church already exists in that sacred locality ... It is now a year since a Hebrew bishop again, after a lapse of many centuries, took up his seat in the Holy City ... Why have the efforts of Christians not been concentrated upon that one spot, which prophecy, Providence, memory, hope and every sacred association, point out as the most important upon the earth's surface?[50]

This important article, representing the heart and attitude of the parent Society, the LJS, concluded with an exhortation for the friends of Israel to support the strengthening and fostering of this new entity in Jerusalem. There is little doubt that this attitude was very much bound up with the presence of one man – Michael Solomon Alexander. It was he who exemplified the expectations of the LJS, and even larger sections of the British, German and world-wide Protestant communion.

Church of England Quarterly Review Article
The expectations upon Alexander spread further than just the LJS. A very prominent Church of England paper, the *Quarterly Review*, published a positive five-page article about Alexander and his mission in its April 1843 edition. It stated:

Whatever obscurity may hang over the *future* condition of the Jewish people, there is no doubt concerning what our duty towards them is at the

---

[50] *Restoration of the Churches of Jerusalem and Judea,* in *JI*, 1843 pp. 45-48.

present time … It is unquestionably our first duty towards the Jews to encourage them to believe, and teach them to understand, all the promises of God: to speak to them in their own way, and to speak by acts when words fail to reach their hearts … Moreover, though the Jews are a very hard people to deal with, and seem to us as if preternaturally blinded, we should remember that but for them, and, humanly speaking, but for their rejection of Christ, we might have been now in a condition farther removed from salvation than they are …

And where we cannot lead the Jews beyond the mere letter of the promises made to their fathers, we should encourage them even in this; and we may rest assured, that it is not without a purpose, and not without an end still to be accomplished, that God has kept them thus far faithful, and thereby a separate people for so many ages, and under such unprecedented scattering and persecution.

A Bishop of the Hebrew race and a Bishop of Jerusalem, cannot but excite attention among the Jews, and if it lead to nothing farther than provoking to jealousy, in the first instance, even this is preparation for another step, whether that be for their gathering into the Christian Church, or reinstating them in that land which was so often promised to their fathers …[51]

Sir Moses Montefiore steps in

Another British medium, the *Morning Herald* newspaper carried an article on 3 February 1843 stating that Sir Moses Montefiore was establishing a dispensary in Jerusalem at his own expense and sending a young Prussian doctor, Dr. Simon Frankel, to head up this dispensary and in time to establish a hospital in Jerusalem.[52] Of this decision Albert Hyamson wrote:

Until the beginning of the year 1843 there was no qualified medical attendant of their own community of the Jewish poor of Jerusalem. Those of them who had the courage had therefore when ill, recourse to the medical men attached to the English Christian Missions, to the scandal of their fellow Jews and the indignation and denunciation of the rabbis. Sir Moses Montefiore, recognizing this unsatisfactory state of affairs, sent at his own expense Dr. Simon Frankel, of Ziltz, Silesia, a young Prussian physician, fully supplied with medicaments and other medical necessities, with instructions to place his services at the disposal of all, irrespective of faith, who might need them. Dr Frankel arrived in Jerusalem in February

---

[51] *Church of England Quarterly Review,* April 1843, pp. 374-398, quoted in *JI,* 1843, pp. 151-2.
[52] *Morning Herald,* 3 February 1843, quoted in *JI,* 1843, p. 90.

1843. The first appointment was for three years, but the dispensary established by Frankel continued its activity until it was absorbed into the Bikur Cholim Hospital.

In a letter addressed to rabbi Abraham Chaim Gaguine, Rabbi Moshe Rivlin, Rabbi Abraham Shelomo Zalman and Jospeh Amzalek, all of Jerusalem ... Montefiore described the extreme anxiety and worry caused to him when he learnt that three Jews of Jerusalem had come under the influence of Christian missionaries. He was sending Dr. Frankel, equipped with drugs, to give medical assistance to the Jewish poor of the city and he hoped that with this the risk of missionary influence would be removed.[53]

The *Jewish Intelligence* of November 1842 and July 1843 mentioned Jewish ideas of establishing a hospital in Jerusalem to counter the efforts of Macgowan's medical work. It appears that even the French based Rothschild family had donated 100,000 francs to the scheme. But nothing seemed to come of it. Dr. Frankel himself furthered this proposal, writing in the German *Allgemeine Zeitung des Judenthums* on 31 October 1843:

> It is well-known to you that the Missionary Society strains every nerve to make proselytes; they leave nothing undone. They have erected a hospital in which none but Jews are to be admitted. No Jew, it is true, will enter it, if he can help it; but what shall the poor, unfortunate, sick, and houseless do? Who after all can blame him for it? And what is the consequence? Alas! A very sad one. (During the time I have been here, ten Jews have been baptized. On the 25th instant, a father, mother and daughter). At any time a hospital would have administered relief to the sick and suffering; now, it will likewise counteract the efforts of the Mission – an object which, in my opinion, every one of our brethren should, and will keep in mind.[54]

Macgowan was pleased about Dr. Frankel's arrival. Frankel in fact very quickly sent his card to Macgowan, and, wrote Macgowan, 'I lost no time in calling upon him.' He added: 'I consider his arrival here as a real advantage to the immediate object we have in view which is to afford medical relief to the poor suffering Jews in Jerusalem.'[55]

---

[53] Albert Hyamson, *The British Consulate in Jerusalem*, (London, 1939) Part I, pp. 67-8, Note 2.

[54] *Allgemeine Zeitung des Judenthums*, on 31 October 1843, quoted in *JI*, 1844, pp. 134-35.

[55] Macgowan to LJS London, April 1843, in *JI*, 1843, p. 260.

The LJS was pleased that the Jewish people were taking responsibility in this way, and wrote concerning the proposed new hospital: 'We hope that this will lead many to imitate the good example. It is indeed a matter of thankfulness that the Christian Church was permitted to lead the way in administering to the necessities of the afflicted and suffering sons and daughters of Abraham who now reside in the Holy City ... Although so late, it is gratifying to find that the Jews themselves are willing to do something in this respect for their own nation.'[56]

Debate in Parliament.

An interesting debate took place in the House of Commons on 11 April 1843 concerning Alexander and the Protestant cause in Jerusalem. Dr. (later Sir) John Bowring wanted the correspondence between the British Government and the Turkish Porte to be produced, so as to prove the ineligibility of the bishopric and indeed of the Protestant presence in Jerusalem. Dr. Bowring made some stinging remarks, also referring to the poor witness of a married bishop and with six children as well. Bowring 'thought that the circumstance of the Bishop being married was not calculated to serve him in the estimation of the people amongst whom he went. Amongst the whole east' Bowring continued 'it was impossible to connect the idea of sanctity with the Episcopal character, unless the individual had also the reputation of celibacy.' Dr. Bowring also saw fit to challenge the propriety of sending out a Jew as bishop, and also cast doubt upon the academic qualifications of Bishop Alexander.[57]

Dr. Bowring also commented on the building of the church. He stated that there 'was at Constantinople a convocation called "The Court of the Mechami," to whose decision all questions that involved religious considerations were referred. A decision had lately been come to' he added 'that no new Christian church should be allowed to be erected unless in places where a Christian church existed before.' Dr. Bowring stated that he himself had spoken to Mehmet Ali about this matter, and the Egyptian leader had said that the Court of the Mechami stated that this issue 'had been settled since the period of the Mahomedan conquest, that no new Christian church should be erected.'[58]

Sir Robert Inglis, a known LJS supporter, then arose and addressed these issues. Referring to Alexander's Jewish descent, Inglis pointed out: 'Why, who was the first Bishop of Jerusalem – was he not a Jew? Was not the

---

[56] Editorial Note in *JI*, 1843, pp. 243-244.
[57] *Morning Post,* 12 April 1843, in *JI*, 1843, p. 154.
[58] *Morning Post, ibid*, p. 155.

first Christian church founded in Jerusalem by St. James?' Inglis further added that Alexander was a 'competent Hebrew scholar' and that he had been informed by good authorities that Alexander equipped himself well as Professor of Hebrew and Rabbinic Literature at Kings College.

After Inglis it was the turn of Sir. Robert Peel, the Prime Minister, to contend with Dr. Bowring's accusations. One by one he countered them. Lord Palmerston followed and challenged Dr. Bowring concerning the tone and manner in which his raised his motion, and 'regretted that his Hon. Friend should have treated the subject with ridicule, but it was quite manifest that his Hon. Friend acted on misinformation.'

Dr. Bowring then apologized for having conveyed any idea of ridicule or levity, and stated his belief that the 'Government were not aware of the difficulties with which this Bishop had to contend.' He finally withdrew his motion.[59] The motion may have been withdrawn, but it did reveal the depth of feeling within Britain concerning the presence of the *Jewish* Bishop Alexander in Jerusalem.

The Domestic Bishop

It would be all too easy to view Alexander as a man so immersed in his episcopal functions, and so caught up in all these debates about him and his presence in Jerusalem, that he had little or no family life. Such seems far from the reality. There is every indication that he was very dedicated to his family. Deborah, his daughter, provides numerous glimpses of the domestic Bishop and his family:

> In our time the Holy Land was not modernized ... Gethsemane was un-closed, and on Good Fridays Papa assembled us all to read under those gnarled old trees the chapters describing Our Lord's Passion ... Riding and walking were our only means of locomotion. Papa, Mama and Fanny each had a lovely Arab horse, and I had a beautiful Egyptian donkey ... Her name was Darby, and I had a syce who groomed and fed her till she was quite a picture. My syce's name was Hanna Esau ... One day, I was resting on Darby under a tree, and the syce was sitting on the ground. He took up a straw to pick his teeth with. I said to him, "Don't put that in your mouth; it is like a pig." (Khungseer). To my surprise, he leaped up in a fury and rushed off to tell Papa what I called him – a Khungseer, the unclean animal. It was a long time before he was calmed down, and not until I had apologized to him, by Papa's command.[60]

---

[59] *Morning Post,* 12 April, 1843, in *JI*, 1843, pp. 156-160.
[60] Ransom, *ibid*, p. 19.

It would appear that whenever possible Alexander would take walks or rides with his family, sometimes with Deborah his wife, and sometimes just with the elder children. Again Deborah describes these occasions:

> One of our walks was through the St. Stephen's gate, the reputed Via Dolorosa, the wretched Turkish burial ground, the brook Kedron, then dry, the garden of Gethsemane, the Chapel of the Blessed Virgin Mary.
> The steep ascent of Mount Olivet, on whose brow, the Saviour wept over Jerusalem. Papa always felt this to be a hallowed spot. One night when camping there with Mr. Rowlands, he was discovered at midnight kneeling on the bare ground, in earnest prayer and weeping bitterly.[61]

On another occasion Deborah described that:

> Our daily life was regulated by the climate a good deal. A ride at sunrise, service in Church at 7 a.m. and 4 p.m. Lessons and meals until the cool of the day when we used to ride out, frequently to what we called the ledge of rocks. This was a narrow, long ledge of rock, on the face of a steep hill in the valley of Jehoshaphat. To it the servant took out rugs, fruit, and afternoon tea, and at this delightful spot, truly a shelter in a weary land, we spent many happy days, only leaving it in time to reach Jerusalem before the City Gates were shut at sunset. Visitors often came out to call which cause a pleasant diversion from the usual routine of reading, working and sketching.[62]

After all their trials and sicknesses since their arrival, especially the loss of their baby Louisa, as well as missing son and brother Robert, the Alexander family were able to greatly rejoice on 31 May with the arrival of another baby girl – Salome.

Many and varied were the demands upon the Alexander household in Jerusalem. Young Deborah relates another interesting incident:

> One evening when we children were all in bed, a messenger came to Papa with a letter from the soldiers who kept guard at the Jaffa gate. The letter was one given to them by an English lady, who had arrived after sunset, but did not know she would find the gates shut, and the keys taken to the Pacha's palace, a mile away. The lady was Miss Cooke Yarborough, the letter was one of introduction to Papa. The only thing to be done was to

---

[61] Ransom, *ibid*, p. 31.
[62] *ibid*, p. 22.

send the sentinel on to the Pacha[63] urgently asking for the gates to be opened. After long waiting, the ponderous keys were forthcoming, and the lady arrived at our home between 9 and 10 p.m. Annie and I were roused from sleep and sent into the nursery, and our room given up to Miss Yarborough. The dear lady was travelling for her pleasure, quite alone, and was utterly surprised to find there was no kind of hotel where she could live. So Papa and Mama invited her to stay at our house which she did for a year, eventually marrying Dr. Macgowan.[64]

Repercussions from Previous Events

The episode concerning the three rabbis, the stoppage of the church, Alexander's trip to Beirut and subsequent contact with Consul-General Rose, engendered much response and activity in Jerusalem, Beirut, Constantinople and London.

Foreign Secretary Aberdeen had no choice but to become more pro-active in these affairs, as the debate in Parliament and public interest had increased exposure to what was happening in Jerusalem. He sent a strong message to Ambassador Canning on 20 March, stating that the Foreign Office had been considering for some time information coming from the consul-general in Syria and from the consul in Jerusalem:

> ... respecting the conduct of Turkish Authorities at Jerusalem and Beyrout with regard to the Protestant Church at Jerusalem, the erection of which, after having been for some time tacitly permitted by the Turkish authorities has at length been abruptly and somewhat arbitrarily stopped.
>
> Although that building had certainly been commenced without the express authority of the Porte, which had always declined granting a formal permission for that object, yet, as it had been stated to Her Majesty's Government Ambassador at Constantinople (as appears from a Despatch, dated Sept 18 1841, no 288) that he had reason to suppose that, provided the fabrick should be modest and unostentatious in appearance and should form part of the Consular residence, no obstruction would be thrown by the Turkish Authorities in the way of its erection; as that building had not for many months been opposed or obstructed, Her Majesty's Government had certainly hoped that the further prosecution of it might and would have been allowed.
>
> Her Majesty's Government still entertain a hope that, on a temperate representation of their wishes being made to that effect, the Turkish

---

[63] Pacha or pasha, the Turkish Governor.
[64] Ransom, *ibid*, p. 23.

Government may be induced to permit the building to be recommenced and to continue without further interruption.

Aberdeen then instructed Canning to bring the matter to the attention of the Turkish minister and:

> ... to represent to him the disappointment which has been felt at the sudden interruption of the work after having been so long permitted by the Turkish Authorities at Jerusalem, and that you will request the Turkish Minister to convey such orders to the Pasha of Jerusalem as shall empower him to authorise recommencement and unobstructed prosecution of the Building.
>
> I hesitate to instruct Your Excellency to demand from the Porte a formal Firman for the above object as it appears to me that it might not be prudent to risk a repetition of the positive refusal which has been already given by it more than once to such a proposition.'[65]

It is obvious from this comment that Aberdeen was walking a diplomatic tightrope. He felt he had a right to demand a political favour which Turkey owed Britain, but realized there would probably be a 'positive refusal' again to the proposal.

Shortly afterwards Aberdeen sent further instructions to Canning concerning how to relate to Bishop Alexander.[66] On the same day he also wrote to Consul Young, with instructions concerning both Bishop Alexander and the construction of the church. He informed Young that he had acted properly in not getting involved in the church affair: 'As the parties have acted without the declared sanction of the Porte.' However, Aberdeen stated, should Turkey:

1) agree to the church being built he was to zealously assist,
2) if the works are only tacitly allowed to be continued as heretofore he was to have nothing further to do in the matter than to employ his best efforts to induce the Pasha to give full extent to the tacit permission of the Porte.
3) if the Turks refused permission for further construction of the church, then he must have nothing at all to do with it.

---

[65] Aberdeen to Canning, 20 March 1843, FO 78/513 (No 41).
[66] Aberdeen to Canning, 3 April 1843, FO 78/513.

Aberdeen also informed Young that he perceived there were problems between him and Alexander 'which for the benefit of the public service' the foreign secretary thought 'ought to be corrected.' Aberdeen then provided Young with advice that, should Alexander contravene the laws of the Turkish Government '... in such a manner as wantonly to excite the hostility of the Turkish Authorities, you as British Consul have not the power to protect him, even if you were authorized by your Government to do so ...'[67]

Indeed the relationship between the two senior British representatives was strained. They were tense not so much because of their differing personalities but due to the differing instructions both were operating under. Concerning these ambiguities Young stated to Aberdeen:

> The agents of the Society appear to me to have extravagant notions on the subject of protection, and in regard to their privileges. In these matters I think that the Bishop has been misled by these, and on the other hand the Bishop's position here is rather novel, being charged with the direction of Ecclesiastical Matters, he is at the same time head of a private mission and consequently continually liable to be put forward in questions belonging to this private society, which are altogether of a secular character and have led him into inconvenient discussions.[68]

Relations between the two were so strained that in a communiqué to Aberdeen on 1 May 1843 Young wrote ten pages about their relationship. Young also claimed that both Alexander and Nicolayson had misrepresented him through reports that had subsequently appeared in the *Jewish Intelligence.*

Young had also written to Alexander expressing his disappointment about what he believed to be the slandering of his name. Alexander had responded stating that in the matter of the three rabbis not receiving British protection, Nicolayson was merely expressing that they felt disappointed at being handed over to the Russian Consul.[69] Despite such explanations, as well as attempts to mediate by the Foreign Secretary and Rose, and Alexander's promise to Rose in February to attempt to abide by British Government policies, it was going to be a challenge for Alexander to work with Young.

---

[67] Aberdeen to Young, 3 April 1843, FO 78/540.
[68] Young to Aberdeen, 1 May 1843, FO 78/540 (No 24).
[69] Young to Alexander, 13 April 1843 and Alexander to Young, 19 April, Young to Aberdeen, 1 May 1843, FO 78/540 (No 24).

Young was determined to abide by the guidelines that the present British administration had handed down to him. But he too was insensitive to the bishop's position. On one occasion Young had slighted Alexander when he visited him in an official capacity without *kawasses*[70] - which was contrary to protocol. Rose wrote to Aberdeen: 'The non observance of any outward mark of respect or form was sure to be felt by Bishop Alexander, unluckily sensitive as he is on these matters, more than any more essential matter.'[71]

This observation by such an astute observer as Colonel Rose hints at an aspect of Alexander's personality. It could very well also have revealed the core of the issue – who really was the British representative in Jerusalem – the Bishop or the Consul! Rose made further observations of the situation in Jerusalem in a dispatch to Aberdeen on 4 July 1843:

> I can assure your Lordship that as regards Jerusalem, and considering the state of parties there, the hostility of fierce, semi-barbarous and bigotted sects towards Bishop Alexander and his companions, the sympathy with and secret encouragement given those inflammable materials by clever and intriguing Agents, the jealousy, if not hostility and want of principle of those who were solely responsible for the preservation of the public peace, the Turkish Authorities, these circumstances rendered even more unpropitious by the state of feeling between Her Majesty's Consul and Bishop Alexander and by the over zeal and want of common prudence of that prelate, and his companions, I can assure Your Lordship that these things considered, I most anxiously felt the responsibility to the fullest extent of strict obedience to your Lordship's and Viscount Palmerston's Instructions to superintend and control Her Majesty's Consular Servants and to know and report on events of interest.[72]

From the safe distance of Beirut, Rose was in a good position to act as mediator. But the character of Jerusalem was such that intra-communal problems would rise continually as that was the nature of the Holy City.

Despite their strained relationship, in May Alexander presented Young with a memorandum to be delivered to Her Majesty's Government on behalf of Queen Victoria's birthday. The memo stated amongst other things that Queen Victoria '... has been permitted to become 'a nursing Mother' to Israel, not only in having her Consul in this long neglected and

---

[70] *Kawass* is a Turkish guard. On official business a delegation was expected to be accompanied by at least one *kawass*.
[71] Rose to Aberdeen, 6 May 1843, FO 78/536 (No 41).
[72] Rose to Aberdeen, 4 July 1843, FO 78/536 (No 48).

forsaken City and Country, but moreover by having been made instrumental in causing the pure worship of God to be established on Mount Zion in Jerusalem.'

This memorandum concluded: '… that her majesty may be permitted to see '"the good of Jerusalem - all the days of her life" and that she may see her Children's Children and peace upon Israel.'[73]

Several months later, in September, Young communicated to Aberdeen another problem with Alexander. This time it concerned a letter from the 'Chief Rabbi of the Native Jews' meaning the Sephardim, 'requesting my interference in behalf of a woman, whose husband has connected himself with the Missionaries here, but whom they state to be still a Jewess.' Young informed Aberdeen that he informed the Chief Rabbi that he could not interfere because the subject in question was not a British subject. Young did indicate though that he had communicated with Alexander.[74] This issue did not cause a further impediment in their relationship.

Visit of Prince Albert of Prussia

In late April and early May a very distinguished Prussian visited Jerusalem, Prince Albert[75] (or Albrecht in German). The Prince was the younger brother of the Prussian King, Frederick William IV, and was therefore familiar with the origins of the Jerusalem Bishopric.

The bishop sent a delegation consisting of Nicolayson, Ewald and Macgowan to meet and escort the Prince into Jerusalem on behalf of Alexander. The royal party however decided to encamp near Abu Ghosh,[76] so the welcoming party returned alone.[77]

Several days later however Alexander, Macgowan, Nicolayson and Ewald had an audience with the Prince, who then in turn visited the LJS property and inspected the plans for the proposed Protestant Church building. This meeting was conducted in English – despite the fact that all with the exception of Macgowan were well acquainted with the German language.

The Prince attended the Protestant service on 4 May, where Alexander preached from Romans 11: 25-26: *I do not want you to be ignorant of this mystery, brothers, so that you may not be conceited: Israel has experienced a hardening in part until the full number of the Gentiles has*

---

[73] Memorandum from Bishop Alexander, 27 May 1843, FO 78/540 (No 27).

[74] Young to Aberdeen, 18 September 1843, FO 78/540 (No 40).

[75] Prince Albert was married to Princess Marianne of the Netherlands.

[76] An Arab village approximately ten kilometers west of Jerusalem and on the route from Ramle to Jerusalem, named after the predominant clan.

[77] Nicolayson to LJS London, 1 May 1843, in *JI*, 1843, p. 258.

come in. And so all Israel will be saved, as it is written; 'The deliverer will come from Zion; he will turn godlessness away from Jacob...'[78]

On this occasion the little St. James Chapel was filled to capacity, partly because of the unexpected presence of the Prince and his entourage. A sizeable collection was taken on this occasion.[79] In one way it was fitting that the first visitor of royal status would be from Prussia. But the very fact it was the Prussian royalty and not the British also shows the depth of interest that the Germans showed in this endeavour.

Several days later, on 5 May, a special meeting was held in a room adjoining the St. James Chapel to coincide with the LJS Annual General Meeting (AGM), where addresses were given by Bishop Alexander, Macgowan, Nicolayson, Dr. Thomas Kerns and Ewald. Alexander proposed the formation of an LJS Auxiliary Society in Jerusalem. The proposal passed unanimously.[80]

There were now two special occasions the young community was annually observing, one the anniversary of the bishop's entrance into Jerusalem, and now the annual meeting of the parent society in London.

Opening of Hebrew College, Inquirers Home and School of Industry

In May[81] the bishop officially opened the Hebrew College. Part of the purpose of this College was to train the rabbis who had come to faith, but others also were to benefit from it. Alexander read from Psalms 132 and 133, and then addressed the students in English and German, during which he pointed out to them 'the nature, use, and blessings of such an institution, and the duties of those who may be received into the same.' The first students were Rabbi Eliezer, Rabbi Benjamin, Isaac Hirsch and Jonas.[82]

Rev. Williams, prior to his departure, was the first principal, and later he was followed by his successor, Rev. Veitch. The subjects taught at the Hebrew College were Divinity, English, German, Hebrew, Arithmetic, Music and Translation from English into Hebrew. In September the bishop examined the students. 'His Lordship' wrote Ewald 'expressed his satisfaction at the progress they had made, and exhorted them to persevere

---

[78] The passage concludes with verse 27: 'And this is my covenant with them when I take away their sins.'

[79] See *JI*, 1843, p 280 and Ewald, *ibid*, p. 189.

[80] Ewald, *ibid*, p. 189.

[81] According to Ewald it was 19 May.

[82] Ewald, *ibid*, p. 190.

in their studies, directing them to seek in all things for assistance from above, and closed the examination in prayer.'[83]

The Inquirers Home was established in order to determine which of the prospective believers was genuine or not. Due to the nature of the Jewish community in Jerusalem, where many people depended upon alms and financial assistance from Europe, such an institution was essential for the LJS. For some, it would appear that the Protestants or British offered a better life than the narrow confines of the Jewish community. Someone could suppose they could feign belief and get accepted into the Protestant community, and thereby receive an opening into a world otherwise not open for Jewish people, by undergoing baptism. This was the accusation often leveled against the LJS. The object of this institution was to weed out insincere inquirers. However this was not a complete guarantee that this objective would succeed.

The 'inmates' or students were provided with board, lodging and clothes while undergoing training and observation. If they were deemed to be true disciples, they then graduated into either the Hebrew College or the House or School of Industry.

A very important adjunct to the LJS work was the House or School of Industry. Critchlow, the LJS clerk of works, supervised this work for a season. Here the pupils were provided with board and keep, and were trained in various tasks that were useful for the daily operations of the Mission, as well as providing a trade for the pupils themselves. These included carpentry, joinery and general repairs.

The foundations were now laid for yet another pioneering venture in Jerusalem. This school became famous in later years, especially when under the direction of the skilled German Christian craftsman, Conrad Schick.

Relations with the French and Roman Catholics (Latins) and the attack on Dr. Macgowan

Relations between Alexander and the British with the Roman Catholics and French were quite a complicated matter. Young reported for instance in May 1843, that after the LJS had hired a house from a Catholic, the Latin Convent had 'caused a denunciation to be proclaimed in Church against any of their people who should be discovered to be having dealings with those who are of a different Religious persuasion to themselves.'[84]

---

[83] Ewald, *ibid*, pp. 212-213.
[84] Young to Aberdeen, 29 May 1843, FO 78/540 (No 29).

Ever since Britain opened her consulate in 1838, and then dispatched the Protestant bishop, France had become wary of British involvement in Jerusalem. The French, following the British example, in 1843 also established a consulate in Jerusalem. And why not? For it was very clear from a geo-political perspective that Britain opened her consulate in the first place in order to observe French (and Russian) activities in the region. The new French consul, M. le Comte de Lantivy,[85] arrived in Jerusalem on 16 July 1843.[86]

Shortly after the French opened their consulate, a nasty incident occurred in the market place of Jerusalem. Dr. Macgowan was accosted by Turkish soldiers and very badly mistreated. Thankfully there were some Jews in the crowd who recognized Macgowan and who began to struggle with the soldiers trying to extricate the doctor. 'I shall never forget' wrote Macgowan 'the courageous assistance they afforded me on that occasion, to which, in all probability, my preservation, humanly speaking, is owing.'[87]

More Turkish soldiers then appeared and dragged Macgowan along Jerusalem's streets, including the *Via Dolorosa,* ultimately to the pasha's residence. Here he was thrown into a dirty cell and was continually abused. The pasha was then informed by the soldiers of what occurred, and the pasha informed Macgowan that he was 'accused of having struck the Turkish soldiers.'

Thankfully Young was informed of this outrage and he immediately sent his guard (*kawas*) and Macgowan received the protection of the British consul. Macgowan then went to Young's residence, where he provided the consul with a complete report. Macgowan afterwards retired to Nicolayson's home.

The following day both Young and the Prussian consul, Dr. Schultz, visited Macgowan. Young viewed the incident so seriously that he sent off a messenger to Consul-General Rose in Beirut. Rose then took up the matter with the Governor-General of Syria, Assad Pasha, who agreed with Young's request that the soldiers who meted out the ill-treatment to Macgowan, be publicly punished. On 22 July the soldiers in question were to be flogged, not in the bazaar where the incident took place, but in the Turkish barracks.

---

[85] Comte Gabriel Marie Jean Benoit de Lantivy de Kerveno, (1792-1866).
[86] See T. Parfitt, *The Jews in Palestine 1800-1882,* (Woodbridge, Suffolk; 1987), p. 135.
[87] Macgowan to LJS London, 29 July 1843, in *JI,* 1843, pp. 349-50.

Young intended to witness the flogging. However at the very time when he was informing Macgowan of the decision, a serious riot erupted only a few yards away, at the residence of the newly arrived French consul, de Lantivy. This consul was intending to raise the French flag, an act disapproved of by some local Muslims. Macgowan wrote of this incident: 'The act of hoisting a European flag in the Holy City of Jerusalem was calculated to rouse all their religious prejudices. It was unprecedented since the time of the Crusaders, never having been attempted by any present or former consul.'[88]

Rumours circulated that the flag was soon to be raised, and an infuriated mob surrounded the consulate. Young noted that: 'The fact of the French Flag having been hoisted very soon spread through the City, and caused great excitement amongst the Mussulmans (sic).'[89]

In the eyes of many of the Muslims there was no difference between the French and the British – they were all foreigners, *Franks*. Bishop Alexander's house was next door to the consulate, and the enraged Muslim mob was at the point of seizing the two-year old Benny as hostage, as he was the only available male. Fortunately the bishop and Consul Young arrived on the scene in the nick of time and were able to appease the rioters, and 'Benny, all unconscious of his enormous importance, was left in peace.'[90] This is a good example of Young and Alexander co-operating when they had to.

The pasha then requested that the French consul take the flag down and not fly it again. 'During the following day' Young wrote to Rose, 'we heard that serious excitement had been manifested among the Musulman (sic) population.' The governor himself was summoned to the *Mekhame* (seat of Muslim council in Jerusalem) and 'notified, that if the French Flag was rehoisted, the Musulman population would rise and destroy his own, as well as the French Consul's houses – and threats were held out against all Europeans, but especially against the consuls. Many proceeded to the Mosque, and there swore on the Koran that they would die for their faith, which they considered to have been attacked.'[91]

With this state of affairs the pasha requested that the anticipated flogging of the two Turkish (Muslim) soldiers should take place in Beirut and not in Jerusalem. Young wisely consented. Macgowan for his part was satisfied that justice had been carried out.

---

[88] Macgowan to LJS London, 29 July 1843, in *JI* 1843, p. 353.
[89] Young to Rose, 24 July 1843, FO 78/540 (No 28).
[90] Corey, *ibid*, p. 73.
[91] Young to Rose, 24 July, 1843, FO 78/540 (No 28).

But the effects of this incident lingered for some time, and Macgowan commented on how Jewish people, many whom he previously did not know, offered much sympathy to him.

Very shortly afterwards Macgowan was back at work, and one of his first patients was Bishop Alexander. Macgowan wrote: 'I regret to say, that on July 23, the bishop experienced an attack of fever, which on the following morning assumed an alarming character. Prompt and active measures were necessary, and were followed by considerable relief.'[92] Thankfully Alexander finally recovered. This was another in a sequence of illnesses while in Jerusalem, and indeed in the years prior to his coming.

The French flag incident and the Macgowan affair brought to the surface deep Muslim feelings and prejudices against the foreigners. The French flag incident also revealed the strength of French feelings of superiority and rivalry. Rose connected this French attitude with the establishment of the Anglo-Prussian presence, stating, 'there can be but little doubt that the religious feeling of the Catholic States has been thereby alarmed.'[93] Mordechai Eliav states that by performing this action, the French Consul 'sought to emphasize his country's preferred status as opposed to that of the other powers.'[94]

This was the first time a flag of a European power was flown in Jerusalem. Not even Britain flew her flag, despite her involvement in ousting the Egyptians and restoring the Turks in 1840. This incident put the Turkish governor, Rachid Pasha, in a somewhat difficult position. On one hand, he had to respect the attitude of the local Muslim *effendis*, leaders, who strongly opposed the hoisting of the flag. But on the other hand the pasha was somewhat bound by the credentials the French consul had been granted by the Sultan of Turkey himself. The French consular agents in fact had protested to the governor that in view of the 'superior claims of France to peculiar privileges' they should be permitted to fly their national flag.'[95]

The French consul immediately reported to the French ambassador in Constantinople about his loss of honour in this incident. Despite the fact that only a few years before the French had openly supported the Egyptians against the Turks, the French held a strong position in the Sublime Porte (Turkish Government). Young received a call from de

---

[92] Macgowan to LJS London, 29 July 1843, in *JI* 1843, p. 353.

[93] Rose to Aberdeen, 27 August 1843, FO 78/537 (No 40).

[94] Eliav, Mordechai, *Britain and the Holy Land 1838-1914*, (Jerusalem, 1997), p. 136.

[95] Young to Rose, 24 July, 1843, FO 78/540 (No 28).

Lantivy on 29 September, and was informed by the French consul that Rachid Pasha and five effendis had been banished from Jerusalem 'in consequence of his representations to the French Ambassador at Constantinople on the subject of the French Flag.'[96]

The outcome of these incidents reveals just how much the traditional *status quo* of Jerusalem was being seriously challenged.

Ministry Events

The *status quo* of the Jewish community was also undergoing a challenge. The Jewish leaders were doing what they could to make life difficult for would-be followers of Jesus.

The difficulties which many Jewish believers or inquirers underwent became apparent to Rabbi Abraham, one of the three rabbis who had earlier come to faith in Jesus. He returned to his wife, who, unfortunately then asked for a bill of divorce. According to the law, the party asking for the divorce is not entitled to the dowry. Rabbi Abraham reluctantly gave the bill of divorce and then his wife presented him with her bill of dowry, and the rabbis sided with her against her husband. 'All these things are done' Ewald stated 'to prevent others from coming in contact with us.'[97]

The opposition towards contact with the British mission grew. Sir Moses Montefiore from London became so concerned that he gave an order to Rabbi Israel the printer to reprint the anti-Christian book *Chizuk Emunah*.[98] This book, *Faith Strengthened* was a polemic against the Christian message.

But such negative issues were always balanced by positive events. Mr. Whitmarsh was ordained on 20 August, and then on Wednesday 23 August following the early morning Hebrew service, Alexander confirmed Mr. Michael Weinkauf. Weinkauf who had previously been baptized by Alexander came up from Egypt for the occasion.[99]

Shortly afterwards, on 24 September, Alexander baptised another Jewish person, or as the baptismal register states, 'an Adult Israelite' - Christian Willhelm Hanauer, at the afternoon German service. 'Thus another son of

---

[96] Young to Aberdeen, 2 October 1843, FO 78/540 (No 41).

[97] Ewald, *ibid*, p. 197.

[98] Ewald, *ibid*, pp. 208-09. This book was initially written by a Karaite Jew, Isaac Ben Abraham of Troki (1533-1598). Others modified the original, and it was reprinted for Jewish use at Amsterdam in 1705; and a Yiddish translation appeared in the same place in 1717. Troki is in present day Lithuania.

[99] Letter from Nicolayson, in *JI*, 1844, p. 377.

Abraham' wrote Ewald 'has been added to our community on Mount Zion.'[100]

Hanauer later worked for the LJS in various capacities, while his son James Edward was destined to become one of the LJS's most faithful workers even into the next century.

Alexander's ministry duties occasionally involved some bizarre events. In June, a number of German speaking members of the Jewish community left the city and encamped near the village of Lifta.

A rabbi had predicted that Jerusalem was to be struck by an earthquake, and because many of these people had survived the 1837 earthquake in Safed, their apprehension was understandable. Michael Solomon rode out and visited them before they returned after camping out for six days.[101]

Alexander and the Church (September)

One issue in particular continued to concern the bishop – the building of the Protestant Church. Alexander wrote to Sir Stratford Canning on 20 September, in response to a letter Canning had written to him on 20 May. He stated:

> I am sorry to learn ... that our Church affairs were nor progressing as we had hoped. I trust better prospects are presenting themselves. It would at all events be very desirable to have the matter settled if possible one way or the other, for if the Church is not to be built, we might then proceed with the building of the Houses, which we greatly need, but at present all is at a standstill ... Our Services are being regularly conducted in the small temporary Chapel, and I am on general terms of friendship with all the Authorities of the different Churches ... I need not say, Jerusalem is beginning to attract general and universal notice. The number of Europeans is considerably on the increase, and many, particularly French families are expected to come and reside here. I trust and pray that it may all tend to promote the best interests of this wonderful but desolate country, and that the predicted time may soon arrive, when in the strictest sense of the word Jerusalem shall again become a Praise in the Earth.[102]

In view of the attitude of the French and Russians towards British activities in Jerusalem, it is only understandable that much opposition

---

[100] Ewald, *ibid*, p. 213.

[101] *JI*, 1843, p. 280.

[102] Alexander to Sir Stratford Canning, 20 September 1843, MSS 3397, Lambeth.

towards the building of the British Church in Jerusalem would be encountered. Canning in Constantinople and Alexander in Jerusalem had many obstacles to overcome.

Jaffa in September

Not long after the Alexander family had seemingly recovered from their previous sicknesses they succumbed again. In early September Fanny Alexander had a relapse of ill health. On 2 September Macgowan wrote:

> I recommended the bishop to remove her without delay to Jaffa; upon which he lost no time in making the necessary preparations, and early on the Friday following, accompanied by his daughter and Miss Deborah Alexander, who had likewise for some time been suffering from the same complaint, as well as an English servant, set off for that place. I am gratified to state, that the Bishop himself has quite recovered from his late alarming attack of rheumatism, and determination of blood to the head.[103]

Alexander invited Ewald to join him in Jaffa between 6-13 September. During this time Ewald wrote: 'Many more Jews are now residing at Jaffa … Whilst I was at Jaffa, sixty Jews arrived from Poland on their way to the Holy City: about forty of them arrived with me today.'[104]

Alexander himself remained in Jaffa for some time, visiting Jerusalem occasionally for essential business, and was able to catch up on correspondence. One letter in particular from Steele, seemed to encourage him. Michael Solomon concluded in a letter to the LJS by stating his thankfulness for this change of air and for the house they had found, and rented for five years, which, he stated 'will serve as a place of resort for my family in case of illness.'[105]

Rivalry with the Scottish Mission and Station at Safed

It seems that Bishop Alexander had a somewhat ambivalent attitude towards the Presbyterian Church of Scotland. The Church of Scotland had dispatched a delegation to the Land of Israel in 1839, headed by Robert McCheyne and Andrew Bonar. Their report indicated that the area of Judea was occupied by the LJS, but that the Galilee was still an open field.

The Scottish Committee accordingly approached Palmerston in October 1840 to seek his approval for their plan to establish a missionary station in

---

[103] Macgowan to LJS London, 2 September 1843, in *JI* 1843, p. 387.
[104] Ewald, *ibid*, p. 210.
[105] Alexander to LJS London, 4 October 1843, in *JI*, 1843, p. 417.

the Galilee, especially at Safed.   Palmerston then conferred with his representatives in the region.

By the time these representatives responded, and the Scots then informed by Palmerston's office, the Jerusalem Bishopric had been established, and Alexander dispatched to the Land of Israel.   Alexander seemed to believe that the entire country was his domain, and 'did not relish the Scots mission in Safed, even though one of their missionaries, armed with a letter from Aberdeen to Rose, was already in Palestine.'[106] Rose was instructed by Aberdeen to protect the Scottish missionary as best he could.[107]

Alexander was then commissioned by the LJS to open a missionary station in Safed.   Consul-General Rose was quite aware of the dangers and complexities of a missionary presence in Safed, and warned that such a settlement was 'attended with risk.'   Consul Young in Jerusalem gave similar advice to Bishop Alexander.

It seems though that neither Alexander nor the Scots were willing to listen to reason, and as a result a race began for establishing a permanent mission presence in Safed.   During Alexander's visit to Beirut, Rose asked him 'to check a spirit of intolerance amongst some of his companions' towards the Scottish missionaries.   Rose informed his superior Aberdeen of these matters, and mentioned that such rivalry between the Protestant missions was no better than their accusations against the strife between the ancient churches.[108]

The Scottish endeavour failed to materialize. And only many years later did the Scots attempt again, at Tiberias and Safed, and this time they enjoyed considerable success.[109]

Meanwhile though, matters between LJS and the British Consulate soon came to a head.   When two of the Hebrew Christians, Paul Sternschuss and Alexander Behrens, who had been commissioned by the LJS for service in Safed, arrived in Jerusalem in March, Alexander approached Young for these two, and two other newly arrived missionaries, to receive British consular protection.   Young refused, stating that Sternschuss, an Austrian, had no passport, while Behrens had a passport from the Hanoverian Consulate in London.

---

[106] Tibawi, *ibid,* p. 68.

[107] Aberdeen to Rose, 5 December 1842, FO 78/483.

[108] Rose to Aberdeen, 15 February 1843 and 29 March 1843, FO 78/535, quoted in Tibawi, *ibid,* p. 68.

[109] Ironically after the First World War the LJS sold their properties in Safed to the Scots.

Young stated that he could offer protection while they remained in Jerusalem, but he could not provide protection for them if they removed themselves to Safed. Young actually informed Alexander 'of the difficulties of them establishing missionary stations in such remote places.' But, Young concluded: 'They seemed determined to proceed.' Young seemed to have a mature grasp on the issues at hand, and then added:

> ...Their zeal on the present occasion is roused from the fact that the Scotch Presbyterian Church is about to establish a Mission to the Jews in Palestine, and that Saffat is one of the stations they have decided upon for the residence of one of their missionaries, who is already arrived in Beirut.
>
> The London Society is desirous of occupying the ground ... before the Scotch missionaries can enter the field ...[110]

Towards the end of May Nicolayson left Jerusalem to accompany Sternschuss and Behrens to their new station in Safed. Nicolayson had secured the services of a local Christian Arab, Tannous Kerm, to acquire a suitable house in Safed. The three men arrived on 2 June, this being Nicolayson's first visit there since the earthquake of 1837, which destroyed much of the city on the hill.

As was so often the case in the land, the house procured was not yet available, as the Muslim family was still lodging there. Nicolayson was then offered help by local families whom he knew from his previous residence in Safed. This problem was immediately followed by rumours put round by some local Jewish people that these men were in fact Freemasons, and opposition came against the family in whose house they were staying. Nicolayson then decided to take temporary leave of Safed, and visit the sources of the Jordan until the promised house was ready.

Nicolayson and his friends were finally able to occupy the house on 16 June, and that same evening, after having received certain Christian and even some Muslim visitors, Nicolayson, Behrens and Sternschuss 'commenced the regular course of daily Hebrew service, which the Bishop had directed the brethren to keep up among themselves ... The next day, being first Sunday after Trinity, we had the full service in Hebrew.'[111]

Once satisfied that his brethren were firmly settled, Nicolayson took leave of them and returned to Jerusalem. Another of Bishop Alexander's endeavours had now been accomplished – the establishment of a mission

---

[110] Young to Aberdeen, 31 March 1843, FO 78/540 (No 21).

[111] Nicolayson to LJS London, 28 June 1843, in *JI*, 1843, pp. 319-322.

station in a centre of Jewish mysticism. But it would be difficult for the two young Hebrew Christian missionaries to fulfill their task there.

And it was a difficult task. The Jewish community closed rank against them ostracizing anyone who had contact with the Hebrew Christian *apostates,* and even withholding *halukah* funds from any who had dealings with them. Of this predicament Sternschuss wrote: 'The Jews here are complete slaves to the persons who have the management of the rent for distribution; and if anyone displeases them in the least, he is immediately threatened with the loss of the weekly and monthly charity-money.'[112]

The pressure continued to mount. On 1 July Tannous Kerm arrived in Jerusalem, and, as reported by Nicolayson 'stated that the populace of that place had raised such a clamour against him for bringing English Missionaries there that the *kadi* himself had insisted upon his giving up the house on receiving back the purchase money.'[113] Tannous claimed he hadn't done so yet, but that unless there was a counter order from the governor-general in Beirut, then he would do so.

Alexander subsequently wrote a letter to Behrens and Sternschuss about this persecution, 'encouraging them to persevere in it, unless the local Authorities should take upon themselves the responsibility of positively ordering them to quit the place.' Alexander also wrote to Rose and von Wildenbruch asking for their assistance in this matter.[114] The two consuls-generals seemingly declined to get overly involved, and eventually Sternschuss and Behrens vacated Safed for a season.

Later Behrens wrote that with but one exception when the bishop was sick, he always sent letters of encouragement to them. 'At the commencement of the present month' he continued 'we received another very kind letter from the Bishop, containing a donation of 200 piastres, which he desired us to distribute among our poor Jewish brethren ... The Bishop is pleased to call the offering a mite, but this mite has gladdened the heart of many an indigent Jewish family, who lack bread to eat and fuel to warm their rooms.[115]

Arrival of German colonists
On 13 October three Germans arrived in Jerusalem, who had been sent as a deputation representing sixty German families then living in Georgia.

---

[112] Sternschuss to LJS London, [no date] in *JI*, 1843, p. 388.
[113] LJS Local Committee, 46th Meeting, 5 July 1843, Minute 174, *ibid,* Schick Library.
[114] *ibid,* Minute 174.
[115] Behrens to LJS London, 30 November 1843, *JI,* 1844, p. 51.

They came to determine if they could become colonists in the Holy Land. All these Germans came originally from Wurttemburg, who in 1817 had begun on a journey to the Holy Land, but had become waylaid in Georgia. The Germans, Ewald wrote 'had of late heard that a Protestant Bishopric was established in the Holy Land and they came to believe –"The time is near at hand."'[116]

At Constantinople they heard of the near impossibility of them being able to settle effectively in the Holy Land, yet they decided to continue on with their journey. Ewald wrote: 'I introduced them to the Bishop, who felt greatly interested in them. There they met with Dr. Schultz, His Prussian Majesty's Consul, who gave them a great deal of information.'[117]

Several days later it was the turn of the king of Prussia himself to be honoured. On Sunday 15 October, the occasion of the king's birthday, Alexander preached a sermon in the morning service and made special reference to that fact. The Prussian consul, Mr. Schultz attended the service in full Prussian uniform. Alexander again alluded to this occasion during the afternoon German service. The following day, 16 October, a delegation led by Bishop Alexander paid an official visit to Dr. Schultz to 'congratulate him on this occasion.'[118]

Nicolayson to Constantinople

On 1 November Nicolayson left Jerusalem for Constantinople to present information to the British ambassador in connection with obtaining a *firman* for building the church.[119] Young actually communicated to Aberdeen:

> I learn indirectly that one of his objects is to obtain permission to purchase, if not my present dwelling, such property as will annex it to the Society's premises and thereby give to the whole the appearance of being part and parcel of the Consular Residence.[120]

Young also stated that Nicolayson had failed to consult him about the trip.[121] In fact the initiative did not actually come from Alexander and Nicolayson, but from London. The LJS Committee, frustrated by the lack of action concerning the church building, had requested the direct

---

[116] Ewald, *ibid*, p. 224.

[117] Ewald, *ibid*, p. 225.

[118] Ewald to LJS, 2 November 1843, in *JI* 1843, pp. 24-25. Ewald, *ibid, p.* 225.

[119] Alexander to Sir Robert Inglis, 21 December 1843, pp. 187-9, Lambeth .

[120] Young to Aberdeen, 2 January 1844, FO 78/581 (p. 17).

[121] Young to Aberdeen, 2 January 1844, FO 78/581 (p. 17).

assistance of Bunsen.[122] Bunsen had stated that Nicolayson's presence in Constantinople to assist Canning was imperative. In fact the Prussian Ambassador, Count Koenigsmark and his successor M. Le Coq, were both instructed by Berlin to support Canning in this quest.[123]

En route to Constantinople Nicolayson was requested to visit Rose and the Prussian Consul-General von Wildenbruch in Beirut (which he failed to do) and that in Constantinople he was to 'use every means according with his instructions to obtain this object, which is so essential to the completion of the Church.'[124] But, wrote Ayerst, the secretary of the LJS, despite all this Prussian assistance, 'you will do as far as may be to attend to British interests in arranging with the authorities. The more the English form and appearance our church and establishment & arrangements can wear the better.'[125]

A memorandum, from Bunsen and the LJS, was sent to Nicolayson at Constantinople, requiring him to urge Ambassador Canning 'to obtain the Firman' and to assist him in refuting the 'allegations contained in the hostile petition got up at Jerusalem & sent up to Constantinople.' The two allegations sent to Constantinople in a petition from the Muslim and Turkish authorities were that the purchase of the LJS property was illegal and invalid, and also that there was no precedent for giving a *firman* to build a new church where there had not been an old one previously.[126]

In view of such accusations, Nicolayson, who purchased the property in 1838 during the Egyptian period was the best able to answer the first accusation. As pertaining to the second accusation, the argument they intended to use was that there had been a church on that property, albeit a Jacobite one. They were unsure, however, if this argument would succeed.

Realising that the chances of being granted permission to build a church were very negligible, a new plan had begun to crystallise in late 1843. Young explains this move in a dispatch to Aberdeen:

> Some time back, when Mr. Johns was the Society's Architect here, I found him one morning, measuring one of my terraces, and drawing lines, in such a direction as would pass through nearly a third of my house, taking off two upper and three lower rooms. On my enquiring of him the object of

---

[122] Ayerst to Nicolayson, in *Letters London to Nicolayson, 1843-1856*, 15 December 1843, No 46, Schick Library.

[123] *ibid.*

[124] *ibid.*

[125] *ibid.*

[126] Memo to Nicolayson, in letter from Ayerst to Nicolayson, *ibid.*

his admeasurements, he replied, that in order to render the Society's Premises complete they would require of me a part of my Dwelling ...

In October last, I receive a Letter from a friend in England stating to me as a warning that "They (the Society) have it in view to connect "the Society's property with your new "house"; and suppose that this will be "putting the Church under Consular protection.'[127]

So, Ayerst continued:

The ground taken by Lord Ab, & adopted by Prussia, to have a Firman for building a Church for the Consul, or for the Consuls, of Gt. Brit & Prussia. The proposal to be made to the Porte will state: That the Church is no ostentatious building and will not have a prominent object but be contained within a square formed of dwellings - & school houses, enclosing the Church from all sides. The plan of Mr. Habershon has been drawn upon this principle.'[128]

Even so there was uncertainty that the Turks would accept this proposal, and if in fact they would require the consul or consuls to live in the premises attached to the church. The Prussians were actually prepared to fund the building of a house for their consul, while the British Government was not prepared to do the same for their consul. Ayerst stated, though, that from the LJS and British perspective 'it may also seem desirable that the house of the Prussian Consul should not form part of that square but rather be built behind the Church near the Bishop's house or the Hospices.'

'The most desirable', Ayerst added, would be that the Consular residence 'will be near the Church.' He then concluded 'that a room or two in one of the houses forming the square be appointed for the Office (not residence) of the Consular Agents, to demonstrate the official nature of the Church in the eyes of the Turks.'[129] As noble and helpful a gesture as the Prussian offer was, it was potentially harmful to purely LJS and British interests. If the Prussians funded the building of a consulate on LJS property, it could seriously complicate ownership issues later on.

Nicolayson and Canning really were encountering numerous difficulties. But, further confusion was added when Ayerst wrote again soon afterwards, relaying the decisions of a meeting of the LJS General Committee, on 26 December 1843. The Committee stated that it would be

[127] Young to Aberdeen, 30 May 1844, FO 78/581 (No 12).
[128] Ayerst to Nicolayson, 15 December 1843, *ibid.*
[129] Ayerst to Nicolayson, 15 December 1843, *ibid.*

preferable to obtain permission for the church as a mission church rather than as a consular church, and concluded, that if possible 'let it be connected with the Bishop's residence.'[130]

Despite the high profile nature of the issue at stake, Rose was not happy that Nicolayson had journeyed to Constantinople without having informed Young, violating an agreement they had previously made.[131] He was also not happy with Alexander, the head of the work in Jerusalem.

But this was not the only issue Rose was upset with Alexander about. Despite assurances in February, Alexander still seemed determined to challenge Consul-General Rose on numerous issues. Tarkover, with Alexander's consent, had requested a British passport, a request summarily dismissed by Rose as Tarkover was not a British subject. Alexander had written to Rose and stated that because Tarkover was ordained he must be a subject of the British Crown as he swears allegiance to the Queen. Alexander had in fact, so he informed Rose, written to the Archbishop of Canterbury on this point. It was in one sense a good case Alexander was presenting.

Rose quickly rejected the idea in his letter to Aberdeen where he stated that Alexander was making a mistake and giving a wrong impression by making Tarkover a priest. Rose informed the foreign minister that, if conversion to Protestantism makes a person British, then 'if it were known that the fact of a foreigner becoming a British clergyman rendered him a British subject, I really believe, My Lord, that nearly the whole Druse people and a great many Maronites and Syrian Christians would eagerly profess conversion to Protestantism and become Ministers of their new creed.'[132]

Again the young bishop experienced the ambiguities of living and ministering in the East. It seemed that nearly everything he did carried with it a potential offense or ramification to one party or group or another.

Ending the year on a Positive Note

On 21 October Alexander addressed his second annual letter, in which he stated:

> I feel daily more convinced that the establishment of a Protestant Bishopric in Jerusalem is the work of God; and as such we cannot be surprised at the opposition, experienced during the past year. No

---

[130] Ayerst to Nicolayson, 4 January 1844, *ibid*, No 47, Schick Library.
[131] Rose to Aberdeen, 26 December 1843, FO 78/537 (No 77).
[132] Rose to Aberdeen, 26 December 1843, FO 78/537 (No 77).

Divine work has ever prospered without opposition, it is in the very nature of things, it being opposed to all works of darkness; but nothing has occurred in the slightest degree to shake its foundations.

The suspension of the building of the church could, under all the circumstances, be scarcely avoided, but in all other respects no interruption has taken place in the usual work of the Mission ...[133]

His sentiments that no interruption had taken place in the usual work of the mission may be open to question, for it seemed that there had in fact been considerable interference with the work in the course of the year. But this was the ever optimistic side of Alexander revealing itself – and besides, it was what the LJS and the German constituency wanted to hear.

Perhaps Alexander's final correspondence for the year was in a letter sent to Sir Richard Steele on 29 December. In it he alluded to the somewhat colder and wetter winter than usual, adding 'and as we have but very inadequate means of keeping either our persons or our rooms, warm, it is really, especially to Europeans, quite trying to endure such weather, which is so unusual in this Climate, many have suffered and still suffer from fevers.'

Alexander also mentioned how Christmas Day was quite gloomy due to the death of Robert Bateson, son of Sir R. Bateson of Londonderry, who had died quite suddenly the evening before. But on a more positive note, he added:

The same day, interesting everywhere to Christians, but particularly so in Jerusalem, was also marked by six Israelites being joined to our Church by Baptism,[134] and by our having met for the first time in a new place of worship[135] which we have been obliged to fit up, as our former Church (an upper chamber) gave way after the late rains and is no longer safe for meeting in it. Our present one is much larger and more commodious, and if the Sultan should still persist in not granting a firman for the building of a new church, I shall be gratified if we are only allowed to go on as we are ... Amongst the Jews there is a decided movement and notwithstanding the peculiar difficulties and obstacles in their way. Individuals and families break through the shackles of rabbinism, and join themselves to our Church, and it is a really strikingly interesting fact that a very decent

---

[133] *Jewish Intelligence [JI]*, 1844, pp. 2-3.
[134] Dr. Anton and Mrs. Marie Kiel and their daughter, Sophia; Mr. Max Ungar; Mr. Judah Levi and Miss Christina Ducat. In all some fifteen Jewish people had been baptised during the year.
[135] The present day Alexander lounge at Christ Church Centre.

respectable Congregation of Protestant Christians now meet for divine worship on Mount Zion, composed chiefly of Christian Israelites. On Xmas (sic) Day we had 33 Communicants. This is surely a sign in addition to many others, that the 'set time is come.' May we all be found amongst God's servants, who take pleasure in the stones of Zion and favour the dust thereof.[136]

The renovation of the new worship building caused work on the new hospital to be delayed, a matter which Dr. Macgowan summed up quite philosophically: 'Interruptions of this nature are constantly occurring.'[137] Nevertheless Macgowan was compensated with the arrival of an assistant, Mr. Manning, who was to be the steward of the dispensary in the new hospital, plus 'a respectable Englishwoman as matron, or head-nurse.'[138]

Another new arrival at the end of the year was Rev. William Douglas Veitch, who was replacing Williams as the Head of the Hebrew College and chaplain for the bishop.

Perhaps now with a chaplain closer theologically to his own position, and with Nicolayson and the ambassadors sure to obtain permission for the continuance of the church, things augured well for Alexander in the coming year.

In fact Alexander seemed optimistic about many things for the coming year, even for a further development in his relationship with the other Churches, except with the Roman Catholics. He wrote also to Steele:

I am also on very friendly terms with the Authorities of the Greek Church, and also of the Armenian, the two principal Bodies of Christians in Jerusalem. I have only this day had a visit from the Greek Bishop ... with several of his clergy, and I feel were no one would venture to raise his voice in England on this score if the facts were generally known. The Armenian Patriarch is quite like a father to my family, and so far my children being obnoxious to the eastern clergy, as has been publicly said in England, the case is quite the reverse and it is the opinion of all rightminded persons here, that the fact of the Anglican Bishop having a family is one of the most important facts in their Appointment as it is a testimony against the error, which satan has succeeded in introducing among the eastern Churches and the Church of Rome. The celibacy of the

---

[136] Alexander to Sir Robert Steele, 29 December 1843, St. Anthony's; and Bishop Alexander to LJS London, 3 January 1844, in *JI*, 1844, p. 77. This building is the present ground floor of Alexander Building.
[137] Macgowan to LJS London, 2 January 1844, *JI*, 1844, p. 79.
[138] Macgowan to LJS London, 1 December 1843, *JI*, 1844, p. 46.

clergy. I cannot but hope and believe, that our steady course here, will have a most beneficial effect upon the Churches in the east, who certainly in many respects are in a very interesting state, but are much exposed to the dangers of Popery, which is working amongst them mightily by the political and ecclesiastical agents of the Papacy.[139]

These concluding comments reveal the tensions and obstacles under which Alexander had to operate. It seemed there was a political agenda or problem attached to every issue. Those political agents he referred to included the 'agents' of the French Consulate. Alexander also mentioned to Steele the problems caused recently by the French Consul about the raising of the flag and how, despite a cordial relationship with the French Consul personally, the event had raised the standing of the British in the eyes of the locals.[140]

The big question for the upcoming year would be – could Britain's standing with the local population, especially the Muslims, finally lead to a granting of the *firman* to build a Protestant church in Jerusalem?

---

[139] Alexander to Sir Robert Steele, 29 December 1843, (f.85), Alexander Papers, MSS 3393, Lambeth.

[140] Alexander to Sir Robert Steele, *ibid,* Lambeth.

Chapter 12

The *Kingdom* Expands: 1844

Young's Pragmatic Observations

Of all the colourful characters forming the Jerusalem Protestant community perhaps Consul Young was the most pragmatic. And Young had some serious difficulties with Bishop Alexander, who he often saw as having a narrow perspective. This narrow perspective of Alexander and many of the Protestants at times ran contrary to the official policy of the British Government, which Young was attempting to uphold.

In his communiqués to the Foreign Office Young has left us with a record that places Alexander and his 'mission' in a larger context. On 8 January 1844 Young wrote to Sir Stratford Canning, British ambassador at Constantinople, about the various groups of people and communities in Jerusalem, and provides below his analysis of the Protestant community, which was mostly, but not exclusively, British:

> But Your excellency is no doubt aware that there is another party, which is looking to Jerusalem and Palestine as the great Theatre on which the fulfillment of Prophecy is speedily to be accomplished respecting the Jews.
>
> After a residence here of 5 years, I am induced to come to the conclusion, that to attempt to shape a course in order to meet the views of a popular reading of Prophecy it is necessary to cast plain and obvious duties and sound reason overboard.
>
> If the student of Prophecy would regard the actual condition of these Countries in a calm and practical point of view, endeavouring to respect the privileges and prejudices of them equally with his own, I think he would feel the desirableness of studying the real position and wants of their present Inhabitants before he indulges in Speculative Theories regarding a superhuman view of the future, which, if ever to be accomplished, he is perhaps more likely to retard than hasten by his premature zeal.
>
> Much jealousy is likely to be excited against us in the minds of both Latin and Greek by the publication of so many speculative opinions on this

Subject, nor is it unlikely to bring the Jews, whom they desire to serve, into danger and increased contempt amongst all classes of natives.[1]

It is clear from Alexander's own writings, and the LJS's comments upon these, that the fulfillment of biblical prophecy was an important component of the LJS's mission in Jerusalem.[2] There were obviously others, visitors primarily, who were more extreme in their prophetic viewpoints than the LJS staff.

Alexander's Second Anniversary letter

Despite being written during 1843, Alexander's second anniversary letter was published at the beginning of the 1844 edition of the *Jewish Intelligence*. In this anniversary letter he mentions the 'extraordinary attention' that his previous letter had received in Prussia.

Alexander explained the need for such a letter, in order 'to afford you from time to time authentic information respecting this place, which of late has become almost universally the object of attention ...'[3] This indeed was the case, although it was often his activities that were a cause for the other European powers, as well as the Turks and local Muslims, giving more attention to the affairs of Jerusalem.

Consul Young shares Alexander's sentiment in a communiqué to Aberdeen on 20 January 1844, in which he wrote about agents of the French and Russian Governments operating in Jerusalem.[4] He also stated to Ambassador Canning in January 1844:

> Jerusalem is now become a central point of interest to France and Russia because both Governments have adopted, according to their respective creeds, the Character of Protectors of the native Christians ...[5]

This observation concerning the opposition of France to the Protestant endeavour was also made by one of Britain's most seasoned politicians, Sir George Rose, former British Ambassador at Berlin, Member of Parliament from 1818 and father of the British consul-general in Beirut. Rose observed within the context of the problems facing this endeavour:

---

[1] Young to Canning, 8 January 1844, FO 78/581 (No 1).
[2] See for example the Bishop's circular letter of 1842 (chapter 10) and the LJS editorial in response to it, see page 149 of chapter 11.
[3] Alexander, *Second Annual Letter*, in *JI*, 1844, p. 1.
[4] Young to Aberdeen, 20 January 1844, FO 78/581 (No 2).
[5] Young to Canning, 8 January 1844, FO 78/581 (No 1).

... we have had to meet there difficulties arising out of the subtleties of our adversaries, and the emissaries of the Church of Rome – who, I know, had concerted their plans in Paris, where the utmost alarm at our enterprise prevailed.[6]

Alexander continued firm in his belief about the viability of the Protestant bishopric, despite the opposition. He stated:

I feel daily more convinced that the establishment of a Protestant Bishopric in Jerusalem is the work of God; and as such we cannot be surprised at the opposition experienced during the past year. No Divine work has ever prospered without opposition, it is the very nature of things ...

Concerning the spiritual affairs of the mission, he added:

The testimony of God to the simplicity of the truth as it is in Jesus, is borne on Mount Zion, in its true, scriptural, and ecclesiastical form ... A Mission in compliance with the Divine command, that "Repentance and remission of sins should be preached among all nations, beginning at Jerusalem," is maintained among the numerous Jews ... The attendance at the daily morning Hebrew service, of converts and inquirers, is truly encouraging. At the monthly celebration of the Lord's Supper, there are not unfrequently upwards of twenty Hebrew communicants, who, together with their Gentile brethren, partake of that blessed ordinance; thus testifying on the hill of Zion, that through him, who, in this very place, broke down the partition wall, having abolished in his flesh the enmity, that he might reconcile both (Jews and gentiles) unto God – "both have now access by one Spirit unto the Father."[7]

Alexander here emphasizes his goal of working to create a new community of believing Jews and gentiles in Jerusalem, a new and revolutionary concept never previously seen in the Holy City.

Summarizing the state of the community, Alexander continued:

We have, indeed, had much to try us in the way of sickness, but on the whole, considering that we were totally unaccustomed to such a climate, the remarkable preservation of all the members of the Mission far exceeds our sanguine expectations.[8]

---

[6] Speech of Sir George Rose at LJS AGM, 1844, quoted in *JI*, 1844, p. 169.
[7] *Second Annual Letter from the Anglican Bishop of Jerusalem*, in *JI*, 1844, p. 3.
[8] *ibid*, p. 2.

Shortly afterwards though the community encountered a deep shock.

Sudden Death of Mary Ann Ewald

The small community was blessed on 20 December by a new baby, born to the Ewald family. Mary Ann Ewald unfortunately then became quite ill, but was nursed back to health by Macgowan and the faithful women of the community. Shortly afterwards Alexander himself again succumbed to illness, and was confined to his house for two weeks.

During this period Mrs. Ewald suffered a relapse and died on 16 January, leaving behind a distraught husband and three young children, including the newborn. Alexander wrote:

> I need scarcely say what a sympathizing sensation this caused in our little community. It was truly a time of trial, to which other circumstances added. Both Mr. Veitch and myself were at the same time confined to our beds, the former with a severe attack of sciatica ... I had an attack of influenza, and poor Mr. Ewald was obliged to read the funeral service himself.[9]

Mrs. Ewald was buried in the newly consecrated burial place situated close to the Mamilla Pool, the service being conducted by the unfortunate grieving Mr. Ewald.[10] But in Jerusalem even such a simple matter of having a funeral would engender complications.

As he was about to accompany the other Protestant residents for the funeral service, Young received a note from the new governor, Haida Pasha, 'requesting that I would find another spot for the internment of our dead, complaining that our present Burial Ground was too near to that of the Moslems.'[11]

Young, alarmed by this act, sent the pasha a note in response, and then decided to proceed with the funeral. And in order to ensure there would be no interruption from the Turks and Muslims, he donned his full uniform – thereby turning the event into an official British function. The message was plain for the pasha to see – and there was no further action that day.

It seemed that in life and in death whatever the British did, was bound to upset one party or another.

---

[9] Alexander to LJS London, 3 February 1844, *JI*, 1844, p. 116.
[10] Ewald, *ibid*, p. 234. The bodies in this small British cemetery were later transferred to Mount Zion where the Bishop Gobat School was built in the 1850's.
[11] Young to Aberdeen, January 1844, FO 78/581.

Journey to the Galilee
In February, following the bishop's recovery from ill health, the Alexanders, accompanied by Macgowan and his son (on sick leave from his base in Aden) journeyed north. On the second night they pitched their tent between Ramle and Haifa. Mrs. Alexander wrote in her diary: 'I was truly thankful to see how much my dear husband seemed to enjoy his ride and evidently looked forward with pleasure to our proposed journey.'[12]

That night Dr. Macgowan and his son visited the Alexanders in their tent and they conversed on numerous subjects, especially 'on the future prospects of the Jewish Nation.' They obviously dealt quite thoroughly with the subject as Mrs. Alexander commented about: 'The absurdity of persons saying there was not sufficient space for them to dwell.'[13]

En route to Haifa the party enjoyed the beautiful landscape, scarred though on one occasion, as Mrs. Alexander records:

… we passed on to a large village but now in ruins, the Mosque only having been left untouched. About 3 months since the Natives of Nables came down in a body upon the inhabitants of Cahoun and burnt and pulled down every house, the inhabitants having fled to the neighbouring villages where they are now scattered.[14]

Due to inclement weather their plans changed in Haifa, but their hosts at the Carmelite monastery on Mount Carmel compensated nicely. Alexander wrote that this fine convent 'is unrivalled for the beauty of its location' and 'is quite like an European Royal hotel; and the monks who were most kind and attentive, entertained us very hospitably.'[15]

The party proceeded to Acre, where they located a suitable house to sleep in. 'The house' wrote Mrs. Alexander 'had been much impaired by the Late War [16]... was all newly built.'[17]

The following day they continued to Nazareth. Of the city where Jesus grew up Alexander wrote: 'The situation of Nazareth is most striking and affecting to the Christian.' Next they continued on to Tiberias. Alexander

---

[12] Mrs. D. Alexander, *Diary of a Journey to Mount Carmel,* MSS 3396, p. 4, Alexander Papers, Lambeth.
[13] *ibid,* p. 5.
[14] *ibid,* p. 5-6.
[15] Alexander to LJS London, circa February 1844, *JI* 1844, p. 141.
[16] The War of 1840, during which the British navy shelled the city.
[17] Mrs. D. Alexander, *ibid,* p. 15.

seemed to enjoy his experience in this city and wrote positively of his visit to the hot springs and the splendid baths erected by Ibrahim Pasha.[18]

But it was the tour offered by their Jewish guide, which took in the five synagogues, which seemed to most impress Alexander. His conclusion: 'This assuredly would be a most important missionary station for the London Society, independent of Safet ... The sea at Tiberias with all its associations, was almost overwhelming to us.'[19]

At this stage there was a disagreement with Macgowan, primarily due to the son's lack of willingness to accompany the bishop and Mrs. Alexander. Alexander was clearly upset by the young Macgowan's unpleasant attitude towards himself and Mrs. Alexander. Macgowan asked the bishop 'do you command me to go? [with the bishop]' to which Alexander responded: 'No. I have never assumed such a tone towards you although I might have done so.'[20] The Macgowans journeyed to Damascus, while Alexander's party journeyed on to Safed.

The strenuous six-hour journey was interspersed with admiration of the landscape, especially around the northern shore of the Sea of Galilee, with its many Biblical associations. Mrs. Alexander recorded:

> The ride was most romantic, we had the lake with us for a long time, passed a little village called Migdal. Only one hour from Tiberias about a dozen houses in it. A great deal of rice grown here.[21]

The Alexander's arrived in Safed in the evening of 22 February. The bishop wrote:

> The young Missionary brethren, Sternschuss and Behrens, were taken by great surprise, as you may imagine, but it was soon turned into joy; and it is with pleasure I state that I was much gratified with all I heard and saw. It is impossible to describe the wretchedness of the place generally, and of their house in particular; but the brethren seemed contented, and quietly pursuing their work. [22]

The bishop's visit was such a surprise that they had nothing initially to offer their guests. But 'they soon brought us some cake & liquer' wrote

---

[18] The adopted son of Mehmet Ali, pasha of Egypt, who was governor-general of the province of Syria during the period of the Egyptian occupation.

[19] Letter Alexander, circa February 1844, *JI* 1844, p. 141.

[20] Mrs. D. Alexander, *ibid*, p. 22, Lambeth.

[21] *ibid*, p. 22.

[22] Alexander to LJS London, circa February 1844, *JI* 1844, p. 141.

Mrs. Alexander 'and after a time some very good soup and pigeons which we much enjoyed.'[23]

Sternschuss and Behrens were eager to join the party on their onward journey, and Alexander consented. They returned then to Acre, where the following day Alexander celebrated the eucharist and read the morning and evening lessons. Following this Alexander and his colleagues visited the synagogue, concerning which Sternschuss wrote: 'we found children reading the Scriptures, and examined them in the Hebrew language.'[24] Sternschuss and Behrens returned to the synagogue the following day, and Sternschuss concluded there were about thirty Jewish families residing in Acre. Mrs. Alexander meanwhile was shown around the city and even picked up part of a bomb from the explosion of 1840.

The party left Acre on 28 February and after visiting both Tyre and Sidon, arrived in Beirut on 1 March. The Alexanders stayed with Dr. Kerns, while the others were with the recently appointed LJS worker Rev. Henry Winbolt. During their stay here Alexander preached in the little mission house on two successive Sundays. Their social activities were very full. Mrs. Alexander wrote for 2 March:

> Mr. Whiting and Mr. and Mrs. Moore called to see us. Also Major von Wildenbruck invited us to dinner on Monday. Mr. and Mrs. Heald called. Col Rose sent an invitation for dinner for Tues. Dined at home at ½ past 6. Mr. Heald dined with us. Mr. and Mrs. Winbolt, Behrens and Sternschuss spent the evening with us, spent it very pleasantly, reading and prayers until they left.'[25]

The bishop's activities during this tour, especially in Beirut, were quite intense and stressful, and while in Beirut he fainted, an indication again of his frail health.

Despite this setback, Alexander saw the value of this tour of his diocese, and believed it right to do so each year. While in Beirut Macgowan returned from Damascus, and recommended that it was not the right time to open a station in that city. As it turned out Beirut would become a vibrant missionary centre, although not for the British.

---

[23] Mrs. D. Alexander, *ibid,* p. 23, Lambeth.
[24] Sternschuss to LJS, 7 March 1844, *JI,* 1844, p. 146.
[25] Mrs. D. Alexander, *ibid,* p. 33, Lambeth.

Relations towards the American Mission

From the beginning there was generally a positive working relationship between the LJS missionaries and the Americans. With the establishment of the Protestant Bishopric this relationship slowly changed, and began to sour, prompting the Americans to seriously considered relinquishing their Jerusalem station.   Then in 1844 Rufus Anderson, representing the American Board, visited the region and enacted this decision.[26]

Concerning this move Lipman concluded:

> The change in the 1840's from the close collaboration and unity of feeling between British and American missionaries in the Holy Land clearly dates from the establishment of the Anglican Bishopric and the arrival of a different type of British clergyman, more concerned with the specific traditions of the Church of England. George Williams, for instance, thought it unfortunate that the first representative of the English Church in Jerusalem had been the Danish Lutheran John Nicolayson.[27]

Rev. George Williams may have indeed been the main British clergyman holding this attitude. He himself wrote concerning Nicolayson:

> It was not to be expected ... that he should faithfully represent the distinctive nature of the Anglican doctrine. It was moreover very natural ... that the Lutheran minister and Congregational missionaries should meet together on a common footing.[28]

An American visitor, and later long-term resident, Warden Cresson, himself somewhat of a controversial figure, wrote:

> When I arrived in Jerusalem in 1844, the missionaries of the Church of England and those of the American Presbyterian Church had quarreled and left Jerusalem, owing to the former calling the latter "Unauthorized Teachers and Schoolmasters", and the latter moved to Beyrout and left the American mission establishment entirely empty, which I occupied.'[29]

---

[26] James. A. Field, *America and the Mediterranean World 1776-1882,* (Princeton, NJ: Princeton Univ. Press, 1969), p. 204.

[27] V.D. Lipman, *Americans and the Holy Land: Through British Eyes,* (Hebrew University, Jerusalem & London, 1989), p. 84.

[28] G. Williams, *Holy City,* (1849), pp. 579-80.

[29] Warden Cresson, *Key of David,* (Philadelphia, 1852), p. 201.

There does not seem to be much evidence that Alexander himself was overly anti-American or opposed to the non-episcopal nature of the American Board. However, it was likely that due to the nature of his position he did give priority to those coming from Britain and Germany and who were fully submitted to the bishopric. Whatever the reasons, the removal of the American mission out of Jerusalem to Beirut provided the Americans with a more suitable base for their operations.

The overly religious and ecclesiastical nature of Jerusalem determined how the Americans would fare as opposed to the episcopally based Anglicans. For all of its faults, the British and bishopric ventures were more assured of acceptance amongst the locals, who were familiar with the episcopal form of church government, while they were nor so familiar with the non-episcopal form of the American non-Conformists. And, while the United States of America was growing then in international importance, it did not have the prestige that Britain had.

To all intents and purposes therefore when a local Arab considered accepting the Protestant message and leaving the security of his or her own *millet* (community) it would be more than likely that he or she would gravitate to the Anglican-British camp rather than to the non-Conformist American camp. Nevertheless, there is no doubt that the American mission did considerable work during its years in Jerusalem. Several years later, under the patronage of the second Anglican Bishop, Samuel Gobat, numerous Arab Christians joined the Protestant 'camp' who had previously been influenced by the Americans.

Beirut indeed offered the Americans more scope. In that city there was not the envy driven interference of the various patriarchs, bishops and church leaders, as was the case in Jerusalem. In fact, in time the Americans played a very important role in developing the educational life of Lebanon, and even of shaping a future important political movement – Arab nationalism.

Challenges in Constantinople

Throughout January, Nicolayson continued his efforts in Constantinople. Both the British and Prussian ambassadors now increased their exertions to receive an imperial *firman*. Canning had received the title deed to the LJS property and asked Nicolayson to draw a sketch from memory. He then informed Nicolayson that the Turkish officials wanted the matter deferred again, but that he, Canning, had insisted it be discussed now. This was agreed to, but Canning informed Nicolayson that a Turkish official stated that although it would go before the Council of Ministers, the *viziers,* there would be opposition and delays, especially from the President of the Council.

It was obvious that the Turkish officials were trying to draw this matter out – and eventually 'kill' it. Nicolayson in Constantinople and Alexander in Jerusalem waited patiently. Then there was a further hold-up due to a minor crisis concerning Admiral Walker, a political matter that caused concern for the Turkish authorities. Once Canning ironed that out, there was another delay.

This time it concerned a letter Alexander had written on 4 October, that was published in the *Jewish Intelligence,* 'which', Canning stated to Nicolayson 'some opponent here had brought to their knowledge.' Canning, very diplomatically, was also able to defuse this obstacle.

Then a major crisis erupted. There were two occasions where Turkish subjects were executed for religious reasons, one being a Muslim who confessed faith in Jesus. Canning had remonstrated with the Turkish government over this. Nicolayson wrote:

> The Ambassadors of course reported both these occurrences to their respective Governments, and about the 10th Inst, the British and the French Ambassadors received instructions to state explicitly and peremptorily to the Porte that unless they pledge themselves to put a stop to all persecution on account of religion their Governments must withdraw from all Alliances with them. A Note to this affect was immediately presented ... and 15 days given to deliberate on the answer ... the Turks in general are in the greatest alarm & perplexity ...'[30]

Nicolayson also stated Austria too added its concern alongside Britain and France. This really was a crisis for the Turks - the Christian European powers challenging their authority to act on affairs of religion within her own domains.

'You will easily conceive' wrote Nicolayson 'that while such a crisis is pending all matters of minor importance must be in abeyance.' Nicolayson did not believe the Turks would do anything that would prejudice its relationship to the Christian European powers 'upon whose support the continuance of the Empire depends.'[31]

Meanwhile however, Nicolayson was able to report that the plan and drawings sent from Jerusalem had given Canning 'a distinct idea of the

---

[30] Nicolayson to LJS London, 26 February 1844, No 87, in *Letters from Jerusalem to London, 1841-1844,* Schick Library.
[31] Nicolayson to LJS London, *ibid.*

need of permission to purchase more (land) as well as of the possibility of connecting it with the Consulate as implied in his instructions.'[32]

Aberdeen's assistant, John Bidwell, sent Young a message on 16 March instructing him to send a sketch of the plan of Young's present dwelling 'showing how or in what manner the Premises now belonging to the Society ... could be made to appear as part and parcel of the Consular Residence.'[33] Herein lay the maturing of an idea. Young complied on 30 May.[34]

In late March, the Turks finally made an offer, but, wrote Nicolayson 'in a form that the Ambassadors could not accept ... and therefore demanded an audience with the Sultan himself.' The sultan was obviously prepared to issue a written order to the local authorities in Jerusalem to permit the building to continue.[35] However this was insufficient, as it was not a *firman*, and therefore was not binding. Canning and Le Coq then pressed their requests again. Canning stated to Nicolayson: 'we must allow them a little breathing space first.'[36] In fact, Canning later told Nicolayson not to call on him again, but to wait until called for by Canning.

Nicolayson finally concluded that there were really only two options left, 1) to leave the matter in the hands of the ambassadors to secure a *firman* or 2) to make do with a written order (not an *Imperial firman*) to the local authorities in Jerusalem to permit the building of the church to re-commence.[37] Frustrated and disappointed, Nicolayson left Constantinople and returned to Jerusalem on 7 June.

The last official correspondence relating to this issue was contained in a dispatch sent by Canning to Aberdeen on 3 May in which 'it appeared that the consent of the Turkish Gov't to the resumption of the works would depend on the report which the Pasha of Saida had been called upon to furnish with reference to the Buildings proposed to be erected at Jerusalem for the accommodation of the British and Prussian Consulates, among which the Chapel was to be included.'[38]

The *Times* newspaper of 17 June carried an article announcing that they had received letters from Constantinople dated 27 May announcing 'that a

[32] Nicolayson to London, *ibid.*

[33] Bidwell to Young, 16 March 1844, FO 78/581 (No 2).

[34] Young to Aberdeen, 30 May 1844, FO 78/581 (No 12).

[35] See Nicolayson to London, 26 April 1844, No 91, *ibid.*

[36] Nicolayson to London, 27 March 1844, No 90, *ibid.*

[37] Nicolayson to London, 26 April 1844, No 91, *ibid.*

[38] Aberdeen to Canning, 20 March 1845, FO 78/592 (No 32). Here Aberdeen was reminding Canning of his dispatch of 3 May 1844.

firman had been at length obtained by the British Ambassador to permit the building of a Protestant Church at Jerusalem.'[39] Alas, this was a false hope. Meanwhile, plans were being considered for building an official home for Bishop Alexander adjacent to the unfinished Church.

Shortly after Nicolayson returned Mr. Alison, the Secretary of Legation at the British Embassy in Constantinople, arrived at Jaffa on 23 June. He had come to see for himself in order to give Canning a first hand report, as well as report to Young what Canning was proposing. He gave those in Jerusalem an optimistic report that upon his return to Constantinople, permission would be forthcoming.

In view of this news, the Jerusalem Local Committee requested the Committee in London to furnish a definite plan so that building could recommence once permission was granted.[40] Mr. Habershon, the architect, was in London and presented fresh plans 'as best he could devise under the circumstances in which that building was left by Mr. Johns and capable of seating 300 persons.' Those plans were accepted, but the General Committee recommended some minor modifications.[41]

Alexander was now expectant that one of the major objectives of his tenure, construction of the Protestant church, would soon be a reality.

Opening of the Book Depot.

Shortly after returning from his long trip to the north, Alexander had the pleasure of opening another pioneering institution, this time the Book Shop or Depot. This institution was located close to the bishop's house, and was headed up initially by Rabbi Judah Levi [Lyons].

The Book Shop was opened to make available the Scriptures in Hebrew, Arabic, Greek, Italian, French, German, and Spanish. It also supplied numerous other materials including Alexander McCaul's *Old Paths,* as well as Bunyan's *Pilgrim's Progress* in Hebrew. The book of Common Prayer in Hebrew, which Alexander had played a significant role in compiling, was also available.

The opening of this institution was of great importance for Jerusalem. It now permitted those Jewish people, and others for that matter, bold enough to enter, the opportunity to quietly investigate the message the

---

[39] *Times,* 17 June 1844, quoted in *JI,* 1844, p. 247.

[40] LJS Local Committee, 58th Meeting, 25 June 1844, Minute 213, *ibid.*

[41] LJS Local Committee, 63rd meeting, 30 July 1844, Minute 227, *ibid.* Mr. Johns the second architect had laid the foundations for the new church. Mr. Hillier had been the first architect but died in Jerusalem in 1840 after a stay of only one month.

missionaries were proclaiming. This was a provocation to the Jewish communal authorities, who became vigilant in hindering and stopping the curious seekers from entering this institution.

Further additions to the Protestant-Hebrew Christian community

On Good Friday, four of the Jewish believers baptised on Christmas Day were confirmed. At the Easter Sunday service two days later there were forty people receiving Communion, twenty of whom were Jewish believers in Jesus. On that same day, Judah Levi [Lyons] was baptised in the afternoon German service.[42]

These events were followed shortly after, on 6 May, with the confirmation of Judah Levi Lyons, Max Ungar, and Christina Ducat, all of whom had been adequately prepared by Ewald. [43] Then the two missionaries from Safed, Sternschuss and Behrens both ventured down to Jerusalem and on 2 June were ordained into Anglican orders.

On 13 July Alexander baptised another Hebrew Christian, Moses Epstein at the Hebrew service. Epstein was a student at the House of Industry.[44] The following day (14 July) Murray Vicars and Henry Aaron Stern were both ordained by Alexander in preparation for further work in the mission field.

Missionary journey to Nablus.

Towards the end of May, Alexander journeyed north to visit Samaria. He was accompanied by a host of companions, including the Earl of Mount Charles, Mr. Acworth from India, Rev. Mr. Wait and Rev. G. Hatchard. At Nablus they visited the Samaritan synagogue of which Alexander wrote:

> We were soon surrounded by nearly the whole community; all seemed to speak Hebrew, more or less, but they do not read it in the square character.[45]

From various comments he overheard, Alexander surmised that the Samaritans still resented the Jews. They even considered the Jewish burial ground as unclean.

One day the party was guided by a Samaritan guide to the top of Mount Gerizim. Here, Alexander wrote: 'It being Ascension-day, we read part of

---

[42] Ewald, *ibid*, p. 246.

[43] *ibid*, p. 254.

[44] *ibid*, p. 257.

[45] Alexander to LJS London, 3 June 1844, in *JI*, 1844, p. 264.

our Church Service, on the very spot where the Samaritan temple stood, and where they say it will be rebuilt.'[46] The remainder of that day was taken up by visiting the Well of Jacob, 'where our Lord conversed with the woman of Samaria, and declared the great truth, that "salvation is of the Jews."[47] This was followed by a visit to Joseph's Tomb, and then in the afternoon to Sebaste, ancient Samaria.

Alexander greatly enjoyed this trip, due to the scenery, the history and also to the company. He wrote that he would like to repeat the trip as it is only two short days ride from Jerusalem.[48]

Extension of the Diocese

The May edition of the *Jewish Intelligence* carried with it a colour *'Map of the Diocese of the Protestant Bishop of Jerusalem.'* The editorial began by stating: 'The Protestant Bishop of Jerusalem exercises spiritual jurisdiction over the most interesting countries on the face of the earth. His diocese ... extends over Syria, Chaldea, Egypt, and Abyssinia.'

The editorial continued: 'The first mentioned of these countries includes that land, once denominated, and again destined to be, the "glory of all lands"... The land of their forefathers is still sacred in the eyes of every Jew: and God seems now to be fulfilling his promise – "I will take you one of a city, and two of a family, and I will bring you to Zion."[49]

One of the next locations to be filled by the LJS as Alexander attempted to occupy his vast diocese, was Jaffa. Here a small Bible Depot was opened and manned by C. W. Hanauer.

Then on 2 September Murray Vicars, Henry Aaron Stern and Paul Sternschuss left Jerusalem for Chaldea – to open a station in Baghdad. This must have been a site to behold, as they travelled via Damascus as part of a caravan of 450 camels.

Another of Alexander's charges had now been fulfilled – although the venture in Baghdad had numerous obstacles to clear. Their initial work was hindered by the issuing of a strong *cherem* against them by the rabbis.

Further Jewish Reactions

The initiatives of the LJS were causing a considerable reaction within the Jewish community. Ewald recorded in May:

---

[46] Alexander to LJS London, 3 June 1844, in *JI*, 1844, pp. 264-5.
[47] *ibid*, p. 265.
[48] *ibid*, p. 265.
[49] *JI*, 1844, pp. 129-130.

There has been a considerable commotion among the three Jewish communities here, viz., the Sephardim, Ashkenazim and Chasidim, on account of Sir Moses Montefiore's proposal to establish a school, manufactories, and a hospital in the Holy City. Most of the chief rabbies and leaders are decidedly opposed to that generous offer.

On the 8th of May the leading members of the three congregations met together to consider these matters. A warm correspondence has been carried on between those who have most influence here, and those in Europe on that subject.[50]

In a circular letter sent to their Jewish brethren in Europe the rabbis stated: 'We, the seed of Israel, the holy nation, have nothing to do with foreign sciences, wisdoms, works, thoughts, and medicines, and such like, which would destroy our chief occupation.'[51]

The peace between the various congregations in opposition to the modernization proposed by Montefiore was short lived, and Ewald wrote in July that the German congregations were prepared to listen to reason and were putting a house in order to become some form of a hospital.[52]

Undoubtedly, it was the activities of Dr. Frankel that assisted with this undertaking. Frankel had written a letter to the major European Jewish newspaper *Allgemaine Zeitung des Judenthums,* which was printed on 4 March. Frankel stated:

It is well-known to you that the Missionary Society strains every nerve to make proselytes; they leave nothing undone. Thus they have erected a hospital in which none but Jews are to be admitted. No Jew, it is true will enter it, if he can help it: but what shall the poor, unfortunate, sick, and houseless do? Who, after all, can blame him for it? And what is the consequence? Alas! A very sad one. (During the time I have been here, ten Jews have been baptised. On the 25th instant,[53] a father, mother, and daughter.) At any time a hospital would have administered relief to the sick and suffering; now it will likewise counteract the efforts of the Mission – an object which, in my opinion, every one of our brethren should, and will keep in view.'[54]

---

[50] Ewald, *ibid*, p. 252.

[51] *ibid*, p. 257.

[52] *ibid*, p. 259.

[53] A term often used by writers of the time to designate the same month or the previous month in which they were writing.

[54] *Allgemeine Zeitung des Judenthums,* 4 March 1844, quoted in *JI* 1844, pp. 134-135.

Complications with Children

While en route to Jerusalem from Constantinople, Nicolayson visited Mr. Cohen in Smyrna. There a Jewish widow asked Nicolayson to take custody of her three children. In Jerusalem, these children were accepted into the community and placed into the custody of a Jewish believer in Jesus, Christian Hausner.

But in June 1844, a man showed up in Jerusalem claiming to be the father of these children – a man in fact the children themselves did not recognize.[55] Young informed Alexander that as these children were in fact *rayahs*, local children, and therefore not under the protection of European consuls and subject to the Capitulations, it was reasonable that they should be restored to their father.[56] Alexander in turn stated that if the man presuming to be the father is in fact the father 'the children must of course be given up to the Father who is the natural guardian.' However, Alexander stated, if this happens, the father should pay for expenses incurred by LJS in rearing these children.[57]

The situation was partly complicated in that the eldest boy, Isaac, was of age, and refused to return to the father. In fact he worked as an assistant to Rev. Douglas Veitch. The other two 'were restored to the father through the Turkish authorities.'[58] This event took place at the Seraglio, Turkish official residence, attended by Young who attested to how painful it was to see the young boy, John, resisting all effort to take him away from Christian Hausner to be given to a man he did not know. Young was actually sympathetic to the child and to the LJS.[59] The young girl, Clara, was quickly married off to a Jewish man in Hebron. Shortly afterwards Isaac also left, enticed, Veitch believed, by financial inducement.[60]

Only a few weeks later Young reported another situation concerning the two children of former Rabbi Yehuda Levi Lyons. While he was attending church Yehuda's wife absconded with the children. Young stated that the Jews supported the mother, and as they were Austrian subjects, he declined to be involved.[61] In fact, Rabbi Isaiah was also the Austrian consular agent! The mother and the two children were then induced by the

---

[55] Young devotes twelve pages to this matter in his communiqué to Aberdeen on 10 June 1844: see FO 78/581 (No 16).
[56] Young to Alexander, 1 June 1844, FO 78/581, p. 126.
[57] Alexander to Young, 1 June 1844, FO 78/581, p. 126b.
[58] Young to Aberdeen, 10 June 1844, FO 78/581 (No 16).
[59] Young to Alexander, 4 June 1844, FO 78/581, p. 127b.
[60] Letter Veitch to LJS London, 27 June 1844, in *JI*, 1844, p. 304.
[61] Young to Aberdeen, 26 June 1844, FO 78/581 (No 17).

rabbis to leave Jerusalem and go to Aleppo.[62] It so happened though that when Lyons went to Beirut to put his case before the Austrian consul-general, he was reacquainted with his wife and sons who were there also en route to Aleppo.[63] Lyons then went to Aleppo to further his claim to his children.[64]

Initially the authorities ruled in favour of the father, but then because the father was a Hebrew Christian, the authorities then ruled in favour of the mother. In what was a long drawn out affair, the Austrian consular officials persuaded the mother to return to her husband with the children, and some time later the entire family returned to Jerusalem.[65]

These two events furthered the already deep gulf separating the two distinct Jewish communities in Jerusalem – the Orthodox and Hebrew Christian.

Shortly afterwards, Ewald, the faithful co-worker of Alexander since the beginning, was forced to return to England. Since the death of his wife, Ewald had not been able to successfully combine his domestic and work responsibilities. His departure was a blow to the fledgling Hebrew Christian-Protestant community. This sad event was partly compensated by the happy occasion of the marriage between Dr. Macgowan and Miss Yarborough.

Domestic
There seemed to be one perpetual problem with Alexander and indeed with the entire family – sickness. On 25 July Mrs. Alexander wrote to Rev. John Coleman:

> Both the Bishop and myself have suffered during this month from fever of which we are but slowly recovering. The heat is intense ...[66]

Taking care of such a large family was always a burden for the Alexanders. Mrs. Alexander also confided to Coleman of another quandary for them, 'whether we should have a lady out for our dear children or send them to England.' Deborah then answers her own

---

[62] Young to Aberdeen, 26 June 1844, FO 78/581 (No 17).
[63] Letter Ewald to LJS London, 31 July 1844, in *JI*, 1844, p. 326.
[64] Nicolayson to LJS London, 2 September 1844, in *JI*, 1844, p. 364.
[65] Nicolayson to London, 2 December 1844, in *JI*, 1845, pp. 51-56.
[66] Mrs. Alexander to Rev. John Coleman, MSS 3393 (f.92), Lambeth.

question by concluding that it is best to keep them with her. She concludes that they are 'promising children.'[67]

Bishop Alexander communicated this same quandary to Sir Thomas Baring. After mentioning that they had lost the services of their good governess to Mr. Macgowan, they sorely needed another to replace her. But, he concluded 'the difficulty of obtaining such at this distance is very great.' He also stated they might 'be obliged after all to come to the painful alternative of sending our children to England.'[68]

In early June the Alexander family set out for a visit to Hebron, this time taking Rev. Veitch along with them.[69] Veitch remembers this trip for various reasons, including the killing of a large snake, measuring, so he states, a massive 'seven feet and nine inches.'[70]

The oppressive heat had a negative effect upon the Alexander family. Immediately upon their return both the bishop and Mrs. Alexander were attacked again with fever. Dr. Macgowan attended them with the lancet and other measures. Macgowan reported that: 'The symptoms were violent in both cases, and required an early and free use of the lancet; the active measures adopted were so successful, that in less than a week I had the satisfaction of seeing both of my patients convalescent.'[71]

Macgowan was more concerned with the health of the youngest Alexander daughter, Salome, and in September he wrote that she had a case of infant cholera and that for some days 'her life was in imminent peril.' He was able to report though that her life was saved but that she was in a very weakened disposition.[72]

Towards the end of the year Alexander was again confronted with worrying health problems for his family. He wrote to Rev. Coleman that he postponed his anticipated trip to Egypt 'when two of my children were attacked with a dangerous fever.' One of them some time afterwards, he wrote to Coleman was 'still in a precarious state.'[73]

Macgowan went even further and stated that Deborah and her younger sister, Annie, 'were both seized with feverish symptoms' and 'presented symptoms of high fever and delirium, and required the most active treatment.'[74]

---

[67] Mrs. Alexander to Rev John Coleman, MSS 3393 (f. 91), Lambeth.

[68] Alexander to Sir Thomas Baring, October 1844, MSS 3393 (f.95), Lambeth.

[69] Veitch to LJS London, 27 June 1844, in *JI*, 1844, p. 304.

[70] *ibid*, p. 305.

[71] Macgowan to LJS London, July 1844, in *JI*, 1844, p. 327.

[72] Macgowan to LJS London, September 1844, in *JI*, 1844, p. 403.

[73] Alexander to Rev. John Coleman, 30 December 1844, MSS 3393, Lambeth.

[74] Macgowan to London, 4 November, 1844, in *JI*, 1845, p. 22.

But there were numerous light hearted moments for the Alexander family. Daughter Deborah relates several incidents:

> Music in Jerusalem was thought much of and especially Papa's pathetic singing of the Lamentations of Jeremiah in Hebrew. People loved to see and hear Fanny with her Harp which she played well. One day a caller was announced and on his card was "Mr. Eliot Warburton." When Mama went to receive him she saw at the far end of our drawing room an elegant man in handsome Eastern dress, playing beautifully on our piano. On her appearing, he turned around and introduced himself, and said he could not resist the charm of playing in such surroundings. In his work "The Crescent and the Cross" he mentions us as "the Bishop and Bishopess and all the Bishoplings and our pretty servant maids."[75]

The bishop seemed to revel in the social activities associated with his position. He wrote of the anniversary meeting of the LJS, when he, Veitch, Ewald and a visitor Sir Cecil Bishopp, all spoke. Alexander continued: 'We almost fancied ourselves in England. The Earl Mountcharles has been here for some time … We have also had the Rev. Lord Thomas Hay and Lady Hay with us; likewise his Prussian Majesty's Consul-General from Beyrout, with his lady and family. We felt, therefore, the comfort of more enlarged church accommodation, as we can now seat nearly 150 persons.'[76]

Alexander's daughter Deborah relates a sad accompaniment to the visit of the Bishopp family:

> Among other people, I remember Rev. Sir Cecil Bishopp and his wife and baby boy. Lady Bishopp was very musical and sang well, and played well on the Harp. She was at a party one night and sang "Weep not for me" very charmingly, and scarcely had she finished when arrived a messenger from the Latin Convent where they were staying to say the baby was very ill. They left at once, but the child died, to their intense grief. He was their son and heir.[77]

The year ended on a high note domestically for the Alexander family. The Bishop wrote to Coleman in December:

---

[75] Ransom, *ibid*, p. 21.
[76] Alexander to LJS London, 4 May 1844, in *JI*, 1844, p. 231.
[77] Ransom, *ibid*, p. 23.

In the midst of all, Mrs. A was confined ... on the 18th (adding another daughter to our number) but a day or two after she was attacked with the fever which made us ... very anxious about her safety.[78]

Mrs. Alexander thankfully recovered from her fever, and on Christmas Day 1844 Emily Alexander was baptised in St. James Chapel.

Disturbed State of the Country

At that time the province of Syria was divided into *pashalicks*, under the governance of a Turkish pasha or governor. However for all intents and purposes the pasha only really ruled within the main towns – outside of these, local Arab chieftains often ruled.

'The Arabs,' Ewald wrote just prior to his departure from Jerusalem in October, 'are constantly in arms against each other.'[79] According to a report in the *Jewish Intelligence,* Sheikh Abu Ghosh murdered the pashas of Jaffa and Lydda on their way to Jerusalem.[80] The pasha of Jerusalem then went to Jaffa, which was in theory under his control. However the Turkish soldiers in Jaffa, who had not received their salaries for some time, besieged him in the Castle there until they received their dues. Then, upon his return to Jerusalem the same thing happened there as well. When the pasha did not respond positively to their request for back pay, they took over the Citadel or Castle of David (which overlooked the LJS property) and threatened to open fire on the town.

As often happened in such situations, the various Christian institutions and the Jewish people were requested to provide the money, which they collectively refused.

These incidents revealed the weakness of the Turkish administration, and consequently provoked local Arab chieftains to take advantage of this weakness and attempt to usurp control. On 18 October Alexander received information from the French consul de Lantivy 'warning them of the danger of going outside the City and recommending to have their houses well guarded at night.' The pasha had in fact informed Lantivy 'that the Sheikhs were in open revolt, that he had no troops, and that it was not unlikely he might be compelled to abandon the City and to seek refuge for himself and his people in the castle.'[81]

---

[78] Alexander to Rev. John Coleman, 30 December 1844, MSS 3397, Lambeth.
[79] Ewald to LJS London, 31 July 1844, in *JI* 1844, p. 327.
[80] *JI*, 1845, p. 4.
[81] Young to Rose, 19 October 1844, FO 78/581 (No 32).

Young consulted with Alexander and the leading British subjects, and it was collectively agreed 'that we should show little symptoms of alarm as possible but rather wait patiently and see the development of affairs.' Young then informed Rose in Beirut that a British warship stationed off Jaffa would be beneficial.[82]

Young in fact had suggested to Alexander that they all retire to the coast 'until sufficient measures are taken by the Turkish Government to render to secure the life and property of her majesty's subjects in case of popular tumult.'[83] When remembering the outburst of feeling toward the *Franks* only a year before, this advice was perhaps quite appropriate.

Alexander thanked Young for all of his endeavours and advice, but replied to the consul that: 'I sincerely trust that whilst there is evident cause of alarm He who rules and guides all the affairs of men, will overrule everything for the good of this Land and of His people.'[84]

Alexander made a similar statement to Sir Thomas Baring at this time, writing:

> The state of the country is at this moment very disturbed and it seems to me important political changes are inevitable. All things are ... working together to bring about the fulfillment of God's purposes.'

He also stated to the President of the Society that he 'laments the lack of British protection.' But such concern was soon alleviated. Rose quickly responded to Young's request, and on 29 October Captain Nugt Glascock of *HMS Tyne* was anchored off Jaffa, and sent word to Young in Jerusalem.[85] Young happily was able to respond to Captain Glascock that two battalions of Turkish troops had entered Jerusalem on 3 November, and that all now seemed well.[86]

Although it was a relief for all foreigners to see the arrival of the Turkish troops, no one was more relieved than Alexander. He had taken a gamble by not acting on Young's advice to leave for Jaffa and therefore had the welfare of his own family and the members of his community to worry about.

When those Turkish troops arrived in Jerusalem they were headed by none other that Sheikh Abu Ghosh, the leader of the bandits on the road to

---

[82] Young to Rose, 19 October 1844, FO 78/581 (No 32).

[83] Young to Aberdeen, 23 October 1844, FO 78/581 (No 37).

[84] Alexander to Young, 22 October 1844, FO 78/581 (p. 229).

[85] Captain Glascock to Young, 29 October 1844, FO 78/581 (No 32).

[86] Young to Captain Glascock, 4 November 1844, FO 78/581 (p. 257).

Jaffa! This provided little comfort to many of the citizens, and it was reported that one Karaite Jewish man was murdered and his head severed from his body, while his wife was savagely beaten, to the point where her life was endangered.[87]

The security in Jerusalem was still somewhat precarious – but the dispatch of the British warship was a clear sign to any would-be troublemakers to be wary of harming British subjects. How accurate were the forecasts of the LJS pioneer missionaries, Lewis, Dalton and Nicolayson, who saw in the early to mid 1820's the need of a British Consul in Jerusalem.

Opening of the Hospital

The 12 December 1844 was a momentous day in the history of the LJS, for on that day the first *modern* hospital was officially opened in Jerusalem. Although the success of this venture is rightfully attributed to Dr. Macgowan, a fair degree of credit must also be given to Alexander. This was one of the important issues in his initial instructions. He encouraged and supported the medical work fully during his almost three years in the Holy City.

Nicolayson recorded that there was opposition to its opening by some Sephardic rabbis. He also stated that in their efforts to oppose the hospital, the Ashkenazim opened a 'hospital' of their own, through the efforts of Rabbi Isaiah Bak and generosity of Sir Moses Montefiore.   But, Nicolayson wrote: 'The order and comfort of ours is so much superior, and the confidence felt in Dr. Macgowan's experienced skill so much more influential, that it is quite full already.'[88]

Macgowan himself wrote of the hospital:

> To have provided a place of refuge for the sick and suffering Israelite in the city of his fathers, has been the distinguished honour and privilege granted to the London Society, and which next to the erection of a Christian Church on Mount Zion, seems to have been uppermost in the thoughts and wishes of a large portion of the Lord's people.[89]

Macgowan also alludes to the death of an aged Jewish lady in the hospital on 31 December. The rabbis had threatened not to bury her body in order to offer an example against any Jewish people using the hospital.

---

[87] *JI*, 1843, pp. 4-5.

[88] Nicolayson to LJS London, 31 December, 1844, in *JI*, 1845, p. 89.

[89] Macgowan to LJS London, 4 January 1845, in *JI*, 1845, p. 90.

Thankfully, Macgowan was able to relate, there were enough Jewish people who spoke well of him, that this threat was not put into effect.

Opening of station at Hebron
Bishop Alexander seemingly had boundless energy and vision – despite his frequent ill-health. No sooner had one crisis passed or project been established, than he entered into another scheme. Young reported in private to Colonel Rose on 17 December 1844 that Dr. Veitch and a Mr. Keavus had departed that day for Hebron to determine its suitability for establishing a missionary station. They had requested a letter from Young to present to the Governor of Hebron, but Young politely declined 'because,' he wrote 'I could not make myself a party to a measure, the success or failure of which, did not directly affect my office.'[90]

Young had stated in his letter some caution towards the enterprise:

> I pointed out to Mr. Vietch the violent and fanatical character of the people of Hebron, and also the danger of opposition from the Jerusalem Jews, who would probably influence their brethren at Hebron to view Mr. Keavus' closeness with our movements with suspicion, added to this I thought the closeness with which our movements generally are watched here by Foreign Agents, was another cause for caution in extending the Society's efforts in this neighbourhood at the present juncture, when the question of the Church is still a subject of Sir. Stratford Canning's solicitude at Constantinople.[91]

Young was able to report to Aberdeen, on 20 December, quite thankfully, that both Veitch and Keavus had returned from Hebron, and that the venture had been abandoned.

French Reactions to Anglicans Initiatives
Young's comment, 'I thought the closeness with which our movements generally are watched here by Foreign Agents, was another cause for caution in extending the Society's efforts in this neighbourhood at the present juncture' sums up his perspective of the happenings in this region.

The British in particular were concerned with French ambitions in the region, and the Peel/Aberdeen administration was inclined to avoid any possible conflict with France.

---

[90] Young to Rose, 17 December 1844, FO 78/625.
[91] Young to Rose, 17 December 1844, FO 78/625.

But the French were also very concerned with British ambitions. The French consul, de Lantivy, Alexander's neighbour, had for a year now closely kept an eye on British-Anglican activities. Through correspondence to Baron James Rothschild and to his foreign minister in Paris, he proposed to counter this British activity through increased French cultural activity – and of even offering more consular support to the Jewish people.

Tudor Parfitt brilliantly sums up the French concerns:

> The fear that many Frenchmen had of British ambitions in the Middle East can be seen from a passage from the writings of a French historian of the period.
>
>> L'Angleterre, ce terrible vautour du monde politique s'est abattue sur le Liban, aux bords du Nil de la mer rouge et de l'Ocean indien; la civilization pour elle, c'est l'exploitation de l'univers a son profit.[92]
>
> The time was ripe, thought de Lantivy, to extend the scope of French influence and to increase the scale of French cultural activity.[93]

In a long communication to the French foreign minister, de Lantivy summarized Anglican activity, highlighting that they 'had a doctor, architect and chemist working for them as well as a well-equipped hospital.'[94]

And in order to highlight that this was a British initiative, including both Anglicans and Jewish endeavours, he also included the present initiatives of Sir Moses Montefiore. He concluded that the French had to increase their influence in order 'contrebalancer les influences rivales des Anglicans et des Russo-Grecs.'[95]

Young wanted to ensure there was no cause of major conflict with the French over issues developing in the area under his jurisdiction. His

---

[92] 'England, this terrible eagle of world politics, has beaten on Lebanon, from the borders of the Red Sea at the Nile, and the Indian Ocean; its civilization is the exploitation of the universe for its profit.' M. Poujoulat, *Histoire de Jerusalem* (Paris, 1848), ii, p. 486, quoted in T. Parfitt, *The Jews in Palestine 1800-1882,* (Suffolk, England, The Boydell Press, 1987), p. 144.

[93] Parfitt, *ibid,* p. 143.

[94] Parfitt, *ibid,* p. 144.

[95] '…to counter balance the influence of their rivals, the Anglicans and the Russo-Greeks.' From A.E., Dir. Pol. 75 (188), de Lantivy to Minister, Jerusalem, 28 July 1844, quoted in Parfitt, *ibid,* p. 144.

caution often brought him into conflict with Bishop Alexander. Young had in view the 'bigger geo-political' picture, and he critiqued each of Alexander's moves as to how it affected Britain's relationship with Turkey and the other European powers. All of these entities looked at each of Alexander's initiatives as being endorsed by the British Government.

On the other hand Alexander was largely motivated by religious concerns. His primary motivation was to extend the Kingdom of God - to present the message of the King and Kingdom wherever Jewish people lived. In the coming year Alexander anticipated expanding his work even more.

Chapter 13

Death at the Moment of Victory: 1845

Alexander's Optimism

Alexander's annual circular letter written to commemorate his entry into Jerusalem, was full of his usual optimism. He mentioned how 'the enemy has ventured at a distance to insinuate the complete failure of the Jerusalem Anglican Episcopate,' but, he contended 'we who are on the spot and have the best means of judging, are strongly convinced of the contrary.'

The bishop reiterated that his main objective for being in Jerusalem was to be connected with 'that people who are still beloved for their fathers' sake, who are to obtain mercy through the mercy of the Gentile Churches (Romans xi), and who are destined again "To blossom and bud and fill the face of the world with fruit." (Isaiah xxvii.6)'[1]

In a letter to Sir Thomas Baring in late January, Alexander provided further details about the progress and state of the Mission's activities:

> We now have quite a respectable congregation on the Lord's Day, comprised chiefly of Israelites and when on the 21st January ... we had a Sacrament after the early morning Hebrew service, we had no less than 36 communicants! At our usual monthly Communions we have generally between 40 and 50. It is indeed to us no small privilege thus to be permitted to worship the God of our Forefathers on Mount Zion, and, to friends of Jerusalem generally it can be no less encouraging that through their instrumentality a Church has been established in the City of the Great King in which the Truth is exemplified to the Church at large, that through it both (Jews and Gentiles) have access by one Spirit unto the Father; an important and interesting work has been commenced here, which the friends of pure Scriptural Truth in general, and the friends of Zion and Israel in particular, ought to countenance and support by every means. Our enemies are numerous and various and also Powerful. I cannot but mention

---

[1] *Third Annual Letter from the Anglican Bishop in Jerusalem*, in *JI*, 1845, p. 1

that in a paper which the Jews (I ought to say the Rabbis, for the people are differently minded) have lately printed for general circulation among their Brethren throughout Europe they actually call upon their European Brothers' who have influence with the Governments to use every effort to get us removed.[2]

Opposition to the Hospital
It wasn't long before renewed efforts were being made to get rid of the Anglicans. On 19 January Dr. Macgowan informed the leading Sephardi rabbi, Abraham Chaim Gaguine, that one of his patients was seriously ill in the hospital. The same day the servant of this rabbi called and picked up the property belonging to the patient, which included a handkerchief holding money.[3]

The patient died on 21 January, and when informed, the senior rabbis refused him a Jewish burial. These leading rabbis then sent a note to Dr. Macgowan, stating 'that unless I shall promise to dismiss all the Hebrew servants from the hospital, and like-wise the patients who are actually in the hospital, and moreover unless I shall engage not to receive any more Jews into the hospital in the future, that they the Rabbis will not allow the interment of the patient who died this morning in the hospital.'[4]

Macgowan and Nicolayson then asked Young for his assistance. Young advised them that he had no authority to act in this matter, but he did act as a channel for communication. As no steps had been taken by the leading rabbis for burial by the next day, Macgowan informed Young that after proper preparation according to Jewish customs, the body was interred in the British burial ground near the upper or Mamilla pool.[5]

Within a few days both the Sephardi and Ashkenazi rabbis had issued very severe *cherems* or excommunication bans against any Jewish people using the English Hospital, and the patients were induced to leave. The rabbis then issued statements that were dispatched to Europe, casting a very negative light on the activities of Alexander's mission. This was the most severe test the small Protestant community had had to endure since the crisis with the three rabbis in 1842.

Alexander, at his philosophical best, wrote of this situation:

---

[2] Alexander to Sir Thomas Baring, January 1845, St. Anthony's.
[3] Macgowan to Young, 21 January 1845, FO 78/625.
[4] Note from Chief Rabbis to Dr. Macgowan, FO 78/625.
[5] Macgowan to Young, 22 January 1845, FO 78/625.

Our first month of the new year has been characterized by ... a mixture of joys and trials. The Lord in his wisdom knows that such is the safest state for his people, to keep them from being unduly elated, and from despondency, both alike to the Church's best welfare. In the midst of the enjoyment of restored and perfect health ... we celebrated the third anniversary of our arrival in the Holy City ...

Soon after arose upon this our joyful and hopeful horizon, the rabbinical thunderstorm ... All is sure to work for good. But I must say a few words as to what I conceive to be the immediate causes of the present opposition of the rabbies. First of all, it must be traced to the *offense of the Cross,* and the natural hatred of the human heart generally, and of the Jews in particular, against the truth as it is in Jesus ... At the same time I trace the present proceedings of the rabbies more particularly to the recent publication here of the blasphemous book חזוק אמונה[6]... [7]

In his letter to Sir Thomas Baring, Alexander also stated:

Rabbinism has begun to raise its hand against us, encouraged by a visit the Jews here have lately had from a rich member of the London Synagogue, a Mr. Samson. A strong Anathema was proclaimed during his presence here in the Synagogue against the Hospital which had been opened just before, in which a poor Jew died ... This was followed by the thunders of Excommunicating etc. The effect of which is already subsiding: since the departure of that Gentleman poor sick Jews are beginning again to enter the Hospital. To him also we cannot but ascribe the difficulties which have arisen at Safet, which place was visited by him previous to his coming here.[8]

Opposition in Safed

In his letter to Baring Alexander also complained about the lack of protection offered by the British consuls in Beirut and Jerusalem for the missionaries in Safed, (Behrens and the family of Dr. Kiel) because they were not British subjects. The bishop asked Baring to use his influence to rectify this situation, stating that it was imperative that members of a British society should receive British protection, even if they were not British subjects themselves.

In January serious problems beset the work at Safed. Behrens was seriously attacked by a deranged local, and had requested the assistance of

---

[6] *Chizzuk Emunah* (Faith Strengthened).
[7] Letter from the Bishop of Jerusalem, 4 February 1845, in *JI*, 1845, p. 107.
[8] Alexander to Sir Thomas Baring, January 1845, St. Anthony's.

the British consular agent at Acre, Mr. Finzi. Finzi turned to Young for advice. In desperation, Behrens finally withdrew from Safed and sought the personal aid of Finzi in Acre.[9]

Alexander informed Young on 8 February that Mr. J. O. Lord was being dispatched to Safed, so as not to allow the work there to discontinue, and 'to protect the Society's property there.' Lord was also to encourage the LJS workers in Acre to return to Safed.[10] Alexander felt that Lord, being a British subject, would be satisfactorily protected, but even so Young advised Alexander against sending Lord (and an accomplice Mr. A. Tymmim) to Safed.[11]

Lord had been dispatched from London to be the London Society's worker in Hebron. He had approached Young in early February for a letter of recommendation to the governor of Hebron, a request which Young politely refused. Two days later Young wrote that Lord and an Austrian, Mr. Zimim, had gone up on their own accord to establish the work in Hebron. In this they failed. Eventually Lord went to Safed.

Petition to Lord Aberdeen
Despite all the efforts of ambassadors Ponsonby and Canning, there were no breakthroughs in gaining a *firman* for building the church.

In desperation, the LJS solicited a petition. They obtained the signatures of the Archbishop of Canterbury, the Bishop of London, many other bishops, nobility and dignitaries in the church, 1400 clergy and over 14,000 other citizens. It was in many ways a unique phenomenon.

Led by Shaftesbury, the delegation presented the petition to Aberdeen on 18 March. Although primarily requesting permission to build the church, the delegation also requested the granting of official recognition to the Protestant bishop in Jerusalem, and for those professing the Protestant faith. The heart of the petition is found in these words:

> ... the Society most deeply regret, that whilst the Greeks, Roman Catholics, Armenians, and other minor sects of Christians, enjoy the permission to worship God in their respective temples, and whilst no privilege is withheld on the representations of French and Russian diplomacy, - the pure Reformed religion of the British nation, to whom, under God, Turkey is indebted for the recovery of Syria, should be alone proscribed, and her Protestant children alone denied the possession of a

---

[9] Various correspondence relating to the subject, FO 78/625.
[10] Alexander to Young, 8 February 1845, FO 78/625.
[11] Young to Alexander, 8 February 1845, FO 78/625.

consecrated building for the service of God, and especially that recognition of the Protestant faith which is indispensable to ensure protection.[12]

Aberdeen sent a copy of the petition to Ambassador Canning on 20 March, stating also the Government's eagerness to obtain permission for the Protestant church to be built. He also stated that the last reference he had on the matter was the communication on 3 May 1844 when the Turks informed Canning that the advice of the pasha of Saida (Sidon) was sought.
    Aberdeen asked Canning to follow this matter up, emphasizing:

> I have to desire that Your Excellency will now ascertain from the Turkish Government whether the report in Question has been received from Syria, & the course which in that case the Porte is prepared to take on this matter.[13]

At this point Aberdeen expresses quite clearly the importance of the submitted Memorial, stating to his ambassador at Constantinople:

> In the event of any further hesitation being shown by the Porte to grant the necessary permission for the resumption and completion of the works, Your Excellency will call the attention of the Turkish Ministers to the enclosed Memorial, and take such further measures as may appear to you best calculated for giving effect to the wishes expressed in it.
>   You will at the same time express the earnest hope of Her Majesty's Government that no further impediment may be opposed to the completion of the Buildings, and that the Porte will no longer object to grant the formal sanction of a Firman for that purpose.[14]

The matter had now been expressed forthrightly from the highest level. The public voice in Britain had forced even this less than sympathetic government to take heed of the immense interest in having a British and Protestant church in Jerusalem. There is little doubt that this move was heavily influenced by the lead taken by Shaftesbury, the leading clergy, as well as knowledge of the debt Turkey still owed to Britain from 1840.
    And such an initiative would also greatly encourage and assist the endeavours of Alexander and Nicolayson to receive the necessary

---

[12] *Presentation of a Memorial from the Society to Lord Aberdeen*, in *JI*, 1845, pp. 125-127.
[13] Aberdeen to Canning, 20 March 1845, FO 78/592 (No 32).
[14] Aberdeen to Canning, 20 March 1845, FO 78/592 (No 32).

permission, an Imperial *firman*, and then complete the building of the church.

Visit to Damascus

In mid April, the bishop, Mrs. Alexander, Fanny Alexander and Rev. Veitch, joined the British warship *HMS Warspite* in Jaffa and sailed to Beirut. From there they journeyed overland to Damascus. Alexander stated of this visit: 'I have at length been able to accomplish a long-cherished wish, and almost a feeling of duty, to visit this place …'[15]

Setting out from Beirut the party stayed one night at Morad, and the next day continued onto Damascus. The following day a severe skirmish broke out between the Maronites and Druse – at Morad! This conflict caused the British Consul, Mr. Wood, to insist upon the party remaining in Damascus a bit longer than they had anticipated, in order to ensure the return trip was safe and secure.[16]

Not only did Alexander enjoy visiting the various sites of Damascus, but he enjoyed visits by the principal Jewish people of the city, with whom he entered freely into conversation on matters of religion. With many of these he was able to give copies of the Hebrew New Testament. 'I never wish to lose sight of the missionary character' he stated, adding 'I do not leave home without taking with me some of the missionaries best weapons.'[17]

On one occasion Alexander and the party, which included Mr. Wood, as well as a Druse prince and one of the chief rabbis as guide, was able to visit a small village near to Damascus, site of a cave in which it is believed Elijah the prophet dwelt. Alexander's eagerness to do the work of evangelism is portrayed in his description of this visit:

> We found the synagogue full of Jews. One of the Chachamim[18] sat on a low stool, surrounded by a large group of hearers, to whom he was said to preach. They all immediately rose, and made us sit down before the Ark. The book which the [19]הכם had in his hand was entitled 'Words of the Covenant.' This led me to ask them whether it referred to the old or to the new Covenant? The question startled them, and at once gave me an opportunity of referring to Jeremiah xxxi.; explaining to them the nature of the new Covenant. They took out of a special Ark a very beautiful MS. of the whole of the Old Testament, which was written in the twelfth century,

---

[15] Alexander to LJS London, 6 May 1845, in *JI*, 1845, p. 260.

[16] Veitch to London, 4 June 1845, in *JI*, 1845, p. 292.

[17] Alexander to London, 6 May 1845, in *JI*, 1845, p. 260.

[18] Wise one or rabbi.

[19] *ibid.*

and is greatly prized by them. We read in the same the passage in Jeremiah, and some others connected with it; all the others listening most attentively to a long and interesting conversation carried on under such remarkable circumstances, in a Jewish synagogue, near Damascus, and which I hope has not been in vain. There were at least 200 present.[20]

A lighter side of the trip, although not perhaps very light at the time, is related to us by Fanny's younger sister Deborah:

The young Druse Chief of the Escort fell desperately in love with my dear and beautiful sister Fanny, and urgently asked Papa to give her to him in marriage, and in exchange offered Papa one of his boys!! So angry was he at being refused, that Papa was very glad to dispense with his escort.[21]

While in Damascus Alexander had a friendly visit with the Greek patriarch, who seemed assured that the object of Alexander's appointment was not to disturb them. In conclusion Alexander summarized the character of the Jewish community:

Nothing seems, humanly speaking, likely to make an impression upon the Jews here, excepting a public Hebrew service. Our Hebrew Prayer Book is quite unknown; they were quite astonished when I told them, that in Jerusalem we had every morning prayers in the Hebrew language, into which our Liturgy has been translated; a copy of which I promised to send them.[22]

The return trip was not without incident, with a large snake crawling into Fanny Alexander's tent. It was spotted and killed, then found its way into a bottle and became part of Mr. Veitch's snake collection. At Djebail, on the coast, the Bishop became very unwell, and was quite ill for several days.[23] Then Mrs. Alexander became unwell and was forced to remain an extra day in Ramleh.[24]

Installation of a Greek Orthodox Patriarch
One of the many by products of Bishop Alexander's appointment was the provocation to other sects and ecclesiastical orders. The Roman Catholic

---

[20] Alexander to London, 6 May 1845, in *JI*, 1845, p. 260.

[21] Ransom, *ibid*, p. 34.

[22] Alexander to London, 6 May 1845, in *JI*, 1845, p. 260.

[23] Veitch to London, 4 June 1845, in *JI*, 1845, pp. 331-332.

[24] *ibid*, p. 292.

Church, only a month after Alexander arrived, had issued an order to restore their patriarch to Jerusalem.

The Greek Orthodox Church was soon to follow suit. The Orthodox patriarch of Jerusalem had, for some 100 years resided in the comfort of Constantinople. However it was decided to reinstate this dignitary to the seat of Jerusalem, and on 28 March, the former bishop of Lydda, was installed as the new Orthodox patriarch of Jerusalem.

Nicolayson organized an official visit between Alexander and the new patriarch. The patriarch then invited the bishop and others of the Protestant community to participate in the installation the following day. The patriarch later commented that the Latins were the only Christian community not participating in that event.[25]

Around the same time a delegation of Greek Orthodox (from outside the country) also approached Alexander with a request to join the Anglican Church. Alexander advised them to return home, while he evaluated their case. He ultimately was not convinced that their motives were pure.[26]

Visit of Rev. Dr. Abeken

As these were the days before Cook's Tours, fewer people visited Jerusalem than in later decades, and most of those who did travel were people of means and renown. The Alexanders continued to open their house to visitors, and Michael Solomon was always on call. Of this part of his ministry Alexander's daughter Deborah wrote:

> Papa had to show hospitality extensively in Jerusalem as there were no hotels and resorts for travelers there at that time, except the Convents. Travellers in those days were of a high class. People of culture – of wealth – and many of high birth brought letters of introduction to Papa ... During the months of January, February and March our house was full of pleasant visitors. Among many may be mentioned Dr. Lepsius, the German Egyptologist, Dr. Strauss, Dr. Abeken, Under Secretary for Foreign Affairs at the Court of Berlin, Count Pourtenberg, Count von Wildenbrook, the Marquis of Sligo, Lord Eastnor, W.F. Makepeace Thackeray, Eliot Warburton, Eastlake, author of Eothen, also that marvelous man Arthur Kavanagh who, with neither arms or legs, was able to ride fearlessly.[27]

---

[25] Nicolayson to London, 1 April 1845, in *JI*, 1845, pp. 262-263.

[26] Veitch to London, 28 March, 1845, in *JI*, 1845, p. 261.

[27] Ransom, *ibid*, p. 21a.

In June a special German visitor was Rev. Dr. Hienrich Abeken.[28] Abeken had served as chaplain of the Prussian legation at Rome with Bunsen some years before, as well as assisting Bunsen in the deliberations to establish the Protestant Bishopric. He confided some of his impressions of Jerusalem to Chevalier Bunsen on 22 June. After attending a Sunday morning service at the Church of the Holy Sepulchre, Abeken then attended the Protestant service, and wrote:

> The more refreshing it was, therefore, to attend our church on Mount Zion, and find myself in a very decent church-like place, filled with an assembly of upwards of sixty persons. There I felt more than ever the blessing of Christian fellowship in worshipping, "in spirit and in truth." Truly it is no small thing to find a Protestant Church established in Jerusalem on Mount Zion.
>
> After the service I went to the Bishop, who, with his whole, in every sense of the word, amiable family, received me as an old friend. It was a meeting which could not but be touching and affecting, when we remembered how, nearly four years ago, we took leave of each other in London.[29]

Dr. Abeken in his next letter wrote a fuller account of the bishop himself, stating, rather candidly:

> I found, above all, the labourers in the vineyard rejoicing and of good cheer, undaunted and not depressed, active and persevering, and full of hope and confidence; especially the worthy Bishop himself. I feel more than ever convinced, that through the providence of God we have been permitted to find in him the proper, I might say the only proper person for this office ... You cannot imagine how difficult it is to form and keep together a congregation consisting of Germans, English, and Jews; and if all these three had not been united in the person of the Bishop, it would never have been done. As the three nations are mixed here, there has hitherto been no proper cordiality between them. It is the Bishop who feels equal love towards all of them. Daily do I discover some new admirable quality in this man, when seeing as I do with what a candid but dignified manner, with what faithfulness and perseverance, what

---

[28] Abeken, like Bunsen also married an English lady. He was in England at the time of Bunsen's visit and wrote a booklet about the Bishopric. From 1842 he began a journey to Ethiopia and Egypt with the Orientalist Carl Richard Lepsius (1810-1884). They separated in 1844 and Abeken found his way to Jerusalem.

[29] Abeken to Bunsen, 22 June 1845, in *JI*, 1845, pp. 373-4.

circumspection and discretion, and above all, with what cheerful courage, such as only genuine Christian love can inspire, he passes through all difficulties, of which there are not a few, both great and small.[30]

In his third letter to Bunsen, Abeken, concludes:

Much has been done here, but I must add, much more might have been done, if the Bishop had not been ... so limited in his means. Here I see clearly what a centre Jerusalem is for the spiritual life and being of the Orient, and how easily, from here, in all directions, towards east and west, a continual communication might be maintained with Judaism and Christianity.[31]

Deborah, the bishop's daughter, writes with affection of this dear visitor, stating: 'He was a furious rider ... He taught me to ride, and to play chess, and he used to read Shakespeare's Plays to us.' She also recalls a rather humorous incident involving Dr. Abeken while they encamped at Gifna:

On his arrival at our camp in Eastern costume, he sat down cross-legged and being of an unrestful nature, as soon as coffee was handed to him, spilt it all over his full and faultlessly white Turkish trousers. He had to beat a hasty retreat and did not emerge from Papa's tent until soap and water had repaired the breaches [sic].[32]

Another visitor was Dr. J. Aiton, who responded to accusations by the rabbis that Alexander and LJS proselytised in their institutions:

Both in the Hospital and in the House of Industry plenty of New Testaments in the Hebrew tongue are laid on the tables. But while every facility is given to the reading of the Gospels, there is nothing like compulsion, or any indication that the conversion of the inmates is the sole but disguised object of these institutions. On the contrary, everything is done, so far as the funds will admit it, for the benefit of the Jews in Palestine.'[33]

---

[30] Abeken to Bunsen, 7 July 1845, in *JI*, 1845, p. 375.

[31] Abeken to Bunsen, 2 August 1845, in *JI*, 1845, p. 375.

[32] Ransom, *ibid*, p. 27.

[33] J. Aiton, *The Lands of the Messiah, Mahomet, and the Pope: as visited in 1851* (London, 1852), p. 319.

Finally – a *firman* for the Church.

Sir Stratford Canning had an important audience with the Sultan of Turkey and Caliph of Islam on 25 August. At that meeting a high principle of Islamic Law was about to be overturned. Canning recorded for posterity:

> His Highness took occasion to confirm what His Minister for Foreign Affairs had previously announced to me, namely, that he consented to issue an Imperial Firman for the completion of the Protestant Church at Jerusalem and other suspended buildings with which that sacred edifice is connected. I have much pleasure in adding that His Highness particularly requested me to represent this concession as a mark of the cordial satisfaction which he felt in complying with Her Majesty's wishes.
>
> It cannot but gratify Your Lordship to learn that in every thing which fell from the Sultan's lips at this Audience there was a marked expression of good-will towards the British Crown and Nation, as well as of the most friendly consideration for Her Majesty's person, and confidence in the policy of Her Majesty's Government towards this Empire.[34]

Canning received a translation of a special memorandum from the Porte on 2 September. Then on 4 October Aberdeen wrote an important letter to Shaftesbury stating that in response to the petition presented in March on the behalf of the LJS, he was pleased to announce that an Imperial *firman* had been 'obtained from the Sultan by Her Majesty's Ambassador at Constantinople, by which permission is granted for the erection of the desired building within the precincts of the British Consulate.'[35]

The *firman* stated:

> *It has been represented, both now and before, on the part of the British Embassy residing at my Court, that British and Prussian Protestant subjects visiting Jerusalem, meet with difficulties and obstructions, owing to their not possessing a place of worship for the observance of Protestant rites, and it has been requested that permission should be given to erect, for the first time, a special Protestant place of worship, within the British Consular residence at Jerusalem.*
>
> *Whereas, it is in accordance with the perfect amity and cordial relations existing between the Government of Great Britain and my Sublime Porte, that the requests of that Government shall be complied with as far as possible; and whereas, moreover, the aforesaid place of worship is to be within the Consular residence, my Royal permission is therefore granted*

---

[34] Canning to Aberdeen, 25 August 1845, FO 78/600 (No199).

[35] Aberdeen to Lord Ashley, 4 October 1845, in *JI*, 1845, p. 369.

for the erection of the aforesaid special place of worship, within the aforesaid Consular residence. And my Imperial order having been issued for that purpose, the present decree, containing permission, has been specially given from my Imperial Divan.

This document was also one of the most tangible expressions given of the *Hatti Sherif of Gulhane* of 1839. The sultan was forced to make this compromise for political expediency – but he knew others elsewhere would not understand real-politic. Hence the *firman* continued:

When, therefore, it becomes known unto you, Vallee of Said, Governor of Jerusalem, and others aforesaid, that our Royal permission has been granted for the erection in the manner above stated, of the aforesaid place of worship, you will be careful that no person do in any manner oppose the erection of the aforesaid place of worship in the manner stated. And you will not act in contravention hereof. For which purpose my Imperial Firman is issued.

On its arrival you will act in accordance with my Imperial Firman, issued for this purpose in the manner aforesaid; be it thus known unto you, giving full faith to the Imperial cipher.[36]

It is worth noting several points here. Firstly, immediately after this statement appeared, the LJS made it very clear that the chapel being part of the consular residence would cause them no inconvenience, as legally, the Consular Act held no provision for possessing such chapels. In other words there would be no ownership problems with the British Government over this provision. The Church belonged to the LJS.

The other point is to compare a not too dissimilar event some 2400 years previously – the return of Ezra from Babylon, with permission from the Emperor of Persia, to construct a Temple at Jerusalem. Without taking the analogy too far, Alexander and his movement could almost be equated with Ezra, both being not only heralds of *aliyah*,[37] but also of the introduction (or re-introduction) of a new, reformed Israelite faith system to Jerusalem.

A New Consul and Delivery of the *firman*
Consul Young resigned in 1845, and a new consul, James Finn was chosen to replace him. Finn, a LJS Committee member, and previous

---

[36] Sultan of Turkey to British Government, 10 September 1845, in *JI*, 1845, p. 370.
[37] The Hebrew word for immigrating to the Land of Israel.

acquaintance of Bishop Alexander, was an author of several books on Jewish subjects – and had recently married Elizabeth Anne, daughter of Alexander's long-term friend Alexander McCaul. The signs were there for a promising future between bishop and consul. Both men were avowed restorationists and committed to the Jewish cause.

Until Finn's arrival Henry Newbolt temporarily held the position. Newbolt, who arrived in Jerusalem on 12 October, brought with him the Imperial *firman*. The instructions given to Newbolt were very specific. In order to uphold the terms of the *firman* it was imperative that the British Consulate be as close to the proposed church as possible. Accordingly, on 16 October the archives of the British Consulate were transferred from Young's house to 'a building adjoining the present Protestant place of Worship in the immediate vicinity of the new Anglican church.'[38]

Immediately following the transferal of the archives, Newbolt, Consul Young and the Prussian consu,l Mr. Schultz presented the Imperial *firman* to Ali Pasha, governor of Jerusalem, together with an order from the Turkish governor-general of Syria.

The governor read the *firman*, 'but objected' wrote Newbolt 'to the continuation of the building of the present church on the premises of the Society on the plea that it is not within the British Consular Residence as specified in the Firman of the Sultan.'[39] Newbolt contended that in fact the British Cancelleria[40] was on the same premises of the Protestant church to be built and actually adjoining the proposed church building. The pasha then agreed to visit the proposed church building the following day, a visit delayed until the day after.

On 18 October, the pasha with a large entourage visited the site of the proposed church and closely inspected the premises. Newbolt wrote of the governor's conclusion:

> Although on this occasion His Excellency could not refuse to acknowledge the present Cancelleria as the British Consulate, he still argued that the Firman did not authorize the continuation of the present Church, but a new place of worship for British and Prussian Protestant subjects within the

---

[38] Newbolt to Aberdeen, 4 November 1845, FO 78/626 (No 186). This building, henceforth also known as the *Cancelleria*, is where the present Conrad Schick Library (& CMJ Archive) is located, which itself is attached to the Alexander Lounge, the location of the 'Protestant place of Worship' or St. James Chapel, in November 1845.

[39] Newbolt to Aberdeen, 4 November 1845, FO 78/626 (No 186).

[40] Place where official business takes place and where archives and official documents are located.

Consulate, that the Consulate never having been on the premises before, he could not consider the continuation of the present church as agreeing with the order of the Firman.[41]

Newbolt endeavoured to explain to the governor that he could no longer refer to Consul Young's house as the British Consulate, but that he, Newbolt, had specifically set up the British Consulate on the LJS premises in order to act in accordance with the specifications of the *firman*. But all to no avail, 'and' continued Newbolt 'he further requested (there being at the time laborers employed preparing for the foundation of a house for Bishop Alexander) that the people then employed on the premises should be stopped ...'[42]

Nicolayson's prognosis of this hindrance was:

> The wording of the Firman gave the local authorities here the advantage of founding their opposition at once on the alleged inapplicability of that document, to the resuming of the building previously commenced, as not being "within the Consulate" and the Pasha persisted in demanding a delay till the matter could be referred to Beyrout ... We are fully aware, both of the source of this opposition, and of its extent and object. In order to render the present Firman unavailing for our purposes, a counter-memorial has been addressed by a powerful party here, to the Sublime Porte.[43]

The technicality produced by the pasha and opponents to the scheme was that the British consul at that time had as his office a small room adjacent to the temporary chapel (see footnote No 36), a few metres away from the unfinished church building. This then did not permit, according to the pasha, the literal wording of the *firman* to be fulfilled. In other words, the church had to be constructed within that premise, not atop the foundations of the church already begun.

Alexander in his exuberance after receiving word of the *firman*, had ordered construction to be restarted, and in particular upon his proposed house attached to the church. Consul Newbolt, after consulting with the governor, informed Alexander on 18 October:

> His Excellency then requested that the workmen who are now employed and at work on the grounds might be stopped, giving as his reasons, that the arrival of the new Consul with the Firman was fully known in the City, and that the feeling against building a Protestant Church was so strong that

---

[41] Newbolt to Aberdeen, 4 November 1845, FO 78/626 (No 187).
[42] Newbolt to Aberdeen, 4 November 1845, FO 78/626 (No 187).
[43] Nicolayson to LJS London, 1 November, 1845, in *JI*, 1846, pp. 26-27.

he apprehended difficulties should workmen be seen employed in the immediate vicinity of the church.[44]

Newbolt implored the bishop to refrain from upsetting the *status quo*, while he referred the matter back to Consul-General Rose. Alexander responded immediately 'I shall of course in compliance with His Excellency's request give directions to suspend that work.'[45] One could imagine Alexander's annoyance by this new obstacle. In view though of his previous poor relationship with Young, it would appear that he was determined to work alongside the new, albeit temporary, consul.

But such temperance was obviously not felt by Alexander's associates. After confiding with them, Alexander wrote the following day to Newbolt, 'I find there is a strong feeling in the Mission against being again stopped proceeding with any work on the Premises of the Church, and I would beg of you to submit to His Excellency the Pasha that what is now being done, is only in a small preparatory manner, and cannot possibly lead to any realization of the Pasha's fears.'[46]

One could feel some sympathy for Consul Newbolt, so very quickly thrust into the middle of what was potentially an explosive situation. Yet he stuck to his convictions, and responded to Alexander, that he would pursue his endeavours to meet with the pasha and further discuss this issue, but in the meantime, he requested 'I hope you will not resume the work on the premises of the Society, or if so, I cannot be responsible for any consequences.'[47] Alexander agreed and replied that he would indeed stop any further construction work.[48]

Newbolt finally met with the pasha on 20 October, and laid before him the bishop's requests. The governor was unmoved, and requested Newbolt to desist from any further building until the messengers had returned from Beirut – with a reply from Consul-General Rose, and also one from the Turkish governor-general there.[49] He explained to Newbolt that although he anticipated no disturbance, yet 'the people here were hasty, and easily excited, and ... there would still be great talk about the English building a

---

[44] Consul Newbolt to Bishop Alexander, 18 October, 1845, FO 78/626 (No 190).
[45] Bishop Alexander to Consul Newbolt, 18 October, 1845, FO 78/626 (191).
[46] Alexander to Newbolt, 19 October 1845, FO 78/626 (No 192).
[47] Consul Newbolt to Bishop Alexander, 19 October 1845, FO 78/626 (No 192).
[48] Bishop Alexander to Consul Newbolt, 19 October, 1845, FO 78/626 (No 192).
[49] Newbolt to Alexander, 20 October 1845, FO 78/626 (No 193).

church, that this reaching the ears of his superiors, he would be blamed for allowing the work without being certain that he was right in so doing.'[50]

The governor was being extra cautious, for he knew from the events of the previous year, that opposition from the local sheikhs could easily lead to civil unrest, as was also apparent with the much less serious issue of the raising of the French flag in 1843. Such were the sensitivities of the local Muslim population of Jerusalem. And Alexander did well to listen to this sound advice – as frustrating as it was for him.

Rose's reply reached Newbolt on 2 November – a mere five days before Alexander was due to begin a trip to Egypt and England. Rose, Newbolt stated, had 'failed in his endeavours' with the Turkish governor-general 'for the execution of the Firman, but obtained a letter from him, directing Ali Pasha to cause no hindrance to the work that he had stopped on the premises, unless there could be assigned some legal and regular obstacle for his hindrance of such work ...'[51] The work being referred to here was not on the construction of the church itself (the subject of the counter complaint sent to Constantinople), but the work on Bishop Alexander's private house adjacent to the church.

Newbolt again sought and received an audience with Ali Pasha. And again the governor procrastinated, stating that the order did not permit Bishop Alexander 'to build on the premises of the Church, or, that he was allowed to build a new house...' Newbolt responded that according to his translation received from Rose, it says that 'Bishop Alexander having undertaken to build a house for himself, that should it be in accordance with the law and rule, no hindrance was to be made to such building, or, if any legal or regular obstacle, that such should be given in writing.'[52]

Newbolt's request for the objections to be placed in writing were adhered to – but they were in Turkish, which Newbolt had no capability in Jerusalem to adequately translate. These were then sent back to Rose in Beirut. Newbolt wrote of these presumed objections:

> It is true that at present the Cancelleria is but one small room forming part of the building of the present Protestant place of Worship, but His excellency cannot object to it on account of its size. The church cannot literally be built within it, but I should hardly take such to be the real meaning of the Firman ...'[53]

---

[50] Newbolt to Alexander, 20 October 1845, FO 78/626 (No 193).

[51] Newbolt to Aberdeen, 4 November 1845, FO 78/626 (No 186).

[52] Newbolt to Aberdeen, 4 November 1845, FO 78/626 (No 186).

[53] Newbolt to Aberdeen, 4 November 1845, FO 78/626 (No 188).

It was a frustrating period. Newbolt stated to Aberdeen: 'In all my interviews with Ali Pasha on the subject of the Firman there appears to me to have been predetermined opposition …'[54] Indeed there was – and had been from the very outset of the building, and even of Alexander's entrance into the city. Alexander meanwhile was waiting anxiously. He desperately desired to have the issue settled before leaving.

In a sense, on this issue hinged much of the credibility of his presence in Jerusalem. Indeed there were a number of Jewish people who had acknowledged Jesus as Messiah (some perhaps with dubious motives), but in the East it was essential to have a tangible expression of your community, your *millet,* to which a member would feel secure. An officially recognized church building would be therefore be of much assistance for Alexander to accomplish this goal.

Besides, although of German-Polish extraction, Alexander was by now very much a flag-bearer of the nation which had succoured him. And it was the ultimate insult that Britain, which played the leading role in aiding Turkey regain the land of Israel in 1840, was now being denied permission to build a British church in Jerusalem.

Rose failed in his attempts to get the suspension of building rescinded, so he informed Newbolt to demand written information from Ali Pasha as to his reasons for not carrying out the wishes of the *firman.*[55] Newbolt accordingly wrote to Ali Pasha on 24 November requesting written reasons so he could transmit them 'to Her Majesty's Consul General for the information of His Excellency Her Britannic Majesty's Ambassador at Constantinople, and Her Britannic Majesty's Government.'[56]

The letter from Ali Pasha reiterated the claim that the church was not within the consular residence, and that as Alexander's house immediately adjoined the proposed church, it was seen to be contiguous with it – work could not be continued. But what was especially galling in the letter, translated from the Turkish, was the claim that the area where the Church was to be built was in fact *'the property of Wafk'*[57] and was adjoining a Muslim place of worship.'[58]

---

[54] Newbolt to Aberdeen, 4 November 1845, FO 78/626 (No 188).

[55] Newbolt to Aberdeen, 5 December 1845, FO 78/626 (No 201). It so happened that shortly after issuing this suspension order, Ali Pasha was transferred to Damascus, and he was succeeded by Mahamet, former pasha of Acre.

[56] Translation of letter from Newbolt to Ali Pasha, Governor of Jerusalem, 24 November 1845, FO 78/626 (No 203).

[57] Italics mine.

[58] Translation of letter from Ali Pasha to Consul Newbolt, FO 78/626 (No 204-5).

The Muslim opponents in Jerusalem were persevering in their opposition, this time attempting to claim that the LJS property was actually Islamic *Wakf* property.

And so the matter found its way back to Ambassador Canning, who, as much as anyone else, was annoyed by this further hindrance, and immediately set about clarifying the *firman*.

The Bishop's Fourth Annual Letter – 30 October 1845

Although published several months later, the Bishop's Annual Letter was written from Jerusalem on 30 October. As could be expected it was of great excitement and optimism. Alexander wrote:

> It is with no ordinary feelings of joy and gratitude that I would on this occasion offer you my heartfelt congratulations on the fact that at length a firman has been granted, for the erection of the Protestant church in the Holy City. Whatever may be the circumstances connected with this firman, however much opposition may, and still will, be raised against the carrying of the same into effect, it cannot and must not be looked upon otherwise, than as an additional sign of the further development of the Divine purposes of mercy to Zion.
>
> The Protestant Episcopal Church[59] of England will now have "a local inhabitation" as well as "a name," on the rock of Jerusalem; and whatever is ultimately to follow from this planting of the standard of truth in so conspicuous a place, may safely be left to the appointed course of Providence.[60]

Indeed the granting of the *firman* was music to the ears of both Alexander, the leading Israelite in the Hebrew Christian-Protestant community and to Nicolayson, the foremost Gentile in the same community. No one had worked harder than Nicolayson to get to this point.

Yet no one more than Alexander was pleased with the news. Firstly it was one of his main objectives in coming to Jerusalem. And secondly it was one of the chief burdens he had to operate under. In the East a leader was associated with the prestige his position brought with it. Mosques, synagogues and other churches abounded in the Holy City. An imam, rabbi or patriarch could point to a physical edifice as representing the community to which he belonged.

---

[59] This seems to have been the initial name given to the proposed new Church. Johns in his unofficial publication named it the 'Cathedral Church of St. James.'
[60] Alexander to LJS London, in *JI*, 1846, p. 3.

Alexander, bishop of the Protestant Church, could only point to an unfinished building which was a source of contention, and embarrassment. Both France and Russia could point to edifices representing Roman and Greek Christianity. Britain, professing to be the Great Power of the time, had only the foundations of an unfinished building.

This decision, encompassed in the Imperial *firman* – was perhaps the high point of Alexander's nearly four years in Jerusalem. In his last letter to London, dated 4 November, before leaving to Egypt, he stated:

> The Firman has been presented to the authorities here ... It is quite evident that there are parties still working against us; but they cannot succeed, although impediments may still be thrown in our way. The fact of a Firman having been granted, after all the anxiety and trouble, must be viewed as a cause of thanksgiving: and I doubt not that everything will soon be satisfactorily arranged.[61]

In this very same communication, Alexander related the sad news that his servant, James Sumpter, who had been with him since his departure from London in 1841, had suddenly died in mid October. Sumpter who was 'particularly interested in the conversion and restoration of Israel'[62] offered his services to Alexander prior to his departure for Jerusalem, and had proved a more than worthy ambassador in the Holy City.

The funeral service was conducted by the bishop – one of his last official duties before setting off for Egypt.[63] The body was laid to rest in the small British cemetery outside the walls.

Alexander's Death

Since the previous year Alexander had desired to visit Egypt – which had been postponed due to the ill health of his children. It was decided therefore that he would visit there in November, and then continue on to Britain. He was to remain in Cairo for about a week, during which time he would visit the various CMS operations – and to confirm some of the young people. He would then do the same in Alexandria, from where he was due to sail on 10 December. [64]

The party, comprising of the bishop, Mrs. Alexander, Fanny Alexander, Rev. Veitch, and Rev. Dr. Abeken set out from Jerusalem on 7 November

---

[61] Alexander to LJS London, 4 November, 1845, in *JI*, 1846, p. 23.

[62] *ibid*, p. 24.

[63] *ibid*, pp. 23-26.

[64] Mrs. Lieder to Rev. J. Blackburn, 4 December 1845, in *JI*, 1845, p. 36.

and traveled first to Gaza which they reached the following day. Here Dr. Abeken left the party, and after performing the usual quarantine at El Christi, they then went further south via El Arish. Here they were detained by quarantine regulations, but soon after continued along the northern Sinai route, the ancient *Way of the Sea* – the *Via Maris*. Mrs. Alexander recalled of that time

> On setting out through the Desert, each day my beloved husband and myself rode our own horses; we generally were in advance of the caravan, and we used regularly to chant some of our Hebrew chants, and sung the following hymns: "Children of the Heavenly King:" "Long has the Harp of Judah hung:" cxith Psalm; "Glorious things of thee are spoken:" all out of our own hymn-book: and never did his warm and tender heart overflow so fully, as when he spoke of Israel's future restoration. When I spoke to him about his duties in England, he answered, "I hope, if invited, to preach my first sermon in England at the Episcopal Jews' Chapel …"[65]

During this time in the Sinai Desert, the bishop spoke much about his love for the Jewish people, and of his hopes for the future – for the work in Egypt and in Jerusalem.[66] On one occasion he drew his horse up next to Rev. Veitch's camel and enquired, wrote Veitch 'how I liked the prospect of the journey. I replied, that I looked forward to it with pleasure, and he seemed pleased, and said he felt the same, and expected both enjoyment and health from continually being in the open air for so many days.'[67]

In particular Alexander was happy that the clear air was good for the health of Mrs. Alexander, who had suffered numerous bouts of ague (fever). On the evening of 21 November the party had arrived at Abou Suwyreh, where, Veitch recalled 'our sorrows commenced' for heavy rain fell during the night. This change of weather concerned the bishop, not because of any discomfort towards himself, but 'lest Mrs. and Miss Alexander should suffer.'[68]

The following day, Saturday 22 November, the entire area outside the tents was drenched, so much so that it was impossible to light a fire and drink their customary morning coffee. The bishop 'complained of indisposition' and 'of pain in the chest and shoulders'[69] a similar feeling, Veitch recalled that he suffered at the conclusion of his Damascus trip near

---

[65] Communication by Mrs. Alexander, in *JI*, 1846, p. 35.
[66] Mrs. Alexander, *ibid*, p. 35.
[67] Veitch to LJS London, 2 January 1846, in *JI*, 1846, p. 92.
[68] *ibid*, p. 92.
[69] *ibid*, p. 92.

Djebail.[70] On that previous trip Dr. Kerns had advised that this discomfort was caused by 'the strain of the muscles, from riding for so many hours on consecutive days, augmented in its bad effects by the damp of the preceding night.'[71]

So during the day Alexander opted out of riding his horse and rode instead in the litter on the camel. As the weather had cleared up by mid morning they were able to stop, light a fire, and enjoy breakfast. All except Alexander that is. He was 'seized with sickness and vomited immediately after breakfast' recalled Veitch, who added 'but still I confess I felt no serious alarm, as he speedily recovered, and we proceeded.'[72] That evening they arrived at the village of Ras Ovaddi on the eastern branch of the Nile, the area known as Ras el Wady (Head of the Valley) and Alexander was feeling better.

During the evening meal in Veitch's tent, Alexander insisted he was well, and even refused a treatment offered to him by Veitch. He felt that as the following day, being Sunday, they would not travel, he would have sufficient time to recover. In fact he felt so well that he wrote a letter to Mr. Lieder of the CMS Mission in Cairo, with whom they would stay, informing him of their intended arrival on Tuesday. This letter was to be delivered by a Coptic pilgrim who had joined the party at El Arish and who was due to depart soon after midnight.

Following the evening meal in Veitch's tent, Bishop Alexander arranged for the church service to be held the following day, made some remarks about the value of a day of rest, then retired to his tent.[73] Alexander then declared to his beloved wife 'how exceedingly comfortable he felt'[74] then 'prayed most sweetly with his wife and daughter, and then laid down upon his bed, which was placed on the sand.'[75]

Mrs. Alexander then went to bed, and in her testimony related to Mrs. Lieder, recalled 'she was first awoke by the bellowing of a camel, and then by a groan which proceeded from her husband. She thought it strange, and instantly got up, when she saw him sitting up in his bed, with his eyes closed and apparently dead. She spoke to him, but received no answer –

---

[70] Veitch to LJS London, 26 November, 1845, in *JI*, 1846, p. 1.

[71] Veitch to LJS London, 2 January 1846, in *JI*, 1846, p. 93.

[72] *ibid,* p. 93.

[73] *ibid,* p. 93.

[74] *ibid,* p. 93.

[75] Mrs. Lieder to Blackburn, 4 December 1845, in *JI*, 1845, p. 36.

she touched him, but had no reply – then she gave the alarm.'[76] Veitch then describes the events that followed:

> I was aroused by some exclamations from Mrs. Alexander; I ran instantly into his tent, and saw at once that all was over. We tried all we could think of: applied hot water to his feet, chafed the body, and I even ventured to bind up the arm and got a lancet ready, but it was impossible to make the vein rise, so as to see where it was. I also put a cordial between the lips, but it produced no movement of the throat. Death had taken place in a moment.[77]

Veitch, who thought the death occurred about two o'clock in the morning, continued:

> It was truly a heart-rending scene … to see the widowed wife and fatherless daughter, bending over the lowly pallet, on which were stretched the lifeless remains. Never shall I forget the harrowing scene, or the fortitude with which so awful bereavement was endured. I persuaded Mrs. and Miss Alexander to retire; and after waiting an hour, I returned again to the scene of death, and with the assistance of my servant disposed the body as decently as I could, in the bed on which it was lying.[78]

The sad party set out about eight o'clock the following morning for Cairo, and by traveling continuously, arrived early in the morning of Monday 23 November. Here Mr. Lieder and other members of the CMS station in Cairo, who had been warned of the bishop's death by the Coptic messenger, met them. The camel carrying Alexander's body was brought into the courtyard of the CMS Mission-house, and thereupon placed in the Bible-room. Mrs. Lieder describes the scene:

> I received Mrs. Alexander, with Mrs. Kruse, in Mr. Lieder's study. She was, as might be expected, in much grief. We did all we could, all that human beings are able, to soothe and comfort this afflicted lady. She is evidently a strong-minded woman, for she talked with much calmness and affection of the lamented dead. Poor Miss Alexander seemed greatly cast down, yet resigned. Neither of them could take the least refreshment, nor

---

[76] Mrs. Lieder to Blackburn, 4 December 1845, in *JI*, 1845, p. 36.

[77] Veitch to LJS London, 26 November, 1845, in *JI*, 1846, pp. 1-2.

[78] *ibid*, p. 2.

would they go to bed, although they had traveled and fasted for upwards of twenty-four hours; and through a whole night.[79]

Later that afternoon, Monday 24 November, the British consul - general Colonel Barnett, alongside Mr. Kruse, Mr. Murray Mitchell and Mr. Lieder, consulted, and decided they would perform an autopsy, and then afterwards conceal the body in three coffins – one of wood, one of tin or lead, and an external one of wood, covered with black cloth.

Mrs. Lieder persuaded the two Alexander women to go to bed at eight o'clock in the evening, although how much they really rested is debatable, as the sound of the carpenter making the two wooden coffins drifted up from the courtyard to their window directly above.

A nine o'clock in the evening the English physician, Dr. Abbott, as well as the French physician, Dr Chedafan and their assistants, came to the Lieder home to perform the autopsy. Mr. Lieder, Mr. Kruse and Mr. Veitch were also present. 'It seems' wrote Mrs. Lieder 'that the life of his Lordship had been for some time of doubtful length, and that Dr. Kerns and Dr. Macgowan had both thought him a subject for sudden death.'[80]

The conclusion of the autopsy revealed 'the immediate cause of death was pronounced to have been a rupture of the descending aorta, which caused an effusion of blood into the thoracic cavity.'[81] Or, as Mrs. Lieder stated in more layman's terminology: 'The immediate cause of death was the rupture of one of the largest blood-vessels near the heart; but the whole of the lungs, liver, and heart, were found in an exceedingly diseased state; and had been so for a length of time.' The doctors however clearly stated that Alexander's death was not due to fatigue from the trip across the desert, which by accounts was actually a wonderfully enjoyable and stress-

---

[79] Mrs. Lieder to Blackburn, 4 December 1845, in *JI*, 1846. p. 35.

[80] Mrs. Lieder to Blackburn, 4 December 1845, in *JI*, 1846. p. 36. Macgowan later recorded that while in England Alexander had suffered gout, and in Palestine had suffered several attacks of congestive fever. But, Macgowan stated 'there were other attacks to which I always considered to be of an alarming character. These were fainting fits, which came on without notice, and during which he remained in a state of entire insensibility …

But in all these attacks there was a total absence of all local symptoms that could create suspicion of organic disease of the aorta. My fear was apoplexy – an apprehension which led me to consider the Bishop's life as a very precarious one, and which I had long ago intimated as my own opinion.' Macgowan to LJS London, December & January Report, in *JI*, 1846, p. 115.

[81] Correspondent of the *Times*, dated Cairo 5 December 1845, in *JI*, 1846, p. 40.

less journey, but, as Mrs. Lieder continued 'it was a complaint that he might, in like manner, have been called away in Jerusalem.'[82]

Mrs. Lieder, in describing the results of the autopsy, then gave her diagnosis - '... the accelerating cause, doubtless, was great and continued anxiety – such as the Bishopric of Jerusalem and its cares can best account for. I heard it said on this occasion that had his Lordship not come into the East, he might possibly have lived to a good old age; but the mitre of Jerusalem, like the wreath of our blessed Lord, has been to him a crown of thorns.'[83]

Several pressing matters now weighed upon Mrs. Alexander - whether or not to continue her journey to England, wait in Egypt for her children to join her, or return to Jerusalem. She finally opted to continue to England.

The other matter concerned where to bury the bishop. Some, including the Lieders, had desired for the bishop's body to be interred in their new graveyard. However Consul-General Barnett thought Jerusalem, as this was Alexander's wish. In one of those ironies of history, it was former Consul Young, who being in Egypt at the time 'decidedly thought that his Lordship's great wish should be gratified, and he said he felt sure that most of his Lordship's English friends would also desire it.'[84] Mrs. Alexander then concurred with the opinions of Her Majesty's envoys – and to Jerusalem the body would go.

Then there was a further complication – how to get the bishop's body to Jerusalem, and who would convey it? There were two options, by sea through to Jaffa, or overland along the same route they had come. Either option was fraught with difficulties. Sailing along the coast in November or December could be complicated with a sudden storm, and, there were likely to be major problems with quarantine in Jaffa. The other option, the land route also had its problems – Bedouin, the long distance, and the quarantine at Gaza.[85] However Mr. Lieder had a friend at the head of the *Sanitario* there, and felt this would help.

It was finally decided to adopt the second option. The body would be conveyed on a *tatarwan*, which was to be carried between two camels. But who would do it? Rev. Veitch was the obvious choice. But he had initial grave misgivings about this undertaking, confessing, 'I had almost decided that it was wrong in my position as father of a family, to run the

---

[82] Mrs. Lieder to Blackburn, 4 December 1845, in *JI*, 1846. p. 36.

[83] *ibid*, p. 36.

[84] *ibid*, p. 37.

[85] Not only was Gaza a seaport, but also the first major stop after the Sinai, and so for these two reasons it had a quarantine station.

risk I knew I must run, liable as I am, if exposed to damp, to very dangerous attacks.' His decision was finally made when witnessing the distress this issue was causing the bereaved widow, and of the sound advice and assistance of Mrs. Lieder.[86]

The memorial service was held on Sunday 30 November, which Mr. and Mrs. Lieder organized. During the week Mr. Lieder had managed to have the bishop's mitre made by their architect, Mr.Wild, and this, as well as the bishop's Bible and pastoral staff and cap, were all laid on the coffin.

A very sizeable congregation gathered, including the British and Russian consuls-general, the wife of the French consul-general, many dignitaries of the local churches, and all of the English residents. 'The music' wrote the *Times* correspondent, 'was performed by a numerous choir of Coptic pupils of the Mission – lineal descendants of the subjects of the Pharoahs, raising their voices in a Protestant temple.'[87] Rev. Veitch preached the sermon, from Deuteronomy 34:5: 'So Moses, the servant of the Lord, died there in the Land of Moab, according to the word of the Lord.'[88]

Mrs. Lieder concluded her letter to Rev. Blackburn, with these most appropriate words:

> The Indian mail is in, and Mrs. Alexander will start for England this day (Saturday, 6th); the remains of the Bishop have just left the house on their way to Syria. We have had a dreadful stormy scene with the extortionate Bedouins. However, Mr. Veitch and the Bishop's servant are both off – a large party accompanied the bier as far as Heliopolis, in carriages and on asses. I cannot help comparing the present position of our excellent friend, Mr. Veitch, to that of Joseph, when he took the bones of good old Jacob through the same identical wilderness of Shur; for Jacob prayed them not to bury him in Egypt, for, he said, "I will lie with my fathers, and thou shalt carry me out of Egypt, and shalt bury me in their burying-place." – (Genesis xlvii. 20).[89]

This situation was as close as one could get in the modern age to a re-enactment of that Biblical event. But Michael Solomon Alexander was being returned to Jerusalem, not Hebron like Jacob, for burial. The receivers of God's covenantal promises, Abraham, Isaac and Jacob, were all buried in Hebron. But Michael Solomon Alexander believed that the consummation of those promises would take place in Jerusalem.

---

[86] Veitch, to LJS London, 2 January 1846, in *JI*, 1846, p. 94.

[87] The *Times* correspondent, Cairo, 5 December 1845, in *JI*, 1846, p. 40.

[88] Mrs. Lieder to Blackburn, 4 December 1845, in *JI*, 1846. p. 38.

[89] *ibid*, p. 38.

Alexander's presence in the Land of Israel and Egypt, in 1845, was also very much due to the geo-political reality of the time. Britain coveted the preservation of her link to India. This was proved by her campaign to oust Napoleon and the French between 1798-1801, and by her subsequent moves to keep abreast of all French initiatives – hence the establishment of the British Consulate in Jerusalem.

This scenario led an enterprising Englishman, Thomas Waghorn, in the 1830's to develop an overland mail service, between Alexandria and Suez and onto India.   He maintained that this was the quickest and most efficient means of communication between Britain and India. And indeed this proved to be the case – so that in December 1845, mail had just arrived by steamer at Suez, from India, transported overland to Cairo, and from there by ferry up to Alexandria – and by ship to London. Deborah and Fanny Alexander as well as Mrs. Lieder's letter would then join this ship, and sail onto England.

The bitter and the sweet

When news of Alexander's death arrived in Jerusalem, it was Nicolayson's duty to inform all about it. Daughter Deborah describes how the news came to her:

> One afternoon I was ready dressed for a ride with Mr. and Bessie Nicolayson; very hurriedly Mr. Nicolayson arrived at our home and without taking notice of me, went into the drawing room to interview Miss Cecil. I was eventually sent for and saw that something was wrong and asked at once if any news had come of Mama. She was the one I naturally expected might be ill. I was told that a messenger had just come from Egypt and that Papa had been taken very ill, before they reached Cairo. Later on, the sad – and most overwhelming event of his death in his sleep – was broken to me. I was simply stunned. I tried to cry but tears are never my relief in sorrow. I was roused by a fearful commotion in the nursery where I found all my dear little sisters and brother in floods of tears, and Margaret, our English nurse, in hysterics on the floor. I threw a glass of cold water over her, and then tried to comfort the dear little ones.[90]

Nicolayson's was an unenviable task, as he states:

> How deeply and tenderly the departed was beloved as well as revered by all here, the effect of the painful announcement I had to make, in the

---

[90] Ransom, *ibid*, p. 35.

opening of my sermon on the Sunday morning after its receipt, most affectingly showed. Scarcely any present who was not dissolved in tears.

I may mention that, having waited yesterday on both the patriarchs here, the Armenian and the Greek, to make the melancholy announcement to them, they both expressed their deep sympathy, particularly for the afflicted widow and orphans; and the former (the Armenian patriarch), sent the Bishop Procurator, and the Dragoman of the convent, to my house to-day to express still more emphatically his sincere condolence. He was personally much attached to our late beloved Bishop, who, indeed, was universally esteemed by all who knew him personally.[91]

In one of those bittersweet ironies of history, at the very time when people were mourning for the passing of the bishop, two Tartar messengers arrived at sunset on 9 December, bearing fresh dispatches from Constantinople containing, wrote Nicolayson 'fresh, most explicit, and peremptory orders to our new Pasha here for the instant removal of all impediment to "resuming the erection of the English Protestant Church already commenced here," and of other buildings.' He continued:

> While this is highly gratifying, it serves, too, to renew the grief still so fresh, by the very thought of how our dear Bishop would have rejoiced in it, had he still been among us.[92]

Bishop Alexander's Last Journey

About eleven in the morning of 6 December, Bishop Alexander's coffin, draped in black and carried on the *tatarwan* between two camels, left the CMS home. Various people, including Coptic pupils of the mission school, and other British residents accompanied it.[93] The British Consul-General Colonel Barnett also assisted much, by requesting letters of recommendation from the Pasha of Egypt, Mehmet Ali which Veitch produced along the way where necessary.

At various points after leaving the ancient city of Cairo the people in the entourage turned back, most of them at Heliopolis. Thereafter the journey was continued by the faithful Rev. Veitch and his servant.

Veitch was extremely grateful for the good weather he encountered, except for one occasion when torrents of rain engulfed him. Yet even with this discomfort he could still offer thanks, for he realized that this could have been his lot for the entire trip.

---

[91] Nicolayson to LJS London, 9 December 1845, in *JI*, 1846, p. 97.

[92] *ibid*, p. 97.

[93] Veitch to LJS London, 2 January 1846, in *JI*, 1846, p. 94.

On passing Bir-el-Abd, half way to El Arish, he received warning of a conflict between rival Bedouin parties and was advised to proceed *poste haste* to El Arish – which meant foregoing his Sunday rest. Veitch wrote:

> My fear was that if a party of Arabs ... should come upon us, they would break open the coffin in the hope of obtaining plunder. All we had met had eyed it most wistfully, and we had overheard their speculations as to the value of its contents, and it is very unlikely that here, where truth is a thing unknown, they would have credited any assurance of ours on the matter.[94]

In El Arish his letters of recommendation were of great assistance and the Turkish governor provided him with nine soldiers for the onward journey to Gaza. From this location to Jerusalem, Veitch and his special cargo were accompanied by several Albanian soldiers. 'The name of the redoubted Pasha of Egypt' wrote Veitch 'worked wonders.'[95]

Veitch was extremely grateful to the Albanian soldiers. 'Well acquainted with the road' he stated 'they secured me from the tricks of the camel drivers, who are for ever going out of the way for their own purposes; and provided me with a most comfortable room in the seraglio at Migdal, the first resting place from Gaza.'[96]

Apart from a few testing moments the journey had proceeded well – and except for the sand of the northern Sinai, the route was flat and passable. But towards the end of the route, the terrain changed considerably, and the most difficult part of the journey began. Veitch recalls:

> Our last day was dreadfully fatiguing, owing to the exceeding difficulty of transporting the coffin, - itself of no inconsiderable weight, - up the mountain passes between the plain of Ramleh and the Holy City. It was carried on poles between two camels. I left the convent of Ramleh about four o'clock in the morning, and did not reach Jerusalem until seven o'clock in the evening.[97]

Veitch had sent word forward already to Jerusalem from Ramleh of his impending arrival. He requested Nicolayson to seek permission to bring the body inside the city for the evening, and to have the body buried the

---

[94] Veitch to LJS London, 2 January 1846, in *JI*, 1846, p. 94.
[95] *ibid*, p. 95.
[96] *ibid*, p. 95. Seraglio is basically an inn.
[97] *ibid*, p. 95.

following day,[98] and provided Mr. Critchlow the surveyor, the exact measurement of the bishop's coffin.[99]

Nicolayson knew that it would not be possible for the body to enter into the walled city that evening due to quarantine regulations as well as the 'invincible prejudice arising from superstition which the Moslem population has against this.'[100] He thus requested that the gates be kept open as long as possible so that the body could be interred that evening.

With this news, Nicolayson, along with Newbolt, Dr. Schultz and Critchlow started out to meet Veitch along the Camel Road. Between two to three o'clock in the afternoon they met the party near the village of El Geel. Nicolayson and Critchlow then hurried back to Jerusalem to announce the probable time of arrival.

Later, Nicolayson proceeded out to the Tombs of the Kings, where the party had already arrived, 'attended by crowds of people of all classes from town.' Nicolayson continues:

> The coffin fastened on two long poles, and carried between two camels, was now covered with the pall, and all belonging to the mission walked as mourners, after it, until near the burial-ground, where it was taken off the camels and carried on men's shoulders. I then met it in the surplice at the limit of the cemetery, and preceded it, reading the sentences, to the grave broken into the rock, and regularly built up with masonry. It was now quite dark, and we had only the light afforded by a few lanthorns. I therefore only read that part of the service which is appointed to be read at the grave, and thus we had the last melancholy satisfaction of committing the mortal remains of the *first* Anglican Bishop of Jerusalem to their resting place, in "sure and certain hope of the resurrection of eternal life." The next morning I preached from 2 Corinthians v.1, &., on the glorious hope of immortality set forth in living reality in Christ.
>
> We now indeed all feel like orphans, yet we continue to pursue our work, as far as possible, in all respects as before.[101]

Indeed as the fledgling Hebrew Christian-Protestant community contemplated what they had just witnessed, they were a stunned group, and one could well understand Nicolayson's sentiment that they felt like orphans. The big question now confronting them was – would there be hope and vision without their recognized leader?

---

[98] Nicolayson to LJS London, 31 December 1845, in *JI*, 1846, p. 96.
[99] Veitch to LJS London, 2 January 1846, in *JI*, 1846, p. 95.
[100] Nicolayson to LJS London, 31 December 1845, in *JI*, 1846, p. 96.
[101] *ibid*, p. 96.

Chapter 14

The Day After – Alexander's Legacy

The Immediate Shock

To say that the family, close friends, colleagues, supporters, and even opponents, of Bishop Alexander were stunned, would be an understatement. They were in deep shock.

Shaftesbury recorded the event in his diary for 15 December:

> Just received, in a letter from Veitch, intelligence of the death of the Bishop of Jerusalem at Cairo. I would rather have heard many fearful things than this sad event; it buries at once half my hopes for the speedy welfare of our Church, our nation, and the children of Israel! What an overthrow to our plans! What a humbling to our foresight! What a trial to our faith! Alas! This bright spot, on which my eyes, amidst all the surrounding darkness, confusion, and terrors of England, have long been reposing, is now apparently bedimmed.
>
> I am quite dismayed, and enter fully into the Scripture expression, 'amazement.' We were rejoicing in his expected arrival in England to aid our efforts, and advance the cause; he is cut down as suddenly as a flower by the scythe!
>
> But what is our condition? Have we run counter to the will of God? Have we conceived a merely human project, and then imagined it to be a decree of the Almighty, when we erected a bishopric in Jerusalem, and appointed a Hebrew to exercise the functions? Have we vainly and presumptuously attempted to define 'the times and seasons which the Father hath put in His own power?' God, who knows our hearts, alone can tell. It seemed to us that we acted in faith for the honour of His name, and in the love of His ancient people; but now it would appear that the thing was amiss, and not according to God's wisdom and pleasure.

And yet. Short-sighted, feeble creatures as we are, all this may be merely a means to a speedier and ampler glory! [1]

In a sense, Shaftesbury was looking at Alexander as the representative of the restorationist vision. The following comments of Dr. Macgowan however, summed up the feelings of many who knew Bishop Alexander as their leader, their spiritual guide, and their personal friend:

> To those Christian friends who take part or feel interested in those efforts which have been made of late years for the spiritual regeneration of God's ancient people, the removal of the first bishop of the Protestant Church in Jerusalem, himself a Hebrew, and thus forming a connecting link with the primitive Hebrew Christian Church, this must be considered as a public calamity. But to us, who have enjoyed the privilege of being under his pastoral care, of sharing his intimacy, and of appreciating his kind nature and simple-hearted piety, the loss is attended with deeper and more personal feelings ... His ear, his heart, his purse, were open at all times to every application for the furtherance of the object dearest to his heart. He was indeed an Israelite in whom was no guile.[2]

These sentiments were reinforced by thirty-one Jewish believers in Jesus in Jerusalem, who on 27 December wrote a testimonial to Mrs. Alexander:

> Madam – We, the undersigned, members of the House of Israel, and brethren after the flesh and Spirit to yourself and our much beloved, highly revered, and deeply lamented Bishop, with the loss of who it has pleased the mysterious and inscrutable providence of God to afflict us all, beg leave to express to you our sentiments of the most sincere and heartfelt sympathy in your late bereavement. We will not attempt to comfort you under your severe affliction, for we need ourselves to be comforted; but we will rather pray to the God of all consolation, who has graciously pledged himself never to leave nor to forsake his own, that he may verify in you the precious promises of the Gospel, so that it may become your privilege to realize all those blessings, which to bestow is the sole prerogative of Him, who is emphatically called the Comforter.
> Next to yourself and your dear family, we consider *ourselves the chief mourners*; for we feel both collectively and individually that we have lost

---

[1] Earl of Shaftesbury, K.G., *The Jerusalem Bishopric*, (London, 1887), p. 13.
[2] Macgowan to LJS London, December and January Reports, in *JI*, 1846, p. 114.

not only a *true father in Christ*, but also a loving brother and a most kind friend. The *suavity and benignity of his manner,* which so greatly endeared him to all, and which gained him the highest and most entire filial confidence of every one of us, tends much to increase the keen sense we feel of our loss. *The affectionate love he bore to Israel,* which peculiarly characterised him, could not fail to render him beloved by every one who had the privilege of being acquainted with him: while his exalted piety, and most exemplary life and conversation, inspired the highest reverential esteem. He was a burning and a shining light; and when he was raised to the highest dignity in the Church, he conferred the most conspicuous honour on our whole nation, but especially on the little band of Jewish believers. With him captive Judah's brightest earthly star has set, and the top-stone has been taken away from the rising Hebrew Church. But shall we repine at God's dispensations, because they are trying and painful to us? We know that we dare not, and all we can do now is, that we implore the Father of all mercies to grant us grace to glorify him, by a dutiful submission and calm resignation to his holy will and pleasure.

Our greatest consolation is, the firm conviction and blessed assurance we feel, that our beloved Bishop is with Christ: he had, indeed, fought the good fight of faith, and come off more than conqueror through Him who loved us, and gave himself for us: may we have grace given to us, so to follow his good example, that when we shall have finished our earthly course, we may together with him be made partakers of Christ's heavenly kingdom.

As an apology for thus obtruding on your attention, we beg to state, in conclusion, that reluctant as we feel by this means to remind you of your great loss, we think it but due to yourself and our dear Bishop, - whose memory will always be very dear to us, and a small tribute of the sympathy we feel, - thus to express our sentiments with regard to the event which has at once made us mourners and orphans.

That the Lord may be pleased to shower down upon you and your dear family the rich fullness of his choicest blessings, will be the constant prayer of, Madam, your like afflicted and sympathizing servants.[3]

The following Jewish believers from Jerusalem signed this testimonial:

Alex. J. Behrens.	Rose Ducat.
Eramus Scott Calman.	J. Lisschiltz Marcussohn
Melville P Bergheim.	Jacob Saleeh.
Maria D. Bergheim.	M. Levy Mallis.

---

[3] Testimonial to Mrs. Alexander, 27 December 1845, in *JI*, 1846, pp. 127-128.

Chas. S. Rosenthal.	Abraham Joseph.
Emily H. Rosenthal.	J. M. Franz.
James Schwartz.	Giorgio Abraham Gional.
Christian L. Lauria (Chazer)	Johann Wilhelm Rosenthal.
P. J. Hershon.	Judah. L. Lion.
Edward James Jonas.	John Meshullam.
S. P. Rosenfeldt.	Maria Meshullam.
M. J. Eppstein.	Elijah Meshullam.
Herman Marcussohn.	Peter Meshullam.
Tege Christian Ducat.	C. W. Hanauer.
A. L. Ducat.	Ch. Max. Ungar.
J. B. Goldberg (Benjamin).	

Further accolades poured in from many quarters: Anglican, Lutheran, non-episcopal, British, Prussian and other nationalities. The *Times* newspaper, when referring to an accusation that Alexander's appointment was due to political intrigue, stated of Alexander:

> But any man more completely the reverse of an intriguer than the late Bishop of Jerusalem can scarcely be conceived. He was indeed an Israelite without guile. If he had a fault it was that, incapable of evil himself, he was too slow to see it in others.'[4]

Immediate Consequences
Prior to their trip to Egypt the bishop and Mrs. Alexander had entrusted the remaining children to the care of Miss Cecil, their governess, and Alexander's close friend, Scot Calman. To these two now rested the responsibility of preparing the children for their ultimate relocation to England, which occurred some months later. Calman wrote to Mrs. Alexander about his responsibilities with the children:

> My staying with them and the humble service I was able to afford to them in a land of a strange people, I count as one of the greatest privileges I have ever enjoyed.[5]

The loss of Bishop Alexander deeply affected Calman, as indeed it did all the Jewish believers, as well as the non-Jewish members, like Macgowan,

---

[4] *Times,* dated 5 December 1845, in *JI* 1846, pp. 38-39.
[5] Scott Calman to Mrs. Alexander 4 August 1846, p. 201, MSS 3393 [f.139], Lambeth.

of the Jerusalem believing community. Alexander had indeed become a figurehead, a father in the faith. Now there was a vacuum.

It would be some months before the Prussian king would be able to nominate a replacement, someone who would be Anglican enough to satisfy the British, and German enough to satisfy the Prussians. That man was Samuel Gobat, originally from Switzerland, but who had worked with the CMS in Lebanon, Abyssinia and of late at the Protestant College in Malta.

Until Gobat arrived the small believing community needed to cope and somehow survive. How did it fair? Calman added in his letter to Mrs. Alexander:

> The Jerusalem Mission has lost much in my estimation and judgement of what is really true and valuable, by the removal of the Bishop your late husband who acted as a connected link between Jew and Gentile. Since that event, I am sorry to say, everything here has assumed a form of isolation and separation, every one seeking his own.
>
> You lost in him a faithful husband, the children a dutiful parent, and I a much revered friend, the removal of whom left a vacant void in Jerusalem that nothing earthly can fill it up.[6]

Consequences – Long term

Indeed it would be difficult to fill that void left by Alexander's departure. For Shaftesbury, many other Anglicans, Britons, and others, Alexander's death caused a huge setback in the restorationist hope.

It is very clear that everything that was expected of Alexander was not fulfilled – there was no Jewish restoration, and there was, at least in 1845, no world wide Protestant union with Jerusalem as its centre.

If Alexander had survived, things definitely would have gone differently. Whether or not those plans, ambitions and visions of Shaftesbury, the restorationists and of King Frederick William and Bunsen would have been fulfilled, it is impossible to surmise.

But perhaps Alexander's role in them had been only the beginning, and others were to bring those plans and visions to their fulfillment.

A few months after Alexander's death the new British consul, James Finn arrived, with his talented wife, Elizabeth Anne: James and Elizabeth Anne Finn possibly did more for the Jewish people in Jerusalem and the Land of Israel in the nineteenth century than any other Gentiles.

---

[6] Scott Calman to Mrs. Alexander, *ibid,* p. 204, Lambeth.

Indeed their contribution was great. One wonders what would have happened if Alexander had been bishop and Finn consul at the same time. Instead Samuel Gobat arrived as the German nominated second bishop.

Gobat never desired to work exclusively among the Jewish people, as Alexander had, and as intended in the origins of the bishopric. Yet he never completely neglected the vision of Nicolayson and Alexander. By the 1860's there were over 100 Jewish believers in Jesus, adults and children, worshipping in Jerusalem.

Of these two impressive men, Finn and Gobat, prominent Jewish historian Martin Gilbert wrote:

> In 1846 two men reached Jerusalem who were to have a considerable impact on the city: Consul Finn and Bishop Gobat. Finn was to serve as British Consul and Gobat as Anglican Bishop. The two men were to quarrel without respite. Finn believed, in contrast to his predecessor, Consul Young, that Christian missionary work in Jerusalem was the will of God, and that the prime task of all such missionary work in Jerusalem was to convert Jews to Christianity. Gobat, on the other hand, stressed the need to convert the Arab Christians to Anglicanism, to persuade them to forgo the 'errors' of Greek Orthodoxy.[7]

The Finns remained in Jerusalem until 1863, and Gobat until his death in 1879. So they reigned together for seventeen years, from 1846 till 1863.

And perhaps no other foreigner in the nineteenth century did more for the good of the Arab population, especially the Christians, in the Land of Israel, than Samuel Gobat. Despite therefore a change in direction of the Anglican-Protestant Bishopric from its strong restorationist origins, tremendous benefit accrued to the peoples of the Holy Land from its continuance. And under Gobat German interests grew tremendously.

It was during the time of Finn and Gobat that the Hebrew Protestant Church was finally completed. Although its intended name was the 'Apostolic Anglican Church', Gobat requested in 1847 that the designated name be changed to Christ Church.[8] It was consecrated on 21 January 1849. Its presence was a huge statement for the Protestant cause. The following year Protestantism was officially recognized as a community in the Turkish Empire.

---

[7] M. Gilbert, *Jerusalem: Rebirth of a City*, (Jerusalem, 1985), p. 43.
[8] 'Apostolic Anglican Church of Jerusalem,' LJS General Committee Meeting 10 April 1841, M. 1315, Bodleian. And LJS General Committee, 10 November 1847, 'Hebrew Christian Church at Jerusalem,' d 55/1, Bodleian.

Also in 1850 the first person of royalty visited Christ Church, Princess Marianne of the Netherlands, the divorced wife of Prince Alfred of Prussia, who had been a guest of Alexander in 1842.

Geo-politically the Jerusalem Protestant Bishopric provided Prussia (and later Germany) with the ideal launching pad for German penetration into the Levant. It was not by any means the only avenue for such German infiltration, but it was the main one.

In 1842 Prussia was the smallest of the European empires, and needed a back on which to climb. Britain, the Anglican Church, and more specifically the LJS, provided that back. But by the 1880's, Prussia was no more. Now there was the larger and more ambitious German Empire, the Germany of the Kaiser and of Otto von Bismark. It was now a Germany which no longer needed British support.[9]

This German Empire desired more involvement in the Turkish Empire. But in contrast to the more annexationist tendencies of the rival empires, namely France, Russia and Britain, Germany sought quieter ways of penetration, through cultural and economic routes.

By the end of the 19th century while Germany was seeking expansion, Turkey was seeking a new, and more trustworthy European ally. The destinies of Germany and Turkey were slowly being linked.

Michael Solomon Alexander expended much of his energy on one major project while in Jerusalem for those four years – the building of a Protestant church. This church, when finally completed in 1849, was a focal point of national interest, for the Germans as well as for the British. It provided a cover under which to expand.

But with the new Germany, this cover was no longer big enough to shelter two visions, two ecclesiastical bodies, and two nations. The Germans came to view Christ Church as the British Church, the British emblem in Jerusalem. The time had come for Germany to branch out and establish her own independent cover. The growing relationship between Germany and Turkey facilitated this desire.

Already the Germans had obtained through the generosity of the Turkish Sultan property adjacent to the Church of the Holy Sepulchre in 1869. Here they slowly began to develop their own centre, including a small chapel. And here the foundations were laid for a larger complex – including a German church.

Gobat died in 1879, and the third Bishop, Joseph Barclay, was nominated by the British. Barclay died, prematurely, in 1881. The

---

[9] See: *Correspondence respecting the Protestant Bishopric at Jerusalem,* June 1887, FO 406/5460, entire document.

German Government then wanted to cancel the 1841 Jerusalem Protestant Bishopric agreement. The German ambassador at London, Count Munster wrote the following to Earl Granville, the British Foreign Minister:

> It is not only the necessity, springing from its internal needs, of freeing the largely increased German community from dependence on the Anglican sister Church, and giving it an independent organization, but also the fact that the results of the existing Agreement have but in a small measure fulfilled the views and expectations of His late majesty the King of Prussia, which has determined my Imperial Master to take this course ...
>
> At that time a German community can hardly be said to have existed, but it had to be called into life by the side of the English Mission Station already established, and it was only with the humblest beginnings that it first emerged into being. Now, however, that it exceeds the English colony in numbers, that it is provided with a chapel and school, a clergyman and teachers, with a hospital, and with various admirable invalid and orphan homes, it is in no respect inferior, in the extent and perfection of its organization, to the English sister community. The one thing still wanting to make its independent organization clearly manifest to the world is the possession of a church, which shall be able to hold its own with the churches of the other communities, and this, it is to be hoped, it will before long possess.[10]

In 1898 the German emperor, or kaiser, came to Jerusalem to officially open the new German church, the Church of the Redeemer. Everywhere the Turkish sultan laid out the red carpet – and bequeathed the German emperor several large tracts of land in the Holy City where future large German edifices were built – the Augusta Victoria Hospice, and the Dormition Abbey.

And to consolidate that growing geo-political connection, the sultan permitted a readjustment of Jaffa Gate, the entranceway into the Old City, in order to facilitate the entrance of the kaiser and his grand entourage. It was an ostentatious entrance if ever there was one.

On the same trip Kaiser Willhelm met with Theodore Herzl, the leader of the newly founded Zionist movement, which had been formed the previous year in Basle, Switzerland. The Zionists had fully anticipated that Germany would be the modern day Cyrus who would facilitate the return

---

[10] Munster to Earl Granville, 17 July 1882, *Correspondence respecting the Protestant Bishopric at Jerusalem*, FO 406/5460.

of the Jewish people to the Land of Israel. It was Germany they turned to in order to secure a grant from the Turkish sultan to permit a Jewish 'homeland' or national entity to develop in the Holy Land.

But Herzl himself was an unknown person, even within the Jewish community. How was it that he was able to meet the emperor of the German Empire and be permitted to propose such a radical plan? This meeting was arranged due to the intervention of an Anglican minister, William Hechler, then the chaplain of the British Embassy in Vienna. Hechler was a LJS associate, a renowned restorationist, and former tutor for the children of the Grand Duke of Baden, and thus well acquainted with the German royal family.

Hechler was Anglo-German in parentage and orientation, and was even a possible candidate for the vacant bishopric seat following Barclay's death. This never eventuated, but he accompanied the Zionist delegation to Jerusalem, and preached at Christ Church on 2 November 1898.

But despite all the potential for German support of such a vibrant movement, the German kaiser understood geo-politics all too well, and that to adopt or support such a movement would jeopardize his standing with the sultan and Turkey. The Turks had no desire to surrender any of their empire to a minority nationalist movement. The Zionists were rebuffed. This rejection caused them to turn, albeit slowly at first, and in time completely, to the only nation which historically had shown commitment to this hoped for Jewish restoration - Britain.

It was Britain, and not any of the other nations which in 1840 pressed forward the claims for Israel's restoration. And it was this very same period and time of expectancy which precipitated the king of Prussia's proposal for the Jerusalem bishopric. Coming on the heels of the War of 1840, and Britain's key role in delivering the Land of Israel, provided the backing and support for the Prussian proposal from the politicians, bishops and general British populace. Indeed it was this groundswell of interest, and the feeling that Turkey owed a debt to Britain, that created the environment for the Jerusalem Protestant bishopric to emerge.

The presence of the LJS, of the consulate and the bishopric were large factors in hereafter focusing the attention of Britons from many walks of life upon the activities and destiny of the Land of Israel.[11] And this was in

---

[11] For example, perhaps the most prestigious British society in the later part of the nineteenth century was the Palestine Exploration Fund (PEF) – linked to the War Office. The PEF had an office on LJS property adjacent to Christ Church, and many of its local office-bearers were LJS employees.

conjunction with the larger geo-political concern – how to maintain Britain's sea link to India against rival European powers.

And through the following decades a large question began growing in people's minds – in the event of the Turkish Empire falling, which European power would inherit, or take control over the Land of Israel?

That question came closer to being answered with the outbreak of the First World War. Britain found herself allied to France and Russia, and pitted against Germany, the Austro-Hungarian Empire, and Turkey.

Ultimately, in 1917, conquest of the disputed land became inevitable. British, Australian and New Zealand troops entered the Land of Israel and beginning at Beersheva on 31 October of that year, finally ousted the Turks, as well as the Germans and Austrians, from the entire region. The process that began with Napoleon in 1798, and was very much furthered in the events of 1840-1841, had indeed now come to a completion. A European power had in fact taken control over the Land of Israel.

The initial victory at Beersheva was simultaneous with the issuing of the Balfour Declaration,[12] Britain's official commitment to establishing a Jewish homeland in Palestine. Israel was being restored. Several weeks later, on 11 December 1917, General Allenby, representing Britain and the Allied nations, entered the Old City of Jerusalem. He entered on foot thereby providing an intriguing contrast to the ostentatious entrance of the kaiser, some nineteen years previously.

He ascended the steps leading to the Citadel or Fortress of David. The closest buildings to him, in fact only a few metres away and directly opposite, were those of Christ Church, of the LJS (today CMJ), where the St. James Chapel and the British Consulate were both once located.

One very common adage used in 1917 was that Britain was doing for the Jewish people the same that Cyrus the emperor of Persia had done for them some 2500 years before – restoring them to their homeland. Indeed, as the historical record reveals, this was very much the case. But this event of 1917 was preceded by that of 1840. The War of 1840 created the environment for Alexander coming to Jerusalem.

One important component of the Cyrus event was the re-introduction into Jerusalem of a reformed faith system. Alexander and his colleagues around the period of 1840 were involved in a similar aspect. Although this point could be contended, there is little doubt that in the mind of Alexander and his colleagues, the faith system they adhered too, Jewish or Hebrew Christianity, or by today's terminology Messianic Judaism, was

---

[12] This process was assisted by the findings of the *De Bunsen Committee* of 1915, chaired by Sir Maurice de Bunsen, Chevalier's Bunsen's grandson.

challenging the authority of Orthodox Judaism. Alexander's very good friend and mentor, Alexander McCaul, wrote:

SALVATION IS OF THE JEWS. Amongst all the religious systems in the world, there are two deserving of attentive consideration, and they are both of Jewish origin, and were once exclusively confined to the Jewish nation. They are now known by the names of Judaism and Christianity; but it must never be forgotten that the latter is as entirely Jewish as the former. The author of Christianity was a Jew. The first preachers of Christianity were all Jews. The first Christians were all Jews; so that, in discussing the truth of these respective systems, we are not opposing a Gentile religion to a Jewish religion, but comparing one Jewish creed with another Jewish creed. Neither, in defending Christianity, do we wish to diminish aught from the privileges of the Jewish people; on the contrary, we candidly acknowledge that we are disciples of the Jews, converts to Jewish doctrines, partakers of the Jewish hope, and advocates of that truth which the Jews have taught us. We are fully persuaded that the Jews whom we follow were in the right – that they have pointed out to us 'the old paths', 'the good way', and 'we have found rest to our souls'. And we, therefore, conscientiously believe that those Jews who follow the opposite system are as wrong as their forefathers, who, when God commanded them to walk in the good old way, replied, 'We will not walk therein.'[13]

The heart's desire of Michael Solomon Alexander was to point out to his fellow Jewish people the 'good old way,' as the Jewish followers of Jesus did in Jerusalem some 1700 years before.

However, there was one distinct difference between Alexander and those early Jewish followers of Jesus. In the first century of the common era, when the message of Jesus as Messiah was being first proclaimed, the adherents were all Jewish, and the first gentile adherents needed to 'convert' to the Judaism of the time in order to fully and equally partake of this new reformed faith system.

But in time, by a courageous decree of the Jewish leaders of this movement, or 'church' in Jerusalem, 'conversion' to Judaism was no longer a requirement. The way was now open for more such gentile followers of the Messiah from Nazareth. This was a totally new and radical development in the Jewish faith system.

This bold decision was fraught with danger. And it was quickly apparent that such apprehension was right. For in time the number of gentile followers of Jesus outstripped the Jewish, and the gentile followers soon

---

[13] A. McCaul, *The Old Paths*, (London, 1846), p. 1.

appropriated to themselves, often exclusively, the promises and blessings God had given to the Jewish nation.

The second period therefore of the history of this new, Messianic movement became completely synonymous with the gentiles, and Christianity became regarded as a gentile religious system, completely cut off from its Jewish roots.

Alexander was part of a movement in the Anglican and Protestant church which was endeavouring to restore to the church an appreciation of it's Jewish origins. But Alexander and his colleagues were fully aware that it was impossible for the church or believing community to ever be fully restored to that pioneer 'Jewish Church', the Church of St. James.

The spirit energizing the movement which brought Alexander to Jerusalem desired to introduce into the Holy City the historic conclusion of both of these two periods of the church – the Jewish and the Gentile.

Calman's eulogy stated it well when he said that Alexander 'acted as a connected link between Jew and Gentile.' Indeed the spirit of what Alexander represented was not in any way wanting to make the church entirely Jewish again. Alexander and this movement desired to see the church divested of the false assumption that it was gentile. The real purpose for the church in Jerusalem was to be where both the Jews and gentiles in Messiah, would be living as 'one new man.'[14]

This is the essence of the cultural or religious revolution that he was part of, and in many ways he drove, during his short time in Jerusalem. Michael Solomon Alexander was indeed a Hebrew of the Hebrews, an Israelite in whom there was no guile, an upholder of God's covenant promises with national Israel. And yet he professed Jesus as Messiah, and was therefore part of the universal 'church.' His presence was not only a challenge to those who professed that God had finished with Israel, but also to those who professed that Jesus was not Israel's Messiah.

Today these challenges are as relevant in Jerusalem and the Land of Israel as they were during Alexander's time. Christians in Israel today, Jewish, gentile, (British, German, and others), are indebted to this legacy of Michael Solomon Alexander. Indeed Michael Solomon Alexander was the ideal role model: a strong sense of his Jewish identity and yet a firm respecter of the gentiles who were fellow followers of Jesus the Messiah.

I conclude with one of the most touching modern tributes to the role and legacy of Alexander, which was stated by scholar Patrick Irwin, at the Ecclesiastical Historical Society:

---

[14] See the book of Ephesians chapters 2 and 3 and Alexander's letter to the LJS in 1843, quoted in *JI*, 1843, p. 3, found on page. 182.

For the Church Alexander had created something of lasting worth. His modest and hard-won success so beset by controversy in establishing a Hebrew Christian congregation in Jerusalem ensured that Christian Jewry would have a share in the development of the Holy Land.   He had established foundations on which others could build. Mission to the Jews would no longer be the principal activity of the Anglican bishopric, but Alexander's episcopate had bound it securely to the Anglican Church.

The Jews of Jerusalem too were Alexander's debtors.   In his encouragement of the medical mission he had demonstrated that his love for the Jews was not dependent upon their accepting Christianity. Alexander can with justice take his place among the Jews of the nineteenth century who sought to raise up the Jews of Jerusalem from their state of degradation. The activities of these Jewish philanthropists can indeed be regarded as a response to the challenge provided by the pioneer Christian enterprises of Alexander's episcopate.

Thus as Christian pastor and Jerusalem pioneer Alexander has two distinct claims on posterity's regard.   They have survived the evaporation of the unrealistic expectations of 1841. The restoration of Israel was delayed and the link with Prussia faded, but Alexander's modest achievements remain.   Perhaps most appealing, though, is Alexander the man, the convert with a passionate concern for the Jewish people that transcended all difficulties.   An innocent abroad he may have been, but his generosity of spirit is singularly refreshing. The Holy City has never lacked energetic defenders of the faith. Alexander was something rarer in Jerusalem, a tolerant divine.[15]

Postscript

As we enter the 21st century in Jerusalem, Christ Church continues to be a community of Jews and Gentiles believing Alexander's and Nicolayson's teaching and pursuing their vision in the Church, the Heritage Centre, Alexander College, Shoresh Study Tours, Immanuel Book Shop, the Guest House, and the independent Hebrew speaking congregation: the vision of a restored Israel, and of the one new man in Messiah Jesus. And, like Alexander and Nicolayson, they await the coming of Jesus, who, it is believed, will consummate God's covenant relationship with Israel and the redeemed of the nations.

---

[15] Patrick Irwin, *ibid,* pp. 326-7.

Selected Bibliography

Archives Used
Bodleian Library, Oxford.
British National Archives, Kew (FO = Foreign Office files).
Conrad Schick Library, Christ Church, Jerusalem. ITAC Archives.
King's College Archive, the Strand, London (*King's College Calendar*).
Lambeth Palace, Archive, London.
National Library of Ireland, Dublin (*Dublin Register,* 1826 & 1841*).
RCB Library, Dublin.
St. Anthony's Library, Oxford.

Books
Aiton, J. *The Lands of the Messiah, Mahomet, and the Pope: as visited in 1851* (London, 1852).
Alexander, Deborah. *Autobiography,* unpublished manuscript, Alexander Papers, Lambeth Palace Archives, London.
Alexander, M.S. *Memoir of Sarah J.W. Alexander, daughter of Rev. M.S. Alexander. Written by her father,* no publishing details.
Battiscombe, G. *Shaftesbury A Biography of the Seventh Earl 1801-1885.* (London: Constable, 1974).
Bebbington, D.W. *Evangelicalism in Modern Britain,* (London: Unwin Hyman, 1979).
Ben Arieh, Y. *Jerusalem in the Nineteenth Century,* (Jerusalem, 1984), Vol I.
Bicheno, James. *The Restoration of the Jews, And the Crisis of all Nations,* (London, 1800).
Clark, Christopher. *The Politics of Conversion,* (Oxford, 1995).
Corey, M. *From Rabbi to Bishop,*(London, 1956).
Dunlop, Rev J. *Memories of Gospel Triumphs amongst the Jews,* (London, 1894).
Eliav, M. *Britain and the Holy Land,* (Jerusalem: Yad Ben Zvi, 1997).
Eliav, M. *Eretz Israel and its Yishuv in the Nineteenth century (1777-1917)* (Jerusalem, 1978) [Hebrew].
Encyclopedia Britannica. (London & New York, 1926).
Ewald, Rev. F.C. *Journal of Missionary Labours in the City of Jerusalem,* (London, 1846).
Finn, E.A. *Reminiscenses,* (London: Marshall, Morgan & Scott, 1930).
Finn, James. *Stirring Times or records from Jerusalem Consular Chronicles of 1853-1856,* edited by Elizabeth Finn, (London: C. Kegan Paul & Co., 1878).
Friedmann, Isaiah. *The Question of Palestine, 1914-1918: British-Jewish-Arab Relations* (New York: Shocken, 1973).
Gidney, W.T. *The History of the London Society for Promoting*

Christianity Amongst the Jews, (London, 1908

Hatchard, J. *The Predictions and Promises of God Respecting Israel, (Appendix)*, (London, 1825).

Hearnshaw, F. J.C. *The Centenary History of King's College London*, (London, 1929).

Hechler, W.H. *The Jerusalem Bishopric*, (London, 1883).

Hodder, E. *The Life and Work of the Seventh Earl of Shaftesbury* (London: Cassell & Co., 1887).

Hole, C. *Early History of the Church Missionary Society for Africa and the East to the end of AD 1814* (Church Missionary Society, London, 1896).

Hyamson, A. *British Consulate in Jerusalem in relation to the Jews of Palestine 1838-1914*, (London, 1939).

Jocz, J. *The Jewish People and Jesus Christ*, (London, 1962).

Johns, J.W. *The Anglican Cathedral Church of St. James Jerusalem*, (London, 1844).

Lieber, S. *Mystics and Missionaries*, The Jews in Palestine, 1799-1840, (Salt Lake City, 1992).

Maurice, F.D. *Three Letters to the Rev. W. Palmer*, (London, 1842).

McCaul, Alexander. *A Sermon preached in the chapel of Lambeth Palace at the Consecration of the Lord Bishop of the United Church of England and Ireland in Jerusalem on Sunday, November 7, 1841*, (London, 1841),

Newman, J.H. Cardinal . *Apologia Pro Vita Sua*, (London, 1890).

Orchard, Stephen. *English Evangelical Eschatology 1790-1850*, unpublished thesis, (Cambridge, 1992).

Parry, Yarom. *British Mission to the Jews in nineteenth century Palestine*, (London: Frank Cass, 2003).

Ransom, D.R.M. *Life of Mrs. Ransom*, Unpublished manuscript, copy in author's possession. (London, 1913).

Ridley, Jasper. *Lord Palmerston*, (New York: E.P. Dutton, 1971).

Sacher, H.A. *A History of Israel* (New York, 1976).

Schwarzfuchs, Simon. *Napoleon the Jews and the Sandhedrin*, (London, 1979).

Stein, Leon. *The Balfour Declaration*, (London, 1961).

Tibawi, A. L. *British Interests in Palestine 1800-1901*, (Oxford, 1961).

Trevelyan, G.M. *The History of England*, (Longmans Green and Co: (London, 1948).

Wolf, L. *Notes on the Diplomatic History of the Jewish Question*, (London, 1919).

Articles

Blake, Robert, *The Origins of the Jerusalem Bishopric*, in *Church State and Society in the 19th Century*, (Munchen: 1984), pp. 87-95.

Brown, Malcolm, *The Jews of Norfolk and Suffolk before 1840* in Jewish

Historical Studies. Transactions of The Jewish Historical Society of England, vol. 32, 1990-92.

Detzler, Wayne, A. Seeds of Missiology in the German *Erwecking* (1815-1848) . In *JETS* 38/2 (June 1995) 231-239.

Ehrlich, Richard A. *Michael Solomon Alexander, The First Evangelical Bishop in Jerusalem*, in AJR Information, April 1963, London.

Greaves, R.W. *The Jerusalem Bishopric 1841*, English Historical Review 1949 LXIV.

Irwin, Patrick, "Bishop Alexander and the Jews of Jerusalem' in Studies in Church History, Vol. 21: Persecution and Toleration, ed. W.J.Shields, Oxford 1984.

Skinner, James, *The Three Anglican Bishops in Jerusalem,* in Church Quarterly Review, July 1884.

Taylor, B. *Alexander's Apostasy: First Steps to Jerusalem*, in *Christianity and Judaism,* Ecclesiastical Historical Society, (Oxford, 1992).

Verete ,M *A Plan for the Internationalization of Jerusalem* in From Palmerston to Balfour: Collected Essays of Mayir Verete, (London, Frank Cass).

Verete, M. *The Restoration of the Jews in English Protestant Thought 1790-1840;* in Middle Eastern Studies, January 1972, (Frank Cass and Co, London).

Verete, M, *Why the British established a Consulate in Jerusalem,* English Historical Review, LXXXV, April, 1970.

Welch, P. J. *Anglican Churchmen and the establishment of the Jerusalem Bishopric,* in Journal of Ecclesiastical History, Vol 8, No 2, 1957.

Newspapers

Allgemeine Zeitung des Judenthums, 4 March 1844.
Allgemeine Zeitung des Judenthums, 31 October 1843.
Plymouth and Devonport Journal on 11 November 1824.
Norwich Chronicle, 6 July and 28 December 1822.
Christian Observer, November 1841, New Series, xlvii.
Morning Herald, 3 February 1843.
Morning Post, 12 April, 1843.
Times, 5 December 1845.

Periodicals

Jewish Expositor (JE), Monthly reports of the London Jews Society.
Jewish Intelligence (JI) Monthly reports of the London Jews Society.
Jewish Missionary Intelligence (JMI), Monthly reports of the London Jews Society.
King's College Calendar.

LJS Report, Report of the London Society for Promoting Christianity among the Jews.

Journals
LJS Local Committee *Journal 1842-1867.*
Letters London to Nicolayson, 1843-1856.
Letters from Jerusalem, 1834-1842.

Selected Websites
en.wikipedia.org/wiki/Druses
www.bkerke.org.lb/themaronites.html
www.zinzendorf.com/countz.htm
prayerfoundation.org/christian_history_timeline_2.htm
www.polishroots.org/genpoland/pos.htm
en.wikipedia.org/wiki/Schonlanke
faithstrengthened.org/FS_Biography.html
www.aim25.ac.uk/cgi-bin/search2?coll_id
www.royaltyguide.nl/families/hohenzollern/hhzkings2.htm
www.schloss-albrechtsberg.de/index.php
www.bautz.de/bbkl/h/hechler_w_h.shtml
www.factbites.com/topics/West-Prussia
www.norwich.gov.uk/webapps/contact/ContactUS.asp
en.wikipedia.org/wiki/Spice_trade
www.jewishgates.com/file
Thomas Haweis Collection,
www.smu.edu/bridwell/html/ManuscriptCollection.htm#Thaweis
en.wikipedia.org/wiki/Moses_Mendelsohn
www.allaboutturkey.com
www.bautz.de/bbkl
www.zinzendorf.com/countz.htm

Pamphlets
The Jerusalem Bishopric, (London, Hatchard & Son, 1856)

Selective Index

A

Abbasids [Empire], iv
Abbott, Dr., 227
Abeken, Herr Heinrich, 98, 212-4, 223-4
Aberdeen, Lord, 79, 84-5, 93, 106, 126, 129, 130, 142-5, 158-9, 160, 173-4, 176, 181, 190, 201-2, 207-8, 215,
Abood Markos, 107-8
Aboukir Bay, 8
Abraham [patriarch], 67, 93, 114, 117, 138, 151, 153, 168, 229
Abu Ghosh [Abu Ghoosh], village and sheikh of, 161, 198, 200
Abyssinia, 95, 114, 120, 126, 193, 238
Acco, Acre, vi, 8, 64, 184, 186, 208
Acts [book of], 98-9
Acworth, Mr., 192
Addington Articles, 82
Aiton, J, 214
Ali Pasha, 217, 220-21
Albanian, 232
Aldermanbury Conferences, 45
Aleppo, 149, 196
Alexander, Anna [Annie], 105, 115, 156, 197
Alexander, Benjamin [Benny], 105, 165
Alexander, Bessy, 105
Alexander, Deborah (Jnr), 42, 98, 105, 119, 135, 155-6, 168, 197, 230
Alexander, Mrs. Deborah (Too many references).
Alexander, Emily, 198
Alexander, Fanny, 98, 105, 106, 119, 155, 168, 210-11, 223, 226, 230
Alexander, Louisa, 112-3, 156
Alexander, Minnie, 105

Alexander, Rabbi (Brother), 9, 35
Alexander, Rabbi (Father), 1, 9
Alexander, Robert, 51, 105, 156
Alexander, Salome, 156, 197
Alexander, Sarah, 29, 51
Alexander, (Sister), 37
Alexandria, 145,223
Alicarz, Mrs., 24
Alison, Mr., 190
Allenby, General, 243
Allgemeine Zeitung des Judenthums, 153, 194
All Hallow's Church [Exeter], 25
All Saint's Day, 134
Altmann, Mr, 18
Altmark, 36
American Board of Commissioners for Foreign Missions (American Board), i, 108, 121, 186-8
America [United States of America], 3, 28, 78
Amer Pasha, 106-7
Amzalak, Jospeh [Amstek], 121-2, 153
Anderson, Rufus, 187
Anglican [Church of England], 84, 86-8, 113, 212
Anglo Catholic [High Church, see also Tractarians and Oxford movement], viii, 87-8
Antioch, 115, 149
Apostolic Anglican Church [Jerusalem], 239
Arab, Arabs, 107, 233, 239
Arab Nationalism, 188
Archbishop of Canterbury, 81, 84-5, 87, 95, 118, 144-5, 147, 176, 208
Armagh, 28
Armenia, Armenians, Armenian Church, 57, 118, 122, 178, 208

Armenian Patriarch, 118, 178, 231
Ashkenazi, Ashkenazim, 194, 200, 206
Assad Pasha, 164,
Assyria, Assyrian Empire, iii
Augusta Victoria Hospice, 241
Augsburg [Confession of], 87-8, 94
Australian, 243
Austria, [Austro-Hungarian Empire], vii, viii, 58, 61, 85, 111, 189, 243
Ayerst, Rev. W, 33-7, 39-40, 42, 111, 129-30, 173, 175

B

Babylon, [Empire], iii, 216,
Baghdad, iv
Bak, Rabbi Israel, 200
Balfour Declaration, vii, 243
Ballymena, 28-9
Bankhead, Mr., 92
Barante, Brugiere de, 68
Baring, Sir Thomas, 54, 98, 104, 196, 199, 204, 205
Barclay, Bishop Joseph, 240
Barnett, Consul-General, 227
Basily, Constantine, 147-8
Basle [Basle Bible College], 5
Bateson, Robert, 177
Bedouin, 228-9
Beersheva, 243
Behrens, Alexander Isaac, 149, 170, 172, 185-6, 192, 207-8, 236
Beirut [Beyrout], 98, 106, 122, 130-1, 139, 140, 143, 145, 149, 157, 160, 164-5, 170-1, 181, 187, 195, 198-9, 207, 220
Belfast, 28-9
Bergheim, Maria, 236
Bergheim, Melville Peter, 114, 120, 122, 124-5, 236
Berlin, 5, 9, 30, 34, 42, 73, 173, 181
Bethesda Chapel [Dublin], 27, 30

Bethlehem, 115, 123, 138
Bethlehem, bishop of [Lutheran], 83-4
Bethlehem Gate, 109
Bible Depot [Jaffa], 193
Bicheno, Rev. James, 8
Bickersteth, Rev. Edward, 52-3, 116
Bidwell, John, 190
Bikur Cholim Hospital, 152
Bir el Abd, 232
Bishop of Bethlehem [Greek], 115, 123
Bishopric of the Church of St. James at Jerusalem, 96
Bismark, Otto von, 240
Bishopp, Sir Cecil, 197-8
Blackburn, Rev., 136, 229
Black Sea, 8, 46
Blomfield, Bishop [of London], 77, 84-5, 88, 98, 208
Blood Libel, 59, 61
Bonar, Andrew, 169
Book Shop, [Jerusalem], 191
Book of Common Prayer [English & Hebrew], 48, 115, 191, 211
Bordaki, Rabbi Isaiah [Yeshayahu], 128-9, 133, 195
Bosphorus, vii, 46, 78
Bowring, Dr. John, 154-5
Bristol, 41
British Ambassador [Constantinople], 109, 113, 144, 157, 173, 188-9, 191
British & Foreign Bible Society, i
British Consulate-General [Cairo], 54, 229
British Consulate-General [Beirut], 139
British Consulate [Jerusalem], 56, 164, 170, 215, 218, 229, 243
British Fleet [Navy], 17, 103,
Buckingham Palace, 94,
Bunsen, Christian or Chevalier [de], 52-3, 73-4, 76, 79, 80-1, 83-5, 93-4, 96, 98, 112, 141, 174, 213-4, 239

Bunsen Memorandum, 81
Bynes, Benjamin [John Benjamin Goldberg], 127, 133, 139, 148
Byzantium [Byzantine Empire], iv, v

C
Cadi [Kadi], 107, 171
Cairo, 144, 223, 225-6, 229-30, 233
Calcutta, 78
Caliph, v, 55, 69, 215
Callenberg, Johann Heinrich, 3, 6
Calvin, Calvinism, 53, 87
Calman, Erasmus Scott, 63-4, 127, 132, 237-8, 245
Cancelleria, 217
Canning, Sir Stratford, 98, 140, 157-8, 168-9, 174, 175, 180-1, 188-9, 190, 201, 209, 215, 223
Canterbury, 88
Capitulations, 6, 57, 141, 194
Capuchin monk, 59
Carmelite monastery, 184
Cartwright, Rev. James, 10, 31, 48
Castlereagh, Lord, 119
Castle of David [David's Citadel or fortress], 122, 199, 243
Catholics [see Roman Catholic]
Cecil, Miss, 230, 237
Chaldea, 95, 126, 193
Chedafan, Dr., 227
Cherem [excommunication], 132, 206
Cheyne, Dr., 32-3
Chief rabbi, 14
Chizuk Emunah, 167, 207
Chichester, Earl of, 71, 78
Chrisburg, 36
Christ Church [Jerusalem], 240, 243
Christian Zionist, ii
Christmas Day, 136, 177, 191
Church Missionary Society (CMS), i, 4, 71, 78-9, 113-4, 223, 225-6, 231

Church of Ireland Jews Society, 27
Church of the Holy Sepulchre, 70, 213, 240
Church of the Nativity, 115
Church of the Redeemer, 241
Church of St. James, 94, 96-7, 154
Circumcision, 1, 86, 96, 97
Cohen, Mr. [Smyrna], 194
Colchester, 12, 30, 50
Coleman, Rev. John, 196-8
Coleraine, 29
Colonial [Foreign] Bishoprics Act [1841], 75
Colonial Bishoprics Fund [1840], 78, 83
Congress of Vienna, 69
Conitz, 39
Constantinople, v, 58-9, 60, 63, 70-1, 80, 82, 85, 88, 92-3, 113, 130, 139, 140-2, 149, 154, 157, 168, 172-5, 180, 188, 190, 194, 201, 209, 212, 215
Constanz, 50
Convent of Jacobius, 89
Consular Church, 175,
Cooper, Anthony Ashley [see Shaftesbury]
Copts [Coptic Church], 122, 144, 225, 231
Corinthinians [books of], 233
Cork, 28, 32
Courban Bairam, 108
Court of the Mechami, 154
Covenant, 3, 210, 229, 245-6
Cresson, Warden, 187
Critchlow, R. Bates, 140, 163, 233
Crusader, i, v, 164
Cyrus, 63, 98-9, 241-2
Czersk, 39
Czerskier, M, 48

D
Dalton, Dr. George, ii, 56, 200
Damascus, iv, 59, 60, 149, 186,

193, 210-11, 224
Danzig, 34-6, 38-9, 42
Dardanelles, 8, 46
Davis, A, 149
Derby, 44
Derry [Londonderry], 29
Devonport, 17, 20
Dias, Bartholemew, vi
Divan, 91
Djebail, 211, 225
Dormition Abbey, 241
Doyle, Major, 107
Dragoman, 139, 231
Drogheda, 29
Druitch, Rabbi Solomon, 17
Druse [Druze], 106, 176, 210-11
Dublin, ix, 25-7, 32-3, 38
Ducat, A.L., 114, 118, 236
Ducat, Christina, 177, 192
Ducat, Rose, 114, 118, 236
Ducat, Tege Christian, 236
Dundalk, 29
Dunstable, 50
Dutch [Holland, Netherlands], vi, 34

E

Eastern Question, 46
East India Company [English], vi
Eastnor, Lord, 212
Eastlake, Sir Charles, 212
Ecclesiastical Commission, 85
Egypt, Egyptians, v, vi, vii, 7, 8, 46, 52, 54, 57-8, 61-2, 64, 68, 77, 95, 113, 126, 166, 174, 193, 220, 223-4, 230
Ehrlich, Richard, 43
Eichhorn, Karl, 102
El Arish, 223, 232
El Geel, 233
Elijah [the prophet], 210
Ellen [maid], 105
Episcopal Jews Chapel, 32, 42, 49, 99, 224
Epstein, [Eppstein] Moses, 192, 237

Erskine, Rev. H.M., 119,
Ethiopians [Ethiopian Church], 123,
Euphrates River, ii,
Eutychian heresy, 123,
Evangelical, evangelicals, 4,
Ewald, Rev. F.C, 42, 104, 106-7, 114-5, 118, 123-5, 127-8, 133-6, 138, 161, 167-8, 169, 183, 193, 196
Ewald, Mrs., 183,
Exeter, 24-6,
Ezekiel [the prophet], 22,
Ezra, 216

F

Feast of Tabernacles, 36
Finn, Elizabeth Anne [see McCaul]
Finn, James, 39, 216, 238-9
Finzi, Mr., 208
Firman [*Firman*], 88-9, 90-1, 141-3, 158, 173-4, 179, 190-1, 208, 210, 215-8, 220-22
Fisk, Pliny, ii
Fisk, Dr. George, 119-20
Foreign Bishoprics Act [*Jerusalem Bishopric Act*], 94
France, French, vi, vii, 8, 54, 57-8, 64, 67, 71, 85, 86, 104, 111, 130, 153, 163-5, 168, 181, 202, 208, 220, 222, 229, 240
Franciscans, v
Francke, August Hermann, 2, 3
Francke Institute, *Franckesche Stifungen*, 2, 3
Frankel, Dr. Simon, 152-3, 194
Franks, 92, 199
Franz, J.M, 237
Freemasons, 171
Freistadt, 35
French Ambassador [Constantinople], 166-7, 189
French Consul [Jerusalem], 166, 168, 178-9
French Consul [Damascus], 59
French fleet, 8

French Revolution, 2, 3
Frey, Joseph, 5
Friedmann, Isaiah, 63

G
Gaguine, Rabbi Abraham, 153, 206
Galatians, [Epistle of], 86
Galilee [Sea of], 170, 185
Gannon, Miss, 105
Gaza, 224, 228, 232
Gedaliah, 39
Genesis [book of], 229
Geneva, 87-8
Gentile, Gentile Church, iii, 100-2, 182, 204, 244-5
German, Germany, 2, 4, 5, 6, 33-4, 68, 71, 74, 76, 80, 88, 94, 102, 140, 150, 176, 188, 240-2
German Church, 76, 86, 102, 113
'German' Church [Dublin], 26, 30-2
German colonists, 172
German Protestantism [Evangelical German Church], 102, 118
German service [Jerusalem], 114, 136, 148, 162, 167, 191
Gethsemane [garden of], 156
Gibraltar, 106
Giffna [Jifna], 121, 214
Gional, Giorgio Abraham, 237
Gladstone, William, 87, 94, 98
Glascock, Captain Nugt, 200
Gobat, Samuel, 183, 188, 238-9
Golding, Benjamin [Bass], 15, 17, 20, 21, 24-5
Goldberg, J.B [Benjamin], 237
Gosport, 6, 105
Grandanz, 35
Grane, Mr, 49
Granville, Lord, 241
Greece, 46
Greek Orthodox Church, iii, v, 57, 70, 78, 86, 88, 96, 102, 104, 111, 114-5, 121, 138, 142, 178, 180, 208, 212, 222

Greek Orthodox Patriarch [Jerusalem], v, 212, 231
Groves, Mr. and Mrs., 24
Guildford, 50
Guinness, Arthur, 27, 98, 105
Guinness, Hosea, 29
Guizot, Francois, 67-9

H
Habershon, Matthew, 140, 174, 191
Hadrian [Adrian], 134
Haida Pasha, 183,
Haifa, 184
Halle, 2
Halukah, 123, 133, 171
Hanauer, Christian Willhelm, 168, 193, 237
Hancock, Miss, 14, 18, 32
Harcourt, Archbishop of York, 77
Hassidim [Chasidim], 193
Hatchard, Rev. John, 20, 22-3
Hatti Sherif of Gulhane, 58, 71, 216
Hausner, Christian, 194-5
Haweis, Dr, 4, 5
Hawtrey, Mr, 25, 29
Hay, Rev. Lord. Thomas, 198
Heald, Mr., 186
Hebeler, Mr., 98
Hebrew [language, tribes], 14, 48, 61, 67, 120, 162, 192, 197, 214
Hebrew Bishop, 112, 116
Hebrew Christian, 112, 122, 134, 138-9, 170-2, 182, 192, 195-6, 233, 244
Hebrew Christian Church, 149, 150
Hebrew College, 162-3, 178
Hebrew nation, 146, 152
Hebrew Protestant Church, 239
Hebrew service [Jerusalem], 112, 148, 150, 182, 204
Hebron, 138, 149, 150, 201-2, 208, 229
Hechler, William, 71
Heliopolis, 231

Herzl, Theodore, 71, 242
HMS Devastation, 105-7
HMS Hatchet, 112
HMS Infernal, 105
HMS Tyne, 200,
HMS Vesuvius, 107, 122
HMS Warspite, 210
Hernhut, 2, 5
Hibernian Hotel, 26
Hillier, Mr., 191
Hirsch, Isaac [Paul Herschon, Hershon], 148, 237
Hirschel [Herschell] Chief Rabbi Solomon, 12, 18, 19, 136
Hoga, Stanilaus, 48
Holy Land (also Land of Israel, Palestine, Syria – too many references)
Hosea [the prophet], 21
Hospital, English Mission, 200-1, 206, 214,
Hospitum, 103
House of Commons, 83, 154,
House [School] of Industry, 163, 192, 214
House of Israel, 138, 146, 235
House of Judah, 111
House of Lords, 83
House of Simon the Tanner, 135-6
Howley, Archbishop, 77, 98
Hunt, Holman, 122

I

Ibrahim Pasha, 54, 185
Id Al-Adha, 108
India [Indian Ocean], vi, vii, 7, 202, 229-30
Inglis, Sir Robert, 98, 104, 154,
Inquirers Home, 162-3
Ipswich, 50
Ireland, 26-7, 32, 49
Isaac, 117, 229
Isaiah [the prophet], 22, 98-9, 110, 136, 145, 204
Islam, v, 221
Islamic Law [*Sharia*], 113
Israelite, 148, 150, 177, 245

Italy, 7
Institutum Judaicum, 3, 4
Izzet Pasha, 135, 139, 142

J

Jacob [Israel], 117, 192, 229
Jacobin [Jacobite], 174
Jaenicke, Rev. John, 5
Jaffa, 107, 112, 122, 127-8, 132, 135-6, 168-9, 190, 193, 198-9, 200-1, 210, 228
Jaffa Gate, 107-9, 156, 241
James, brother of Jesus [St. James], iv, 97
Koran, 165
Jehoshaphat [Valley of], 156
Jeremiah [the prophet], 21-2, 120, 145, 197, 211,
Jerusalem Protestant Bishopric [too many references]
Jerusalem Plan [*Plan*], 74, 79, 81, 88
Jesus (the Messiah), ii, iv, ix, 3, 16, 27, 28, 37, 123, 127, 184, 221, 244-5
Jewish believers [in Jesus. See also Hebrew Christians], 102, 235
Jewish Bishop, 95, 96-7, 104, 150
Jewish Church, 102, 150
Jewish Operative Institution, 42
Jewish people [too many references]
Jewish Quarter, 125
Jewish Revolts, ii
Johns, James, 108, 118, 124, 134, 174, 191
Jonas, Edward, 124, 237
Joseph, Abraham, 237
Joseph [Patriarch], 229
Judaism [Orthodox], 196, 244
Judea, 102

K

Kaiser William II, 240-43
Karaite, 201
Kavanagh, Arthur, 212

Kaye, Bishop, 77
Kedron [Kidron] Valley, 156
Keavus, Mr., 201
Kemp, Dr. van der, 6
Kerns, Thomas, 161, 186, 225, 227
Kiel, Dr. Anton, 120, 177, 207
Kiel, Mrs. Marie, 177
Kiel, Sophie, 177
King, Jonas, ii
King's College, 43-5, 50-1, 60
King of Naples, 69
King Frederick William III, 3, 9
King Frederick William IV, vii, 70, 73-4, 76, 80-1, 83, 90, 93, 96, 104, 118, 140, 146, 161-2, 172, 239
King Louis-Philippe, 64, 68
Kingston, Rev. Thomas, 29
Kingswalden, 51
Koenigsmark, Count de, 85, 90, 92, 173
Konigsberg, 149
Kruse, Rev.W and Mrs., 227

L
Labouchere, John, 104
Lake Constanz, 50
Lamartine, Alphonse de, 68
Lambeth, 87, 98
Lamentations [book of], 120, 197
Lampen, Mr., 21
Lantivy, de, 164-5, 166-7, 199, 202- 3
Latin, Latin Church [see also Roman Catholic Church], v, 86, 96, 102, 104, 163, 178, 180, 212
Lebanon, 188, 202, 238
Le Coq, M, 173, 190
Lepsius, Dr. Carl, 212
Lessen, 35, 40
Levant [Levantine], ii, iv, 8, 69, 79, 85, 240
Levi, Mrs., 15, 17, 20, 31, 32
Levi, [Lyons, Lion] Judah, 177, 191, 195, 237
Lewis, William Bucknor, ii, 28,

56, 200
Lieder, Rev. J. and Mrs., 225-230
Lifta, 167
Lisbon, 106
Lisburn, 29
Liverpool, 29, 93
London, 15, 32-3, 45, 50, 56, 63-4, 67, 77, 91, 124, 127, 139, 157, 173, 213, 230
London Conference [1841], 75
London Jews Society [LJS;
London Society for Promoting Christianity among the Jews. Too many references]
London Missionary Society [LMS], 4, 5
Lord, Mr. J.A, 208
Loria [Luria, Lauria], Eleazer [Christian], 127, 139, 148, 237
Lutheran [Church], 5, 7, 53, 74, 87-8
Lydda, 198, 212
Lyndsay, Rev. Dr. [Bishop of Kildare], 33

M
Macgowan, Dr. Edward, 104, 106, 114, 119, 120-1, 124-5, 133, 135-6, 148, 153, 157, 161, 163-6, 168, 178, 183-5, 196-7, 200-1, 206, 227, 235, 238
Machpelah, Cave of, 138
Magee, Archbishop Dr. William, 27, 30, 32, 33
Mahometanism, [Mussulmans, Mahomedan], 82, 90, 97, 154
Mallis, M. Levy, 236
Malta, 75. 78-9, 106, 113, 129, 238
Mameluke, Mamelukes, v, 7
Mamilla [Pool], 183, 206
Mamre, Oak of, Plain of, 138
Manners, Lord John, 87
Manning, Mr., 177
Marabuti, Consul M., 128-9, 130,
Marco Polo, v

Marcussohn, Herman, 237
Marcussohn, J. Lisschiltz, 236
Margaret [nurse], 105, 230
Marienburg [Malbork], 35, 39
Maronite, [Church], 106, 176
Marsh, Rev. William, 12, 25, 29-
    30, 38, 117
Mason, Sir Francis, 106
Matback, Yosef Jarash, 107
Matthew [book of], 13
Matthias, Mr., 30
Mattran [bishop], 135
Mayers, John Michael, 30-2
McCaul, Rev. Alexander, 35, 38-
    9, 45, 47-9, 60, 79, 80, 93, 98-9,
    117, 191, 243
McCaul, Elizabeth [Finn], 38-39,
    48, 80, 217, 239
McCheyne, Robert, 169
Mediterranean, iii, 46, 64, 75, 126
Mehmet [Muhammed] Ali, 46, 55,
    57-8, 62, 64, 72, 154, 185, 231
Mekhame, 165
Melbourne, Lord, 74, 79
Memorial for Protestant Church,
    208-9
Mendelsohn, Moses, 36
Messianic Judaism, 243
Meshullam, Elijah, 237
Meshullam, John, 115, 237
Meshullam, Maria [Rosenthal],
    237
Meshullam, Peter, 237
Methodius, Greek Patriach of
    Antioch, 115,
Metternich, Prince, 58, 69, 70,
Mewe [Meve], 35-6
Micah, 22
Migdal [Galilee], 185
Millenialist, Millenarian, 2, 53
Millet, ii, 188, 221
Missionaries [Mission], 146, 152-
    3, 160, 194, 204
Mitchell, Murray, 227
Moltke, Helmuth von, 71
Monastery of the Cross, 120
Moneymore, 29

Monophysite, 86
Montefiore, Sir Moses, 59, 125,
    139, 152, 167, 193-4, 200, 203
Morad, 210
Moravian [Church], 2,5,6,7
Morning Herald, 112, 152
Moses, 20, 229
Mount Charles, [Mountcharles]
    Earl of, 192, 198
Mount Gerizim, 192
Mount of Olives, 120
Mount Tabor, vii
Muhleisan, John, 114, 120
Munster, Count, 241
Murray, Bishop, 98
Muslim, Muslims [Mussulmans],
    v, 55, 57, 108, 110, 115, 164-5,
    171, 179, 181, 183, 222
Mustapha Pasha, 113, 114

N
Nablus, 184, 192
Napier, Admiral, 64, 72
Napoleon Bonaparte, vi, 1, 7, 8, 9,
    46, 229, 242
Napoleonic Wars, 2,7
Naumberg, 73
Nazarene, [movement], 166
Nazareth, iv, vii, 8, 70, 184
Nebuchadnezzar, 39
Nelson, Admiral, vi, 7
Nesselrode, Count Karl, 70,
Newbolt, Henry, 217, 219-21, 233
Newenham, Robert, 27
Newman, John Henry, 86-7
Newry, 29
New Testament, 9, 12-4, 20, 47,
    123, 214
New Zealand, 78, 98, 243
Nicolayson, Rev. John, 1, 46-7,
    52, 54, 66, 88-9, 104, 107, 109,
    111-4, 119, 123-4, 128, 132-4,
    135-6, 139, 141, 143, 147-9,
    159, 161, 171, 173, 175, 178,
    187-9, 190, 194, 200, 206, 209,
    212, 222, 230-33, 239
Nicolayson, Bessie, 230

Niebuhr, Bartold, 52
Nile, 202, 225
Norwich, 13-4, 16, 41
Nuremberg, 35
Nydick, 35

O
Old Paths, 191
Old Testament, 15, 210
Orthodox Christians [see Greek Orthodox]
Orthodox Judaism, 243
Orthodox Patriarch [see Greek Patriarch]
Osterode, 36

P
Paget, Miss, 24-5
Pahlen, Petrovich, 69
Palestine Place [London], 7, 32, 42, 45, 50-1
Palestine Exploration Fund, 242
Palmeira, nurse, 106
Palmerston, Lord, vii, 46, 54, 56, 58-9, 61-6, 69, 71, 75, 77-8, 81, 89, 90, 97, 113, 126, 145, 169-70
Paris, 182, 202
Parliament, 80, 82, 84, 154
Parsons, Levi, iii
Parthian Empire, iv
Pashalik [pashalic], 68, 70, 72
Patriarchs, 138
Peel, Prime Minister, 79, 83, 155, 202
Persia, iii, 216
Pieritz, George, 60, 114, 123
Pietist, Pietist movement, 2,3,5,6
Pilgrim's Progress, 191
Pisani, Mr., 91
Pitt, Miss, 105
Plymouth, viii, 15-7, 19, 24-5, 31, 41
Plympton, 20
Poland, ix, 38, 45, 63, 169
Ponsonby, Ambassador, 65, 80, 88-9, 91, 106, 113, 140, 144,

208
Pool of Hezekiah, 110
Porte [Sublime Porte], 85, 89, 90, 92-3, 96, 102-3, 106, 109, 126-7, 143, 209, 215, 218
Portsea, 50
Portuguese, vi
Posen, 1,9,11, 34-5, 42
Poutenberg, Count, 212
Prince Albert [Albrecht], 161, 240
Prince of Capia, 69
Princess Marianne [of the Netherlands], 161, 240
Prophecy, 15, 41, 100, 180-1
Protestant[s], 3, 28, 47, 57, 71, 86-9, 104, 111, 147, 151, 154, 176, 180
Protestant Bishop, 81, 163, 208
Protestant Bishopric [too many references]
Protestant Church in Jerusalem, 55, 89, 90, 92, 96, 113, 144, 157, 161, 168, 174, 179, 209, 215, 218, 223, 231, 235
Protestant Episcopal Church, 222
Prussia, Prussian, viii, 1, 8, 9, 58, 61, 71, 74, 76, 84-5, 87, 90-2, 102-4, 115, 142, 146, 149, 174-5, 181
Prussian Ambassador [Constantinople], 81, 188
Prussian Consul-General [Beirut], 198
Psalms, 31, 100, 162, 224
Puritan, Puritan revival, 3,6
Pusey, Philip, 52
Pusey, Edward, 53, 85-6

Q
Quadruple Alliance, 77
Quarterly Review, 54, 151

R
Rabbi, iii, 38, 206
Rachid Pasha, 167
Radowitz, Joseph, 71

Ramle, 107, 161, 184, 211, 232
Ras el Wady, 225
Rayah, 194,
Red Sea, vi, 202
Rehden, 35
Reichardt, Rev, 41-2, 45, 47- 8
Reisenberg, 25
Reschid Pasha, 63
Restoration, restorationism,
  [restoration of the Jews [Israel],
  ii, iii, vii, viii, ix, 3, 4, 7, 8, 46,
  54, 56, 61-2, 77, 79, 93, 99, 118,
  235, 239, 246
Rhind, Lucit, 20
Rhodes Island, 59, 61
Rifaat Pasha, 92
Rivlin, Rabbi Moshe, 153
Roman Catholic Church, v, viii, 3,
  57, 70, 88, 104, 106, 111, 208,
  211, 222
Romans (book of), 21-2, 32, 49,
  98, 118, 161, 204
Rome, 52, 73, 87-8, 117, 179, 182,
  213
Rose, Sir George, 98, 104, 181
Rose, Colonel Hugh, 106-8, 110,
  140-2, 157, 159, 160, 164-5,
  169, 170, 172, 175, 181, 199,
  201, 219, 221
Rosenberg, 35
Rosenfelt, S.P, 237
Rosenthal, Chas, 237
Rosenthal, Dorothy [Bergheim],
  122
Rosenthal, Emily, 237
Rosenthal, Johann Wilhelm, 237
Rosenthal, Marie, 124
Rothschild, Baron James
  [Rothschild family] 153, 202
Rowlands, Mr., 118, 122, 156
Russia, Russian Empire, vii, viii,
  8, 46, 57-8, 61, 68-9, 85-7, 104,
  121, 168, 181, 208, 222, 240,
  243

S
Saalbeld, 36

Safed [Safet], 167, 169, 170-1,
  185, 192, 2076-8
St. Andrews Church [Plymouth],
  20-2
St. Anne's [Dublin], 31
St. Peter's [Colchester], 12
St. George's Church [Norwich],
  14
St. George's Church,
  [Stonehouse], 15
St. James Chapel, 162, 198, 243-4
St. Patricks [Dublin], 29
St. Paul [Paul] 99-100
St. Petersburg, 130
St. Sidewell's
  [Exeter], 24
St. Stephen's Gate, 156
Saladin, v
Saleeh, Jacob, 236
Samaritan, 192
Samaria [Sebaste], 192
Samson, Mr., 207
Sandford Church [Dublin], 29
Sans Souci Palace [Potsdam], 73
Sarim Effendi, 92
Satan, 19
Schick, Conrad, 163
Schirnding, Baron von, 4,5
Schleinitz, Baron, 98
Shochet, 11, 14
Schonlanke, 1,9,10, 36
Schultz, Ernest Gustav, 140-1,
  147, 164, 172-3, 217, 233
Schwartz, Rev. C, 149
Schwartz, J, 237
Scotland, Church of Scotland, 65,
  169, 170
Scriptures, 3, 22, 24, 44, 87, 186,
  191
Sea of Marmara, 77
Second Coming (of Jesus), ii, 246
Selwyn, George [Bishop], 98
Sephardi, Sephardim, 194, 200,
  206
Seraskier, 142
Shaftesbury, Lord, viii, 52-3, 55-6,
  61-5, 73, 76-9, 80-1, 83, 85-6,

98, 104, 113, 116, 208, 215, 234, 239
Shochet, 11, 14
Shtetl, 1
Sidon [Saida], 186
Sinai, 224
Singer, Dr., 33
Sligo, Marquis of, 212
Smith, Eli, 78
Smyrna, 28, 194
Solomon's Pools, 138
Spener, Philip Jacob, 2,6
Spice, spices, spice route, v, vi
Stargard, 35-6
Status quo, i, v, 2, 4, 23, 46, 56-7, 126, 133, 135, 166, 219
Steele, Sir Richard [and Lady], 27, 144, 176, 178
Stern, Henry Aaron, 192-3,
Sternschuss, Paul Heimann, 149, 170-2, 185-6, 192-3
Stoddart, Mr., 51
Stoke, 16
Stonehouse, 16-7, 21, 24
Strabane, 29
Straecke, Rev, 5
Strauss, Dr., 212
Stowell, Rev. Hugh, 117
Stuhm, 35
Suez, 230
Sultan [of Turkey], v, viii, 55, 57, 62, 69, 72, 126, 166, 190, 215, 241-2
Sultan Abd-ul-Mezid, 58
Sumpter, James, 105, 223
Switzerland, 5, 238
Synagogue [shul], 1, 15, 31, 185-6, 207
Synge, Mr. John [and Mrs. Synge], 20, 25, 27, 29, 31
Syrian Church [Bishop], 122-3

T
Tahir Pasha, 110
Tallymore, 29
Talmud, Talmudism, 10-11, 12, 37, 39, 43

Tanach, Tenach, 20
Tanoos, Kerm, 171
Tarkover, E.M, 122, 127, 134, 135, 147, 149, 175
Tartar, 231
Tatarwan, 108, 228, 231
Tatitschew, D.P., 70
Temple, 216
Tiberias, 133, 170, 184
Times /[newspaper], 63, 109-10, 190, 237
Thackeray, Makepeace, 212
Thicknesse, Captain, 16-7, 20
Thirty-Nine Articles, 84
Thompson, William, 107
Tombs of the Kings, 233
Tories [Government], 75
Tractarian [Oxford Movement, High Church party, Anglo-Catholic party], 53, 85-7, 145,
Treaty of London [1840], 72
Treaty of Unkiar Skelessi [1833], 46, 54, 77
Treaty for the Pacification of the Levant [1841], 64, 75, 77
Trinity College, 30, 38
Tripoli, 149
Turkish Empire, Turkey, Turks [also Ottoman Empire. Too many references]
Tymmim, Mr. A, 208
Tyre, 186

U
Ulema, 82, 91, 189
Umayyid [Empire], iv
Ungar, Max, 192, 237
United Church of England and Ireland, 99, 126
United Kingdom [Britain. Too many references]

V
Valetta, 29
Vasco da Gama, vi
Veitch, Rev. Douglas, 178, 183, 195, 197, 201-2, 210-11, 223-5,

227-9, 231-2, 234
Via Dolorosa, 156, 164
Via Maris, 224
Vicars, Murray, 192-3
Victoria, Queen, 64, 77, 80, 94-5,
  117, 131, 160, 215
Vincent, Mrs., 34
Vistula River, 39
Vizier, Viziers, 95

W

Waddington, Frances, 75
Wakf [Wakef], 141, 221
Waghor, Thomas, 230
Wait, Mr., 192
Walker, Admiral, 189
Walphen, Abraham, 127, 133,
  139, 166
Warburton, Eliot, 197, 212
Warsaw, 35, 38, 45
Way, Lewis, 7, 38, 53
Weinkauff, Michael, 135, 167
Wesley, Charles, 2
Wesley, John, 2, 3
Whig [Government], 75, 79
Whitefield, George, 3
Whiting, George Bachus, 121-2
Whitmarsh, William, 133, 167
Wilberforce, Samuel
  [Archdeacon], 75-6, 105
Wilberforce, William, 6
Wild, Mr., 229
Wildenbruch, von, 136, 141-2,
  172-3, 212
Williams, Rev. George, 88, 105-8,
  118, 145, 178, 187
Winbolt, Henry, 149, 186
Wolff, Joseph, ii, 16, 28-9, 50
Wood, Consul, 210
Woodfood, Sir Alexander, 106
Wurttemburg, 173

Y

Yarborough, Miss, 156, 196
Young, William Tanner, 57, 108-
  9, 125-9, 130-3, 136, 139, 140-1,
  147-8, 159, 160, 163-6, 170-1,

173-5, 180-1, 195, 200-1,
  206, 208, 216-8, 228

Z

Zalman, Rabbi Abraham, 153
Zechariah, 22
Zempleburg, 39
Zimim, Mr., 207
Zinzendorf, Count, 2
Zion [Mount Zion], 22, 54, 66, 75,
  97-8, 100-1, 112, 114, 121, 134,
  140, 146, 150, 161, 168, 178,
  182, 193, 201, 204, 213
Zionists, 242
Zurich, 87